The Theatre of Marina Carr:

'before rules was made'

The Theatre of Marina Carr:

'before rules was made'

Edited by Cathy Leeney and Anna McMullan

Carysfort Press

A Carysfort Press Book

The Theatre of Marina Carr: 'before rules was made'
Edited by Cathy Leeney and Anna McMullan

First published in Ireland in 2003 as a paperback original by
Carysfort Press, 58 Woodfield, Scholarstown Road,
Dublin 16, Ireland

© 2003
Copyright remains with the authors

Typeset by Carysfort Press
Cover design by Alan Bennis

Printed and bound by Leinster Leader Ltd
18/19 South Main Street, Naas, Co. Kildare, Ireland

Contents

Acknowledgements

We would like to thank the following people for their generosity and support in the compilation of this collection:

The Arts Council of Ireland/An Chomhairle Éalaoin for their support of Carysfort Press; The National University of Ireland for a grant in aid of publication of this volume; The National Theatre Society Ltd., Tom Mac Intyre and Frank McGuinness for kind permission to reprint programme notes for *The Mai*, *Portia Coughlan*, and *By the Bog of Cats...*; Frank McGuinness and Faber and Faber for kind permission to reprint an excerpt from his Introduction to *The Dazzling Dark*; Medb Ruane and Fintan O'Toole for kind permission to reprint their reviews of *Portia Coughlan* and *Ariel* respectively; Anthony Roche and the *Irish University Review* for kind permission to reprint his article 'Woman on the Threshold' which originally appeared in vol. 25, 1995; Mairead Delaney, Archivist at the Abbey Theatre; Lucy McKeever; also at the Abbey Theatre; Loretto O'Donoghoe at Druid Theatre Company; Amelia Stein for her photographs of productions of *The Mai*, *Portia Coughlan* and *By the Bog of Cats...* at the Abbey Theatre; Fergus Bourke (and the Abbey Theatre) for his photograph of *Ullaloo*; Matt O'Brien (and the Irish Repertory of Chicago) for his photographs of *By the Bog of Cats...*; Pan Sok (and RO Theater of Rotterdam) for photographs of *Portia Coughlan* and *By the Bog of Cats...*; Joe Vanek for his photographs of *By the Bog of Cats...* at San Jose Repertory Theater.

Very special thanks to Dan Farrelly for his patience and optimistic determination, and to Carysfort Press for their enthusiastic interest and belief in the project.

Thanks to Alan Bennis for his brilliance and his courtesy; to our colleagues in UCD and TCD; and, finally, thank you to all our contributors.

Cathy Leeney
Anna McMullan

List of Photographs

Section 1 (After page 36)

1. Olwen Fouéré (Tilly), *left*, and Mark Lambert (Tomred) in *Ullaloo*
   at the Peacock Theatre, Dublin (1991)
(Photo by Fergus Bourke, courtesy of the Abbey Theatre Archive)

2. *From left to right*: Joan O'Hara (Grandma Fraochlán), Derbhle
   Crotty (Millie) and Owen Roe (Robert) in *The Mai*
   at the Peacock Theatre, Dublin (1994)
(Photo by Amelia Stein)

3. Olwen Fouéré (The Mai), *left*, and Owen Roe (Robert) in *The Mai*
   at the Peacock Theatre, Dublin (1994)
(Photo by Amelia Stein)

4. Owen Roe (Robert), *left*, and Olwen Fouéré (The Mai) in *The Mai*
   at the Peacock Theatre (1994)
(Photo by Amelia Stein)

5. Owen Roe (Robert), and Olwen Fouéré (The Mai), *left*, and
   Derbhle Crotty in *The Mai* at the Peacock Theatre, Dublin
   (1994)
(Photo by Amelia Stein)

Section 2 (After page 132)

6. Seán Rocks (Raphael), left, and Derbhle Crotty (Portia) in
   Portia Coughlan at the Peacock Theatre, Dublin (1996)
(Photo by Amelia Stein)

7. Act Two, Scene One of *Portia Coughlan* at the Peacock
   Theatre, Dublin (1996)
(Photo by Amelia Stein)

Section 3 (After page 196)

Introduction

Writing of Marina Carr's second play, *Low in the Dark*, which premiered at the Project Arts Centre, Dublin, in 1989, Sarah-jane Scaife notes that: 'even at that early stage in her career Marina was absolutely sure of her theatrical voice'. That voice has become one of the most powerful, haunting voices on the contemporary Irish stage. Since her earliest plays Marina Carr has crossed genres, shifting from the metatheatrical, absurd strategies of *Low in the Dark* to her more recent, strange hybrids of myth, realism and the grotesque. She appropriates the rules of genre, character, dialogue or setting as she has inherited them, and then reinvents them, creating a dynamic space in which the determining social and theatrical norms of gender, property, identity and tradition become ironic, stifling and sometimes monstrous distortions, as if viewed from a dimension 'before rules was made'. Because her work suggests rather than explains, it leaves spaces for what Melissa Sihra terms the agency and imagination of her audiences and interpreters, analytic and creative. This collection of essays aims to stimulate, provoke, and provide material for further exploration of Carr's theatre. While Carr's plays, as she herself approves, are published and read as literary texts, most of the articles here deal with the plays as theatre, embodied in the space-time of performance and mediated both by the specific contexts of location, publicity, expectations or reception, and the broader contexts of cultural or intercultural translation, and historical moment.

Sarahjane Scaife takes us back to some mutual beginnings: she recreates the theatrical context of Dublin in 1989, the year that *Ullaloo*, Marina Carr's first play, was given a reading at the Dublin Theatre Festival, and *Low in the Dark*, her second, was produced at the Project Arts Centre, Dublin. It was also the year of Scaife's own return to Dublin after several years of training in New York. Scaife vividly evokes the experience of performing in *Low in the Dark*, a highly non-naturalist and metatheatrical piece, commenting that: 'You had to be totally and utterly "in the moment", as it happened, and that was extremely liberating. I watch my kids playing with Barbie dolls or Pokemon, or pegs if they have nothing else. They pick up one figure then another but they stick to the truth of each moment and each character as the story unfolds. They are making up the story as they go along, absorbed in each moment, believing it all and passionately acting it out. Each character gets a different treatment and voice and multiple stories can be accommodated at the same time.' Through her own memories of New York she reminds us that Carr had also spent a year teaching there before writing *Low in the Dark*, and comments on: 'the brave way that the play was written, at the time quite radical. It had the mad energy of New York.' Scaife emphasizes both the anarchic humour of *Low in the Dark* and its 'minor chord of dread', and sees the interweaving of these as also characteristic of Carr's later work even though her subsequent plays are in a different genre. What genre though? How do we describe Carr's drama since *The Mai*? While there are apparent elements of realism in setting, they are inhabited by mythical, larger-than-life presences that threaten to explode the parameters of realism with its focus on the material, the contemporary and the individual in relation to social, geographical and historical forces. These are there, of course, but Carr's worlds, as Sarahjane Scaife suggests, incorporate many stories, memories, temporalities and dimensions simultaneously, of which realism is only one. To see Carr's drama as a mimetic representation of the 'real' is to mistake her rejection of the limited way in which the norms of 'reality' are constituted so as to marginalize and exclude vast areas of human experience.

Playwrights work in an ambivalent relation to tradition and to canons, writing within, and against, reacting and critiquing from without. Whoever it was said that houses are dangerous places for women must have heard Ibsen's Nora slamming the front door behind her at the end of *A Doll's House*. Anthony Roche sets a context for Carr's early play *The Mai*, linking it back through Teresa Deevy's work in the nineteen thirties, to foundational images of women on the threshold of the house, as exemplified in Synge's Nora Bourke in *The Shadow of the Glen*. Roche explores aspects of the deep structure of all three plays, and the way that images in performance link them. Synge's presence here is important in de-essentializing the analysis; the figure of a woman in flight from the domestic has also haunted the male imagination. Roche sees the plays as theatre; embodiment in performance before an audience is central to their meanings. The reverberation of that door slam, as Roche explicates with *élan,* resonates along the passage of Irish theatrical tradition until its re-conception in The Mai's desirable residence on the shores of the beautiful, haunted, and doom-laden Owl Lake. The connections drawn across history, gender and space, between Synge's, Deevy's and Carr's plays reveal a secret history on stage of the in-between space, where women are caught between inner security and outer freedom, both painfully elusive, their paradox powerfully theatrical.

At the beginning of the twenty-first century, Carr's reputation has gained an international dimension, with many productions of the plays in Europe and the US. We have therefore included articles on a selection of these productions which sometimes involved an Irish creative team member (Joe Vanek designed the San Jose *By the Bog of Cats...*, for example, and Melissa Sihra acted as dramaturg or creative consultant in several of these productions.) Since this is a trend also of contemporary Irish theatre in general, exploring how Carr's work has been presented and received out of Ireland has implications for contemporary perceptions or constructions of 'Irishness' and Irish theatre.

There have been many more international productions of Carr's work than we have been able to discuss here, such as the U.S. premiere of *The Mai* by the distinguished director Emily Mann at the McCarter Theater in New Jersey in 1997. In Europe, Carr is, as often as not, associated with the younger generation of playwrights in English including Sarah Kane and Mark Ravenhill. Whether current European productions emphasize Carr's Irishness, or ignore it, a steady stream of young companies has been excited by the contemporary energies of her plays.

Clare Wallace analyses the central concept of authenticity that has been critically deconstructed in relation to Irish culture by critics like Gerry Smyth and Colin Graham.[1] Wallace considers how 'authentic Irishness' was denoted in a production of *The Mai* (translated as *Maja*) in Liberec, in the Czech Republic, and has been invoked in relation to Carr through her portrayal in interviews and photographs as: 'dramatic, lonely, isolated, natural, beautiful, feminine'. She also points out Carr's own authenticating strategies as she places herself within a poetic and tragic tradition of inspired authorship. Yet Wallace complicates this by emphasizing that in the work itself the very issues of origins and authenticity are slippery and never verifiable.

Unlike the Czech production of *The Mai* considered by Clare Wallace, RO Theater in Rotterdam produced a double bill of *Portia Coughlan* and *By the Bog of Cats...* in 2002 without any performance references to 'Irishness'.[2] Both plays were translated both linguistically and culturally into the context of contemporary life in the Netherlands. Directed by Alize Zandwijk, the performance style and design moved the plays away from poetic realism towards rawer, presentational performances, paced through ritual actions, and the repeated breakdown of

---

[1] See Colin Graham and Richard Kirkland, eds, *Ireland and Cultural Theory: The Mechanics of Authenticity*, (Basingstoke: Macmillan, 1999), and Gerry Smyth, *Decolonisation and Criticism: the Construction of Irish Literature*, (London: Pluto Press, 1998).

[2] See Cathy Leeney, Review of *Portia Coughlan* and *By the Bog of Cats...*, *Irish Theatre Magazine*, 3 (14) (Spring 2003), pp.82-86.

ritual into chaos. The sense of obsessive passion and estrangement inherent in *Portia Coughlan* and *By the Bog of Cats...* was extended in a number of ways. Fintan Goolan, the slimey barman from *Portia Coughlan*, appeared again in the second play, fulminating against Hester and her kind, a figure of dangerous but pathetic misogyny as he stalked her almost to her death. Ordinary objects were defamiliarized. When Damus brings flowers for Portia, he is bent double under the weight of a huge, heart-shaped wreath, hauling it on his back like Christ with the cross. The focus of the audience was continuously split, and the mood of a scene was counterpointed by action elsewhere on stage. Farce and pathos, poetry and chaos were bound together in one knot. Zandwijk's daring and free approach to Carr's texts released huge energy, and revealed Carr's sinuous dramaturgy, particularly in *Portia Coughlan*. Beyond their 'Irishness', an emotional and theatrical depth was confirmed in both plays.

Carr's love affair with English is at the centre of Eilis Ní Dhuibhne's examination of *The Mai*. Here is an interrogation of 'storytelling' in theatre, of narration and how it works in performance. Ní Dhuibhne connects Carr with Edna O'Brien, and with the insight of a writer, sets out how two registers of language operate in the play to give it a resonance beyond the human/psychological, linking the elemental and poetic aura of certain passages to the archetypal appeal of fairy tales. Yet the power of the story to make the dead live, to recreate the past as the present is overtaken finally by drama, as the power of presence on stage captures and supersedes the word. Ní Dhuibhne reveals the perspective of 'the wronged child' as a crucial thread connecting Carr's major works thus far. In the competing discourses around Carr's work, this view clarifies the contemporary content of the plays as the expression of generational conflict in the face of economic success and emotional failure, while valuing how the plays feed a hunger for the longer view of the ritualized folk tale.

As with any new playwright to emerge on the theatrical scene, the initial mediators and commentators are the reviewers, or those who write the programme notes or introduce published editions. It is fascinating to revisit the immediate, visceral, imaginative and analytic responses of these 'Aperçus' regarding Carr's work as it emerges, and they are often prescient of tensions and preoccupations that recur in later commentaries. In his evocative programme note to *The Mai*, Tom Mac Intyre notes the tension between word and image, the wit and humour, the 'wild imaginings' of the 'walking wounded', the lyric daring and the probing of pain that continue to resonate in Carr's later work. He also notes Carr's delving into the unconscious, which raises questions about gender, self and other in her work. Mac Intyre's programme note to *Portia Coughlan* continues his distinctive meditation on the evolution of Carr's contradictory poetic voice, and places it within a genealogy which for him includes the American writer William Faulkner. He notes the juxtaposition of fierce comedy, the grotesque, and a tenderness untainted by sentimentality. He draws our attention to the quest motif, the 'search energy' of Carr's work: "'When a body goes looking for that which is lost", Marina Carr wisely tells us, "everything becomes a sign"'.

Frank McGuinness's association of Carr's plays and the dark time of the year, All Soul's Night and remembrance of the dead, evokes the spiritual landscape occupied by Portia Coughlan, and by Hester Swane in *By the Bog of Cats*.... He identifies Carr's re-invention of tragedy as a place lit up by 'a fatal excess of self-knowledge', by language that scalds like fire, by a killing truth. McGuinness places Carr's heroines in the gallery of theatre's most powerful and un-self-pitying women. His responses ask us to embark into the borderlands between the living and the dead, to confront, as Portia and Hester do, terror and destiny, sorrow, comedy and death. His words may give us courage in the 'big country' of Carr's imagination.

Medb Ruane's review of *Portia Coughlan* captures and eloquently articulates the sense of energy and the emergence of a new voice in theatre which was palpable following the premiere in the Peacock in the Spring of 1996. Ruane homes in on this 'brutal and passionate drama of family relationships and personal disintegration' and emphasizes that 'Portia Coughlan is all about speaking the unspoken.' Ruane also emphasizes the impact of the play in performance: Garry Hynes's powerful production, the visual clarity of the set, the 'mega, towering performance of Derbhle Crotty as Portia'. While Ruane points to certain weaknesses in the plot structure of the play, which 'eventually opts for a mechanistic, causal explanation of [Portia's] suffering', she concludes that 'you don't often find such passion on an Irish stage'.

Ariel was presented on the Abbey Theatre's main stage in October 2002, as part of the Dublin Theatre Festival, directed by Conall Morrison. It is loosely based on Euripides' *Iphigenia at Aulis*, and follows the rise of a politician who has made a Mephistophelian pact with his god according to which he sacrifices his daughter on her sixteenth birthday in return for political success. Fintan O'Toole emphasizes the ambitious scope of this play, which tries to 'fuse an immediate vision of political crisis with a large sweep of religious and Biblical images'. Carr's vision portrays a world whose foundational structures – Church, State, and Family – are in 'an advanced state of decay'. O'Toole also sees *Ariel* as characteristic of the challenges facing the younger generation of theatre-makers as 'the society that gave form and meaning to the work of their older contemporaries is in disarray'. Indeed, the carnage at the end of *Ariel* underlines the catastrophic working out, not of a curse, but of a culture of sacrifice in private and public life. Interestingly, it was in her play for children, *Meat and Salt*, presented at the Peacock Theatre in February 2003, adapted from a fairy tale with similarities to the *King Lear* narrative, that Carr envisaged a hopeful sense of survival. The youngest daughter is exiled after failing to demonstrate with sufficient excess her love for her power-obsessed father, but manages to survive separation from her 'Big Daddy', and from her long-lost and ever distant mother, and, after many vibrantly presented adventures, creates a pragmatic life and love on her own terms.

Melissa Sihra emphasizes the extension of Carr's plays to new audiences and to mixed responses in the U.S. during 2001, with productions in Chicago, Pittsburg, and San Jose, and her appointment to the Heimbold Chair in Irish Studies at the University of Villanova, Philadelphia in 2003. Sihra places these plays in the context of a changing contemporary Ireland, and comments on the ways in which their performances: 'articulate and explore, perpetuate or contest, received or distinctive notions of "Irishness"'. Sihra draws on her professional experience of working as dramaturg or creative consultant with the above production teams and on her intimate knowledge both of the texts and of their diverse embodiments on stage, contrasting the specific dynamics of each production. She emphasizes Carr's resistance to closure or definition: 'As in *The Playboy of the Western World*, itself a study in absurd reference and poetic anecdote, the countless incidents in *Portia Coughlan* are often referred to without any specific contextualization, imbuing the lives of the characters with both spoken and unspoken histories.' She also provides a perceptive meditation on Carr's recurrent motif of death, arguing that: 'Death *per se*, can offer no resolution unless it is viewed as a symbiotic dynamic of living.'

Reflecting on her own direction of *By the Bog of Cats…* for Irish Repertory of Chicago (2001), M.K. Martinovich teases out the connections between Carr's play and its Greek ante text, *Medea*, which was an important part of her and her team's research, as they sought to connect 'three distinct cultures'. Her interpretation of the play foregrounds the many 'hauntings' which torment Hester. She explores the role of ghosts as liminal beings occupying 'many roles – as the undead, as unconscious, as prophecy'. Martinovich discusses Carr's textual revisions in the scene between Hester and her brother, and comments that: 'In the new scene, the reasons for Hester's murderous actions towards Joseph are more vague. The scene seems to suggest that Joseph's ghost could act as a warning from hell.' She also points out that 'Hester is haunted not only by her absent mother, but also by other maternal figures and associations in the play'. Martinovich reveals the search to materialize on stage these 'liminal realms of the real and the fantastic, the worldly and the spiritual, the corporeal and the intangible'.

As collision points between painful tragedy and ribald comedy Carr's plays yoke together extreme states, moods, and events. Bernadette Bourke spotlights this through a lucid examination of carnival in Carr's work. Bourke's introduction to the ideas underlying carnival bring the reader into an extreme scene of grotesque, of arse-over-tip reversal. Carnival usurps and threatens post-renaissance humanism, and the centrality of the rational individual in a rational, material world. Carr's writing is often spoken of in relation to J.M. Synge's. Here however, Bourke proposes a deeper connection through what Synge called 'the Rabelaisian note, the 'gross' note if you will'. The role of death in Carr's plays is placed as part of a continuity between worlds, between earth and womb, and 'between past, present and future'. Bourke allows a deeper understanding of the warring elements operating in Carr's plays to emerge as she unpicks the overlapping worlds of folklore, of spirits, of soulless contemporary materialism, of nature both sinister and beautiful, and of the individual inside and outside the tribe. Post modernism accommodates Carr's grounded, metaphysical vision. Bourke locates the plays in a theatrical tradition, yet recognizes and highlights how they subvert, disrupt and lay waste the comfort zones of convention. Grotesquerie is acted out as often as described; death stings on stage, placing Carr in relation to the brutal theatrical aesthetic current among other playwrights of her generation.

Victor Merriman jolts us into what he calls the crisis in post-colonial dreaming. Theatre, as he has expressed elsewhere, is a potential site where globalized Irish culture conflicts with 'the egalitarian and communitarian aspirations of anti-colonial nationalism', where post-colonial dreaming of possible worlds might take place outside the terms of the global marketplace. Merriman sees the potential of theatre to be engaged with social and cultural realities, and his vision is deeply idealistic insofar as it credits theatre with the power to interrogate and to critique received structures, complacent assumptions, and disabling exclusions, and to open possible futures. The workings of spectacle and of the grotesque, as an avoidance of real engagement with issues of power, demand debate in current Irish theatre practice. Merriman opens questions of how to read the intensity of Carr's representations in *Portia Coughlan* and *By the Bog of Cats...* as they are framed by current conditions in Irish theatre. *By the Bog of Cats...*, he argues, is a play about land and travellers, and the new wealth in rural Ireland. Whether the reader agrees that the plays damn their heroines for their un-naturalness, or whether they rather see Carr's work dissecting and exposing fearful strata of discrimination and hatred, this commentary slices through the critical complacencies that lie to the east and west of such a formidable writer as Carr when placing her within an Irish playwriting tradition, and invoking the authority of the master narratives of European high culture.

Through a time of unprecedented affluence and of unprecedented recognition of, and demand for, Irish theatre abroad, Carr is the primary female playwright working at the beginning of the twenty first century. She is a writer of epic, comic trage-dies in the midst of value-free, postmodern cultural prolifera-tion, a poet of deep intensity in a Europe and North America in ideological free-fall. All of these framings are fraught with ironies and contests of interpretation that force us to question our valuing of theatre, of performance as a national forum, to question women's place in that forum, and the role of that forum in our civic and personal lives.

The testimony of the performer offers visceral and felt in-sights into the style, form, language, and emotional territory of a play. In measuring and elucidating the demands made on her by Carr's *The Mai*, and *By the Bog of Cats…* Olwen Fouéré, one of the most brilliant actors of her generation, reveals the pas-sionate land Carr's plays occupy, and the epic challenge they pose to performers and audiences. Like footbridges between worlds, Carr creates pathways from recognizable, rooted scenes, to archetypal and savage fields of energy. Fouéré vividly de-scribes the negotiation she made as a performer between the Himalayan scale of Hester's emotional landscape, the material detailing of a living individual, and the technical demands of a hugely intoxicating and draining role. Her insights into both *By the Bog of Cats…* and *The Mai* are informed by her deep under-standing of theatrical language and style, of the characters' impulses, and of the dynamic created with a live audience in performance. Her perceptions combine an intense and often poetic engagement with her subject, and an ability to view even the characters she has played with a penetrating, objective scrutiny.

The epoch of space is upon us, and Enrica Cerquoni links space and gender in theatre as central to her concentrated and eloquent analysis of the phenomenon of theatrical space in *By the Bog of Cats....* Cerquoni foregrounds the vastly different approaches of two accomplished theatre designers, Monica Frawley and Joe Vanek, entering into the matrix of images created between the text of the play and two very different designs for the Abbey Theatre and San Jose Repertory Theatre. She shows the profound effect of theatre space and design in creating the dramatic experience of the audience. Whether it was the performance on the Abbey stage, primal scene of Irish drama, or on the stage at San Jose, *By the Bog of Cats...* conjures unforgettable images of woman, home, landscape, family and nation. As they collide, shatter, and disperse in the play, these themes are dramatized in the visceral relationship between person, territory, and community, between performer, stage space, and design. Carr's 'implosive dramaturgy' as Cerquoni intensely analyses it, is a site of intersection, an inner condition, a state of mind, and a state of nation.

Adroitly meshing his own experiences as a father, as producer and director of new Irish writing in the U.S., and as a critic, Matt O'Brien opens a male perspective on idealized masculinity in Carr's theatre, and relates it compellingly to *The Mai, By the Bog of Cats...* and *On Raftery's Hill.* O'Brien remarks on the tendency for Carr's work to attract interpretation by women directors, and comment from women critics and commentators. In a cultural arena where women's work has rarity value in performance, and yet where audiences at all levels are predominantly female, this is not surprising. The hunger for Carr's work, say amongst female students of drama, measures a longing to see, to understand, to propose a world otherwise. O'Brien draws attention to the role men play in Carr's dramatic universe, and as always when one sex is in turmoil, the other is inevitably and crucially in turmoil too. O'Brien's perspective is completely complementary to the emphasis elsewhere on Carr's heroines; while seeming at first to lead away from their values and struggles as a central concern, in fact he develops the theme of the idealized 'White Knight' to reveal awkward and unpalatable aspects of the women's quest through the plays until its nightmare apotheosis in *On Raftery's Hill*, the play nobody wishes to speak about. O'Brien's startling suggestion of this play as key to earlier works opens up important and challenging questions about the role of the gendered 'other'. The significance of performance in defining meaning (casting of individual parts, balancing casts, and staging) is central here, reinforcing the strong sense in this volume generally of Carr's theatre as a live art form, contributing over cultural and social boundaries, unhinging predictable points of exit and entry in the battleground between men and women.

Claudia Harris discusses the reception of Carr in the U.S. specifically in relation to the touring production of *On Raftery's Hill* at the Washington Festival of Irish Culture, and places the mixed response to Carr's bleak yet darkly comic play in the context of other representatives of contemporary Irish theatre at the festival. She considers the pressures on Irish culture in the global marketplace, but also argues for a complex engagement with the visions and imaginings of a particular culture. She discusses the play not only in terms of the binaries real/fantastic, human beings/ghosts, the material/the intangible, but also in terms of human beings/animals, and sees the animalism of *On Raftery's Hill* as one source of its disturbing power (especially as the gorilla which makes off with the three year old Shalome is seen as more caring and maternal than the humans: 'it was a wonderful, wonderful time' the old woman remembers). Harris quotes Richard Schechner on theatre: 'the interactions played out in the theater are those which are problematical in society, interactions of a sexual, violent, or taboo kind concerning hierarchy, territory, or mating. [...] drama is not a model of all human action, but of the most problematical, difficult, taboo, liminal, and dangerous activities.' Yet Harris also considers whether, in staging these 'violent and taboo interactions', there is a possible danger of reinforcing rather than critiquing the patterns of abuse depicted? Nevertheless, she concludes that: 'Carr's individual voice is a crucial component of the cumulative, cultural story. In her work, Carr cracks open a window onto the ghost world that troubles her sleep and allows her audiences to overhear the tumult. May the scary hauntings continue.'

We are only beginning to respond to this distinctive voice of contemporary Irish theatre. Genealogies and connections suggested here include J.M. Synge, Teresa Deevy, Samuel Beckett, Edna O'Brien, William Faulkner. There will emerge many more perspectives and evaluations, connections to be made and explored. The French philosopher, Luce Irigaray emphasizes the importance of symbolization for women, having been for so long in Western culture associated with the material, the corporeal and the immanent.[3] She emphasizes that women must create a kind of mobile home for themselves within language, a second skin, where other bodies, selves and possibilities can be played out, as well as past traumas, hidden histories. Carr's unflinching vision suggests that what we take for granted as the normal rules blinker us from some very disturbing realities and from diverse possibilities of subversive play and invention.

---

[3] See Luce Irigaray, *An Ethics of Sexual Difference*, trans. from the French by Carolyn Burke and Gillian C. Gill, (London: Pluto Press, 1993).

1 | Mutual Beginnings:

Marina Carr's *Low in the Dark*

Sarahjane Scaife

When approached to write about performing in *Low in the Dark* I wondered how I would recollect in sufficient detail working on a play that had been presented thirteen years earlier. *Low in the Dark* was one of the first plays I worked on when I returned to Ireland having spent the previous four years training in New York. It was written by a then unknown writer, Marina Carr, for a new theatre company, Crooked Sixpence, and premiered at the Project Arts Centre, Dublin, in October 1989. It was considered very experimental at the time, with its non naturalist setting, structure, and characters: BINDER (Sarahjane Scaife), BENDER, Binder's mother, (Joan Brosnan Walsh), CURTAINS, covered from head to toe in curtains, (Brid Mhic Fhearrai, now Brid McCarthy), BAXTER, Curtain's lover, (Peter Holmes), and BONE, Binder's lover (Dermod Moore).

In fact though, as soon as I started reading the play, it brought me right back to the TEAM rehearsal rooms at Marlborough Street in Dublin. No room to move as we were rehearsing in a space that was basically no more than a glorified warehouse. There were bits of sets and props and rubbish all over the place. It was absolutely grotty, damp and cold. Even reading the first few lines I could almost feel the grasp of Joan Brosnan Walsh, who played my mother Bender, as we rolled around fighting each other on the floor during one of our

scenes, both of us screaming insults at each other. Such satisfying insults to scream whilst in the middle of a good ruck. Something a mother and daughter could only normally dream of
doing!

> **BINDER**: (*Whispers*) Menopause, men o pause,
> men…o…pause!
> **BENDER**: Stop it! (*Starts hitting her.*)
> **BINDER**: Menopause, hot flush, empty womb.
> **BENDER**: (*Chasing her*) Stop it! Stop it!
> **BINDER**: The womb will be empty and the tomb will be full!
> **BENDER**: Stop it! (*LITD*: p.78) [1]

It seems childish now when I think of the sheer joy and fun I
got out of that scene. In fact that was the overriding feeling that
came to me when I started re-reading the play. It was like being
a child and 'playing'. You had to be totally and utterly 'in the
moment', as it happened, and that was extremely liberating. I
watch my kids playing with Barbie dolls or Pokemon or pegs if
they have nothing else. They pick up one figure then another
but they stick to the truth of each moment and each character
as the story unfolds. They are making up the story as they go
along, absorbed in each moment, believing it all and passionately acting it out. Each character gets a different treatment and
voice and multiple stories can be accommodated at the same
time. That's what I immediately recalled of the process of
working on *Low in the Dark*: throwing myself totally into whatever action or character I was portraying at the time. I was soon
to find out that the other actors in the play had a similar
recollection.

---

[1] All references are to the edition of *Low in the Dark* in Marina Carr,
Plays 1, (London: Faber & Faber, 1999).

Setting the Scene: Dublin, 1989

The research phone calls that I made were really positive, talking to actors, some of whom I had had no contact with for thirteen years, as if the rehearsals had taken place last week. Everyone seemed so 'back there' in time when we talked about 'the process'. I haven't worked on many productions that have had the same reaction and 'vibe' for want of a better word. It seemed to reawaken a time and place where there was genuine excitement and buzz about something of which they all felt very much a part, and of which they were very proud. Dermod Moore, who is now London based, recollected that it was the only time that someone had ever literally stopped him in the street to demand: 'Are you that guy in that play at the Project?, Jesus, fair play to you if you are.' So what was it I wondered, that was so special about that particular play at the time?

The first person I talked to was Joan Brosnan Walsh, who played my mother Bender. I began to realize that there had been a whole history to the piece before I joined the process. Later, through further discussions with Peter Holmes, Dermod and Brid Mhic Fhearrai (at the time), I started to get an understanding of what that history entailed.

Since I had been in New York training and performing, I had missed what had been developing in theatre in Ireland. In the 1980s in Ireland there was very little money for theatre, and there were few independent theatre companies. There were some, but nothing like the number that developed later. If a company did manage to get a show together, it was usually done on what was euphemistically called 'shares'. Shares consisted of what profit there was left from the box office after all expenses were met, divided out between everyone involved. This could mean next to nothing! I think we got £30 in total for *Low in the Dark*. The training deemed necessary for becoming an actor at the time was likely to include a declaration of that fact, an official 'signing on' of the dole, then a quick trip down to the local to discuss 'theatre'. The dole office often served as the local Equity branch!

Peter, Dermod, Brid, Joan and Philip Hardy were amongst a group of actors, directors, writers and designers who got together under the umbrella of the Independent Theatre Association. This was set up in 1989 at Projects Arts Centre, whose Artistic Director at that time was Tim O'Neill. Those involved felt that, not only was there very little work or money for theatre practitioners, but that when the work did arise they felt rusty, their artistic muscles weren't being worked. They felt a need to workshop together to keep themselves inspired and also hopefully to generate their own work in the longer term.

The Project Arts Centre in general and Tim O'Neill in particular played a crucial part in encouraging this process of continuing the learning curve when not actively 'in work'. Tim's policy was always to be open to good ideas. Many performers and fledgling directors had him to thank for the belief he retained in projects, even when the finances were lacking or, in some cases, nonexistent. There was a very 'open door' aspect to the Project. There was no sense of the awe that one might have felt at some of the main spaces. There was a creative feel about it, despite the rain thundering on the roof, the leaks, the gammy photocopier, the temperamental washing machine that was used for more than costumes. Sometimes it seems to me today that the packaging of theatre has become more important than the worth of the work itself. The Project and other theatres such as the Oscar, despite all their resource limitations, were theatres started by actors, for actors. In 1989, the Project witnessed the emergence of a very different voice in theatre.

Crooked Sixpence, the company that produced *Low in the Dark*, had its inception at that 1989 meeting of the Independent Theatre Association at the Project. They spent months workshopping ideas, developing ways of working together, and playing theatre games to break down personal and artistic barriers. They were basically trying to create a common theatrical language in order to facilitate the evolution of their creative ideas. They had a couple of writers on board, but enlisted the help of Frank McGuinness to give them a simple theatrical scenario from which to start.   He presented them with a simple theatrical idea. The aim of the exercise would be to tease out this idea, using the process they had been employing during the workshopping stage, into a full length piece. This was to be a collaborative effort, employing all the elements of theatre that they had been playing with up until then. The commitment, they decided, was to have a dual purpose. It was to be actor led and it was also to explode conventional forms of theatre. Tim O'Neill was very supportive and enthusiastic about what they were doing. He offered them a two week slot at the Project and limited financial help.

However, as they continued, they found that the co-operative work method was far more complicated than they had appreciated. It would be necessary for one person to take control. Philip Hardy, subsequently Director of Barnstorm Theatre, took over the role of director of the piece. As they weren't progressing satisfactorily with the writing he took it on himself, after discussion with the others, to invite a young playwright, Marina Carr, along to rehearsals. He wanted Marina to take on the writing of the piece. Marina came along to the rehearsals, and was very impressed with the way the group worked and played together. By this stage, the barriers that can sometimes be there at the inception of a production had been broken down. The actors were easily able to jump into improvisation without egos getting in the way. That was an important aspect in the scripting of the play. The first thing I noticed when I became involved was that sense of an 'ego-less' atmosphere. It was so refreshing and exciting. There was an expectation that anything could happen, because what might have blocked it ordinarily, had been removed.

At the end of that first day Marina declared her interest in writing with the group. Her codicil was that she wanted to write from her own premise. She came in the next day with two pages of a play. The setting was a bathroom. The characters were two women, a mother Bender and her daughter Binder. Binder's 'area' was the toilet and Bender's the bath. Tom Mac Intyre's work at the Abbey had prepared the ground for 'a different approach' to the purely literary based work that had dominated up until then, but this scenario was still, by mainstream standards, wacky. The group were all very interested and loved Marina's actor-friendly approach.

This way of working was to become the pattern for the rest of the process. Marina would write at night and come in the next day with a whole new scene. By now, she was under huge pressure. There was a very real deadline to be reached for the upcoming opening at the Project. We would play the scene, then we would play with it. Afterwards we would all talk about what worked and what didn't. Marina would then revise what she felt was necessary. Dermod feels that there was a reason why this extremely pressurized way of writing was possible. It was that, even at that early stage in her career, Marina was absolutely sure of her theatrical voice. So much so that she gave a confidence to the whole process, which validated what the group had already being trying to achieve.

I don't think I was consciously aware of it at the time, but retrospectively, the facts of Marina's sex and youth removed her from the traditional male hierarchy that had been predominant in theatre in Ireland. There were few prominent female playwrights in Ireland at the time. Theatre was run by men for the most part. Plays were directed by men and written by men. The two designers for the show were also female, Leonor McDonagh and Liz Cullinane. They produced miracles. I felt very comfortable creatively in this environment. Because I only entered the fray after the first scene had been written, it was essential that I would be absorbed into the process organically.

I had been asked to replace an actress who had to get a 'real job' as she couldn't continue to work without finance, a common complaint at the time! Due to my recent experience in New York, the scenario as explained to me by Dermod Moore seemed very familiar and not at all absurd. The fact that there wasn't any money was of no real importance as I was used to the notion that you worked to get paid so that you could afford to do what really interested you. I am not recommending this as a professional strategy, it was just the way things were then.

New York

I was used to going to shows done on a shoe string in New York, presented in back yards, lofts and studio spaces. The cutting edge of 'experimental theatre' could be seen in places like LaMama Experimental Theatre Company (La MamaETC) and Theatre for the New City. There was all sorts of cross disciplinary work going on: puppetry, movement, opera, musicians all performing together. At La MamaETC you could see companies such as Eugenio Barba's Odin Teatret. Odin's performances were image-based and exciting. A show would start and you wouldn't even be aware of it. The actors would infiltrate the space with instruments playing hauntingly, and before you had time to prepare your 'audience head' you would be in the midst of an inspiring experience. You would leave the theatre with some haunting image burnt onto the retina of your imaginative memory, such is the power and beauty of the image within a play. They didn't seem like 'the plays' I was used to. Performance artists like Karen Finley would present you with a piece that seemed like a 'play' as one knew it, and would then turn it all on its head. I remember one particular show where, during the 'average family' meal scene complete with the huge American fridge, she lifted up her dress as the 'mom' to reveal her naked genitalia while she yelled some abuse at one of her children. Now it seems like nothing unusual, but to me at the time, it was a revelation.

Marina has refined this method of using a visual image to create a powerful minimalist effect, in her later work. In the opening image of *By The Bog of Cats...*, for example, Hester Swane drags a dead swan through the bog in the half light of dawn. In *On Raftery's Hill*, the glorious vision of the grandmother Shalome descends the staircase in Raftery's horrendously dark, fetid farmhouse, her floating white, chiffon wedding dress offsetting the darkness of her surroundings, suitcase clutched in her hand, ready to journey to a better place. *Low in the Dark* is full of these images.

I went to see a Butoh company from Japan playing in New York's City Hall, and outside in the street entertaining the 'line' were black kids spinning on their heads and back flipping to the accompaniment of a loud rap song on the ghetto blaster. Both performances were terrific. Central Park and Washington Square Park in Greenwich Village were full of performances of all sorts. There were some great shocking 'in your face' black street comedians. The whole city was like a reality performance, particularly for an Irish person at the time, unused to the blaze of difference and multiculture. When I left Ireland in 1983 it was relatively monoethnic, and in terms of the arts in general and theatre in particular there was little cross disciplinary work going on. A play was a play, it was strictly word based and the idea of actors being trained in the use of their bodies was just starting. Chris O'Neill had started off the Oscar Theatre School where his brother Vincent taught movement. The idea of an image-based theatre was very much in its germinal stage and didn't enjoy the popularity it does today. *The Great Hunger*, a piece of physical theatre adapted by Tom Mac Intyre from Patrick Kavanagh's poem, and which premiered at the National Theatre in Dublin in 1983 directed by Patrick Mason, had stretched the boundaries, but they were still holding tight.

I found out years later that Marina had actually been working in New York around the time that I had, for at least a year. She taught girls in a convent school, but carried in her briefcase her Levis for after work and her Marlboro Lights. Being in New York must have affected her slant on things. The streets and bars were full of material for writing and characters. Every hobo had a story. You could be listening to what you thought was a basket case ranting at the corner of 42nd street and Eighth Avenue, (it was a spot!), and after five minutes realize that what he was saying made enormous sense. The hookers, cross dressers and coke dealers who took their break at night where I worked were full of loud colourful theatricality. A situation would flare up, everyone would be involved and then it would be over as quickly as in *Low in the Dark*. Life in New York was extreme, like a drug, the highs not possible without the incredible lows. This sense of the two sided coin of black despair and sharp cutting humour is present all the time in Marina's work.

There is a scene in *Low in the Dark* where Binder and Bender are involved in one of their 'role plays'. Bender plays a cool black dude who approaches Binder asking her where she is from: 'Ireland' she answers 'I'm Irish'. I used to love playing those lines having been that Irish person often. It was the face I used to do that I loved, the open-faced, naive, recognizable 'I'm Irish, just arrived' face that you could spot a mile off in New York then. Now we are far too cool and cosmopolitan, the Irish in New York blend in perfectly. In Act One, Scene Four, Bender talks of the black hobo that she met:

> **BENDER**: God I'm stuck, just like that black hobo on east 51st one evening. 'Lady,' he said, 'Lady I'm stuck here a long time!' 'so am I,' I answered, 'so am I' [...] But I gave him a dollar and he gave me a light, then he invited me to stay with him on the cardboard [...] The pair of us could still be there, a trash can for a pillow [...] His lice ridden head on my breast, maybe I woul' have been happy there, maybe. (*LITD*: p.53)

But it isn't just the above that makes me think of New York. It was the brave and quite radical way that the play was written. It had the mad energy of New York. You could jump into a character and then out into another one, change scene, jump back again. Everything was so colourful and zany: music, dance, tragedy, comedy, crazy costumes, crazy set.

Low in the Dark

The stage was split into two sections. Stage right was the 'men's area', composed of a wall that was in the process of being built – the men's work. Stage left was the 'women's area', a bathroom with a toilet, bath and shower. Curtains was free to wander into either area. A very enigmatic character, she wore what could only be described as 'a set' as a costume. She was literally a walking curtain. She couldn't be seen at all for the duration of the play. The set was cleverly realized by Liz Cullinane, how, we never understood, being aware only too well of the budget involved.

There was an assortment of props that were integral to the action, the main one being THE SCARF. Both Dermod and Peter cite learning to knit as being a definite cool aspect of the whole experience, that and the high heels they had to wear during their various role plays. The knitting of the scarf repre-sented 'female action' and it grew longer and longer throughout the play. Everyone, except Curtains, got to knit as they were all at some stage pregnant. There was always a moment of panic off stage when Dermod and I had to remember which of us was wearing the scarf, (the leader), and which of us was doing the knitting, (being led). Curtains had a carpet beater which she kept hidden behind the curtains, and which she and other characters used to beat her when necessary. The lads had a handbag with various items, for when they played the different women in their respective lives, lipstick being of paramount importance to both the men and women, like war paint in preparation for battle.

There were dozens of babies, made up of wrapped, stuffed cotton, with different colour codes. In the bath, Bender was constantly dropping babies and feeding them, and demanding more. Both Bender and myself had fantastic John Paul Gaultier style boned costumes with cone shaped 'boobs', Madonna style. The 'boobs' unzipped to reveal babies' faces on them. We were constantly unzipping them to feed the babies. Act Two Scene Seven is a poignant scene between Peter 'an other' son who comes to meet his estranged mother Bender in her spot in the bath:

> **BAXTER**: Mother it's Baxter.
> **BENDER**: Baxter…(*Trying to remember*) Baxter…were you the one who raped me?
> **BAXTER**: No.
> **BENDER**: Or the one who used to beat me ?
> **BAXTER**: Used you wear red ?
> **BENDER**: Never wore red.
> **BAXTER**: The one I hit wore red.
> **BENDER**: Bet she deserved it.

BAXTER: No.
BENDER: Stealing a son off his mother like that. I'd hit her as well. A good clout puts manners on them when they're young…what's your name again? (*LITD*: p.86)

In an attempt at motherly contact of some sort, just before he leaves, she offers him her breast:

BENDER: (*offering breast*) Are you hungry?
BAXTER: Not any more.(*Gets out of bath and kisses her*) Lovely to see you.
BENDER: (*going off*). Call again soon, do you hear me now, call again, next time I'll remember you. (*Exit BENDER*). (*LITD*: p.87)

Although the pathos of this scene is offset by its humour, it provides a hint of the themes Marina keeps returning to in her later work, such as the notion that mothers just cannot seem to provide any real sustenance for their offspring: it seems to be part of the human condition that they are unable to help alleviate the suffering of the children that they have been instrumental in creating.

The characters represented general patterns of human behaviour and desires. The women represented the presumed female concerns such as reproduction and attracting men; the men the preoccupations of finding, keeping and to some extent understanding their particular women, whilst maintaining their building role with the wall. Interestingly, the men spent much more time trying to figure out what the women were thinking or acting than the women did in reverse. Throughout the play all the characters were involved in 'opposite sex' role play. Baxter and Bone would take turns in being the woman in 'the relationship', which led to some great fun for them as well as the audience.

Act One, Scene Two

> **BAXTER** and **BONE** *come on stage right.* **BONE** *has his arm around* **BAXTER** *as if they are a married couple.* **BAXTER** *wears high heels, a woman's hat, a dress, and a necklace around his neck. He looks pregnant.*

> **BAXTER**: (*Woman's voice*): You're marvellous darling, you really are.
> **BONE**: (*Pointing to the wall*): So you like it?
> **BAXTER**: (*Examining the wall*): It's exactly what we needed....exactly.
> **BONE**: (*Thrilled*): Do you think?
> **BAXTER**: How high will you build it ?
> **BONE**: Well how high would you like it ?
> **BAXTER**: I don't mind as long as it's higher than everyone else's. (***BONE*** *has begun building*) Can I help ?
> **BONE**: I think you should do your knitting.
> **BAXTER**: I want to help with the wall!
> **BONE**: Knit darling knit. (*LITD*: p.16)

Even in the later plays we can see this divide. The women are obsessed with the artistic or the romantic, the notion of 'the story' that is separate from the here and now. The men are preoccupied with the land or the accumulation of money: 'the wall'. They see the possibility of their redemption through their future achievements or the goals that they hope to fulfil.

Peter remembered that Marina had had an idea for the play, that she got from the notion that there was, in some men, a sort of pregnancy envy, that some old bachelors grew humps on their shoulders as a sort of surrogate pregnancy: by the end of the play everyone has been pregnant except for Curtains.

There is a brilliant, farcical, theatrical humour about the procreation theme. Bender gets some of the best speeches. In Act One, Scene Five she is looking for one of her dozens of babies, the Pope, but she can't find him in the bath. The mother here is the one to select one of her offspring to raise him as a future religious figure: she colludes in the institutional hierarchies and repressions whose effects we hear about today:

> **BENDER**: I want the Pope! Get me the Pope!
> **BINDER**: (*Flings the Pope at her*): He's not Pope yet!
> **BENDER**: Woe betide you when he is! Neglecting him like that! (*She gives reverential and preferential treatment to the Pope.*)
> **BINDER**: You fed him already! (*Exits.*)
> **BENDER**: I'll feed him again. I want him fat and shiny. Holy Father, (*Bows to the baby*) you'll pull your auld mother up by the hair of her chinny chin chin, won't you ? We'll have tea in the

palace and I'll learn Italian and the pair of us side by side,
launching crusades, banning divorce, denying evolution, destroying the pill, canonizing witches. Oh a great time we'll have,
you singing the Latin with a tower of a hat on you, the big stick
in your rubied fist and them all craw-thumping around the hem
of your frock and whispering for miracles. And me sitting there
as proud as punch in the middle of the incense and the choir.
Oh a great time we'll have, the pair of us, we will surely. (*LITD*:
pp.54-55)

This passage doesn't seem at all absurd now, with all the scien-
tific and religious mania and confusion that is going on at the
moment about when exactly life starts? Whose embryos are
whose? When does an embryo become a human? When does a
male become a male or is he just a bastardized female who has
received too much testosterone in the womb? Whose rib was
given to whom? Nature versus nurture? These questions are
being analysed constantly and in great detail. There is a huge
fascination with the genetic versus environmental question.
How much of our lives are we actually responsible for, or have
we any control over? Do we just, as seems an overriding theme
in Marina's work, keep repeating the appalling patterns of
human behaviour despite our attempts to the contrary?

In *Low in the Dark* many issues are dealt with in a general
way that become more personalized in her later work. However
the basic inevitability of human culpability, or the human condition remains constant. In *Low in the Dark* we don't feel so tragi-
cally about the fate or history of the individual characters because they look and act in an 'absurd' way, and display an almost Beckettian appreciation of the humour which is absolutely
integral to our human condition. Baxter and Bone work in
tandem as characters, their theatrical power comes from their
'Laurel and Hardy meets Beckett' exchanges. They are, to me,
forerunners of Maggie May and Senchil Doorley, from *Portia
Coughlan*. In this passage, Bone has become pregnant by Binder,
and Baxter and himself are discussing the problem:

Act Two, Scene Five

> **BONE**: You were a Caesarean baby ?
> **BAXTER**: Of course.
> **BONE**: No wonder you're so balanced. I was a natural birth.
> From paradise I came, through the chink, to this galaxy of grief.
> I'll never forget it and I'll never forgive her for it. Purged from
> the womb, jostled down the long passage, the umbilical around
> me neck, the grunting, the groaning, the blood, the shit, the piss,
> and the first scream, there was the point of no return. A rough
> start to a rough journey I tell you. I wouldn't wish life on my
> worst enemy, I'll have an abortion.
> **BAXTER**: We're all abortions, some later than others, that's all.
> But look on the good side Bone. Life is short, soon we'll be
> dead. (*LITD*: p.80)

Low in the Dark incorporated many aspects of absurd theatre:
fractured characterization, non-linear story and non-sequential
script. Thus at times for the performer it could be a particular
character you were playing, maybe many different characters,
but they each had a sense of logic to them. At other times, there
could be many different stories being told at the same time with
no reference to each other. These parts were most intense when
Curtains was present. We would all have our individual lines
which had no relation to the other actors' lines. Each one's lines
had a logical throughline of their own but not to anyone else's.
Whilst concentrating on your own throughline, you also had to
watch out for the rapid rhythm that the scene was firing along
on and not miss your cue. I dreaded these scenes for fear I
would throw everyone else. The worst of these was the 'eejit'
scene where we would end up screaming 'eejit' at each other
according to a strict pattern. (*LITD*: pp.89-91) It was like rehearsing music.

However, the intensity of performing prevented me at the
time from appreciating the depth of Curtains's story. When I
read the play again I was thrilled by its dark beauty. Marina's
plays read so well. It is in her story as well as in the occasional
monologues by other characters that we hear an echo of the
minor chord of dread that is so much a part of the later plays.

Brid had real difficulty in finding a path to play the part as she could not use her physicality in the normal way, being shrouded in curtains! However, through this restriction she found a new freedom for her voice, which was probably the idea. Beckett used this method very sucessfully. It allows the actor to create a distance from the words in order for them to exist in the mind of the audience long after the show is over. Brid also had to react and interact with Baxter and Bender quite a lot so she had to constantly switch roles. In Act One, Scene Six, she speaks of the journey of the man from the north and the woman from the south:

> **CURTAINS**: They agreed to be silent. They were ashamed, for the man and the woman had become like two people anywhere, walking low in the dark through a dead universe. There seemed no reason to go on. There seemed no reason to stop.(*LITD*: p.59)

It is impossible in an essay to give the full flavour of her story. You'll just have to go and read it, and while you are at it read all the others, as the characters that had their beginnings in this 'absurd' play are developed further in her later ones. Marina's sense of fun and the ridiculous have been retained despite the seriousness of the later subject matter.

My two favourite characters from Marina's plays are Tilly from *Ullaloo* (1991), and Shalome from *On Raftery's Hill* (2000). Both women are so much larger than life. Tilly is on a mission, the mission being to 'save' herself, not at all in the figurative sense, but literally, sensually. She covers one eye as she looks out through the other, trying to save her sight. She tries to close her ears so she doesn't waste her hearing. Speaking becomes a real difficulty and she even shortens words to their almost unrecognizable meaning. She lies in her hammock performing what is like a choreographic ritual, hiding her eyes with her hair, covering her ears, stopping her breath, much to the absolute frustration of her partner Tomred. There is a lovely eccentricity and gentility about her which has flavours of Shalome in *On Raftery's Hill*.[2]

> **SHALOME**: Don't you raise your voice to me! I hate it, young man, I hate it. I hate this world. People are just awful! They're so ridiculous with their noses and their necks and their hands and their stupid, stupid legs! I mean what are legs actually for?

Shalome is a fantastic character in the true sense of the word, she would certainly have been very comfortable in *Low in the Dark*. She reminds me of Curtains wandering across the stage telling her story to anyone who'll listen. She brings a moment of pure theatricality, her appearance generating a visceral sense of humour each time she appears in her wedding dress with her suitcase in her hand, to go back to 'Daddy'. We are rooting for her to succeed, to escape her sordid destiny, but we know that she never will. For me, the fabulousness of her character is what saves the play from being at times too dark to bear.

That sense of pure theatricality and wry humour is what we all loved about working on *Low in the Dark*. Music, lights, a word or a prop and you had transformed yourself for the moment, and the moment was all. As Binder says to Bender during a role play of one of Bender's ex-lovers:

> **BENDER**: Will we talk about us?
> **BINDER**: What about us? We're alive, we're together, we're rotting. (*LITD*: p.37)

---

[2] Marina Carr, *On Raftery's Hill*, (Oldcastle, Gallery Press, 2000), p.29.

2 | Woman on the Threshold:
J.M. Synge's *The Shadow of the Glen*,
Teresa Deevy's *Katie Roche* and
Marina Carr's *The Mai*

Anthony Roche

There have been two productions of Teresa Deevy's *Katie Roche* since the opening of the new Abbey in 1966 and the Peacock in 1967. The first, directed by Joe Dowling and with Jeananne Crowley in the title role, was produced on the main Abbey stage in 1975. The second, with Judy Friel directing Derbhle Crotty, was produced at the Peacock in April 1994. When the earlier production appeared, it did so as an isolated incident, since there was virtually no concurrent production of plays by Irish women playwrights at the time. The context had not changed utterly by 1994 when Irish women playwrights were (and are) still the exception. But a process of transformation was at least under way. Deirdre Ann Hines had won the 1991 Stewart Parker First Play Award for Pigsback's production of her *Howling Moons, Silent Sons.* Glasshouse Productions had not only staged new plays by Trudy Hayes, Clare Dowling and Emma Donoghue; but had also devised two anthology pieces, *There Are No Irish Woman Playwrights One* and *Two.* Where the first surveyed the work of contemporary women playwrights like Anne Devlin and Deirdre Hines, the second brought to light a line of Irish women playwrights through the century and included an extract from Deevy's *The King of Spain's Daughter.* In

1994, the Peacock presented Marina Carr's most accomplished play up to that point, *The Mai,* also named after its central female protagonist. Where Carr's previous plays had met with a mixed reception, *The Mai* was compared by the *Observer*'s Michael Coveney to the work of Eugene O'Neill, was awarded the prize for Best New Play of 1994's Irish Life Dublin Theatre Festival and played to packed houses.

Deevy's *Katie Roche* was consciously presented by the National Theatre's Artistic Director Patrick Mason in tandem with Frank O'Connor and Hugh Hunt's *Moses' Rock* as two Irish plays of the nineteen thirties, both focusing on the dilemma of a young woman whose independence is constrained by the circumstances in which she is placed. The two productions served to underscore the superiority of the Deevy play, particularly in the range and complexity of the woman character, and suggested that it should have occupied the main stage and *Moses' Rock* the Peacock. It was the joint appearance of Teresa Deevy's *Katie Roche* and Marina Carr's *The Mai* at the National Theatre in 1994 that provided the truest and most far-reaching grounds for comparison, a comparison that my article will pursue. Judy Friel's production featured a performance by Derbhle Crotty as Katie Roche which caught the youthful exuberance, contradictoriness and petulance of Deevy's heroine. Crotty also featured significantly in *The Mai,* as the title character's daughter (in the past) and as the figure who assumes responsibility for telling the Mai's story (in the present). The hat trick of Crotty's mercurial passage across the National Theatre's stages in 1994 was completed by her performance as Molly Byrne in Synge's *The Well of the Saints*. And Synge is crucial to my argument as well. His play, intended to open the Abbey Theatre in December 1904, was staged early in 1905 and was chosen by Patrick Mason to honour the seventy-fifth anniversary of the Irish National Theatre Society Ltd.

But the Synge play which is most relevant to any consideration of Teresa Deevy's *Katie Roche* is his *The Shadow of the Glen* of 1903. The controversy generated by *Shadow* accompanied the inauguration of an Irish theatre movement and focused its hostility on the representation of an unsatisfactory marriage

between an older man and a younger woman. What drew the
strongest protest was the action of the wife at the play's denouement. Rebutting as unjust the charge that he had said there
was no such thing as an unhappy marriage in Ireland, Arthur
Griffith went on in the pages of *The United Irishman* to indicate
where his real objection to Synge's play rested:

> Man and woman in rural Ireland, according to Mr. Synge,
> marry lacking love, and, as a consequence, the woman
> proves unfaithful. Mr. Synge never found that in Irish life.
> Men and women in Ireland marry lacking love, and live
> mostly in a dull level of amity. Sometimes they do not –
> sometimes the woman lives in bitterness – sometimes she
> dies of a broken heart – but she does not go away with the
> Tramp.[1]

Teresa Deevy follows up on Synge's play in two important
ways: by reproducing and extending the dramatic situation of an
older man married to a younger woman and by introducing the
figure of the Tramp at a key moment in each of *Katie Roche*'s
three acts. Where both Nora the character and Synge the playwright appear to find satisfactory an ending in which she goes
away with the tramp, Deevy has her own reasons – and they are
very different ones from Arthur Griffith's– for rejecting the
arrival of the Tramp in the Gregg household as a resolution of
the new Mrs Gregg's unhappiness.

A crucial element in both plays' dramatic treatment is the
heroine's positioning within a peasant cottage setting. The
house is what she has married into; and her increasing sense of
claustrophobia and confinement is counter-balanced by the
possibility of freedom beyond the cottage walls. The woman is
poised on the threshold between the security of 'in here' and
the potential of 'out there'. As these symbolic overtones accrue,
crossing over the cottage's front door becomes an increasingly
fraught activity for her, a breaching of boundaries which the
respectable husbands are anxious to keep in place. I will study

---

[1] Cited by Robert Hogan and James Kilroy, *Laying the Foundations
1902-1904: The Second Volume of The Modern Irish Drama* (Dublin:
Dolmen Press, 1976), p.79.

these issues as they are represented first in Synge's play, then in Deevy's, and ultimately in Carr's, where they are re-worked in a contemporary context: the unhappily married couple are now the same age, the Tramp has switched gender and the walls of the rural home have become transparently revealing but no less charged with danger for the woman they contain.

Synge's *The Shadow of the Glen* was only one of several important plays in the emerging Irish Dramatic Movement that fore-grounded a young woman about to be, or recently, married. These works dramatized her ambivalence through the medium of a peasant cottage setting. Synge gave the credit to Douglas Hyde's *Casadh an tSúgáin/ The Twisting of the Rope* when he wrote that it alone 'had the germ of a new dramatic form... [and] gave a new direction and impulse to Irish drama, a direction towards which, it should be added, the thoughts of Mr W.B. Yeats, Lady Gregory and others were already tending.'[2] Hyde's play is set in a cottage on the eve of a wedding and treats of the disruption caused when the wanderer Red Hanrahan has an almost mes-meric influence on the young bride-to-be, Oona. Only by a concerted communal effort is the threatening outsider removed and the wedding allowed to proceed as planned. The Yeats play referred to by Synge must surely have been *The Land of Heart's Desire* where the troubled spirit of a recently married young woman in the house of her husband's people summons up a fairy force to carry her away 'Where nobody gets old and godly and grave,/ where nobody gets old and crafty and wise,/ Where nobody gets old and bitter of tongue.'[3] Yeats and Lady Greg-ory's *Cathleen Ni Houlihan* contains the most politically national-ist version of this scenario: the young man about to be married is instead wooed to embrace martyrdom in the cause of Ireland. Synge's own thoughts were tending in the direction marked out by Hyde and were to achieve their fullest articulation in *The Playboy of the Western World,* a much more elaborate but still

---

[2] J.M Synge, 'The Dramatic Movement in Ireland', *The Abbey Theatre: Interviews and Recollections*, ed. by E.H. Mikhail (London: Macmillan, 1988), pp.54-5.

[3] *The Collected Plays of W.B. Yeats* (London: Macmillan, 1952), p.55.

recognizable working out of *The Twisting of the Rope* scenario: Christy Mahon arrives out of nowhere as the disruptive tramp figure and encounters Pegeen Mike as the young woman about to enter into a far from satisfying marriage with Shawn Keogh.

But *The Shadow of the Glen* also partakes of the same 'germs of a new drama' and develops it in a different direction. It does so by dealing with a young woman who is already, rather than on the verge of being, married. Here the degree of her distress conjures up, not the pre-Raphaelite fairy child of Yeats's play, but the much more sexually dangerous figure of an adult male. As the playwright Denis Johnston once remarked, the Tramp takes the place of the fairies in Synge's plays.[4] The two occasions on which the fairy forces gather close are at those two crucial periods of transition: an impending marriage or a recent death. The Tramp fears such a possibility, seeking to ward off any such visitation by wearing a needle as a talisman ('There's great safety in a needle, lady of the house')[5] and by saying the 'De Profundis'. But this corpse is anything but ethereal and is unlikely to draw extraordinary presences. Synge locates the true drama in the plight of Nora Burke rather than in the grotesque charade performed by her husband, Dan. The ostensible aim of the trick is to catch his wife in the act of adultery. Many cultures have such a folk-tale in their repertoire. The most famous, the Widow of Ephesus, is the one Synge was accused, by Griffith and others, of importing from abroad, from the classically derived and currently decadent milieu of the outside world, into the pure and chaste regions of Irish culture: 'To take the Widow of Ephesus and rechristen her Mrs. Burke and relabel Ephesus Wicklow is not a brilliant thing.'[6] As Synge was able to rebut, his source for the story could not have been more authentic and

---

[4] Denis Johnston, *John Millington Synge* (New York: Columbia University Press, 1965), p.14.

[5] J.M. Synge, *Collected Works, Volume III: Plays, Book One*, ed. by Ann Saddlemyer (London: Oxford University Press, 1968), p.41. All subsequent references to *The Shadow of the Glen* are from this edition and will be incorporated in the text.

[6] Cited in Hogan and Kilroy, p.78.

indigenous in terms of Irish culture, since he had it orally in Gaelic from the storyteller Pat Dirane on the Aran Islands. As he records in *The Aran Islands,* 'Pat told me a story of an unfaithful wife'.[7] In reproducing the story Synge marks it off from his own narrative, attributes it to its storytelling source and observes: 'In stories of this kind he always speaks in the first person, with minute details to show that he was present at the scenes that are described.'[8] Synge has already submitted the story to a degree of translation, by moving from Irish to English, from oral storytelling to a printed prose narrative. But he has preserved the details and sentiments of what he was told. It is in the dramatic version that the sympathies are going to be radically displaced.

In his storytelling, Pat Dirane remains a neutral observer for much of the narrative of the unfaithful wife, a personal witness of the event itself. He is brought in out of the cold by the woman of the house while travelling from Galway to Dublin, given first a cup of tea, then spirits and a pipe. When she leaves, her dead husband sits up and discloses the traditional kernel of the narrative: '"I've got a bad wife, stranger, and I let on to be dead the way I'd catch her goings on." Then he got two fine sticks he had to keep down his wife, and he put them at each side of his body, and he laid himself out again as if he was dead.' When the wife returns with a young man, they head for the bedroom and the narrative rushes to its melodramatic and bloody conclusion:

> Then the dead man got up, and he took one stick, and he gave the other to myself. We went in and we saw them lying together with her head on his arm. The dead man hit him a blow with the stick so that the blood out of him leapt up and hit the gallery. That is my story.

The storyteller's sympathies are implicitly aligned with the old man, once he has been told the situation. The producing of

---

[7] J.M. Synge, *Collected Works, Volume II: Prose*, ed. by Alan Price (London: Oxford University Press, 1966), p.70.

[8] *Ibid.*, p.72.

the two sticks and his acceptance of one of them signals his adherence to a code of behaviour in which wives who do not submit to being 'kept down' must be made to by physical force. The old man's stick figures prominently in Synge's *The Shadow of the Glen*; and in Deevy's *Katie Roche* the play's most shocking action occurs when a man raises a stick *'with surprising vigour … [and] hits her across the shoulders.* KATIE *collapses on to a chair. Groans. Silence …'*[9]. Synge makes a significant alteration in the received tale when he reduces the number of sticks to one and associates the weapon absolutely with the vengeful husband, Dan Burke. As the Tramp does what he is instructed and furnishes the dead man with the stick, his tone of innocent enquiry prompts the justifying statement: 'It's a long time I'm keeping that stick, for I've a bad wife in the house.' (p.43) The appearance of the black stick suggests to an audience that the play is heading in the bloody direction of the original, with the cheated husband despatching his male usurper and teaching his trespassing wife a lesson. But the Tramp then makes a crucial intervention by directing his sympathy away from the self-righteous husband towards the threatened figure of the wife; 'Is it herself, master of the house, and she a grand woman to talk?' Far from maintaining the alignment between the storyteller and the old man, the play has opened up a gap between them and developed a potentially disruptive alignment of the Tramp with the wife that the old man is quick to detect and warn against. He does so by repeating his original claim, not once but twice, that he has 'a bad wife'; each repetition falls like a verbal blow and each carries less conviction, failing to receive implicit assent from the on-stage audience of one. As he hears his wife and Michael Dara returning, Dan asks the Tramp to put the stick 'here in the bed' with him and to smooth out the sheets so it will not be noticed. When he later rises from the bed to denounce the lovers and shake his stick at them, the physical

---

[9] Teresa Deevy, *Three Plays: Katie Roche, The King of Spain's Daughter, The Wild Goose* (London: Macmillan, 1939), p.59. All subsequent quotations from *Katie Roche* are from this edition and will be incorporated in the text.

threat betrays its psychosexual nature: 'you'll see the thing I'll give you will follow you on the back mountains when the wind is high'. (p.53) Dan Burke's marital ambition is giving lumps, not making children, and the stick figures throughout Synge's play as the sign of the old man's impotence rather than the rule by which the sexual regulation of society is administered.

Much of the deviation of the later stages of Synge's *The Shadow of the Glen* from its Aran Island source derives from the crucial intervention made by the Tramp in the direction the plot is going to take. The ground for that pivotal shift of emphasis, away from the punishing husband towards the threatened wife, has already been prepared earlier in the play. The major addition that Synge makes there, while at one level he is following the direction and action of his source, is to introduce a lengthy and revealing dialogue between Nora Burke and the Tramp. Rather than being presented as a grotesque incident in its own right, the device of the dead man stretched out on the table is pressed into service as a psychological index of the relationship between the married couple. Under the Tramp's gentle prompting, Nora speaks of the life she has led across a span of years and of the lack of intimacy afflicting their union: 'Maybe cold would be no sign of death with the like of him, for he was always cold, every day since I knew him, – and every night, stranger'. (p.35) From the beginning of the play, Nora breaks with one of the most binding and enduring taboos in Irish society, of discussion of intimate relations between a married couple. She follows this with an implicitly feminist declaration, that she 'never knew what way I'd be afeard of beggar or bishop or any man of you at all ...' (p.37) Synge's play, then, rapidly establishes Nora's orality as the potential site and source of her greatest freedom, that zone of language in which she builds up an autonomy and self-deriving authority that is most at odds with her social situation. Characteristically, that talk is reduced and dismissed as 'blathering' (p.43) by her husband when he revives and chides the Tramp for encouraging and participating in it.

The figure that serves to indicate the greatest level of shared verbal intimacy between the wife and the Tramp is the enigmatic and recently deceased Patch Darcy. The Tramp's mention of his name provokes a jolt of recognition in Nora, who then gives the basis of their relationship: 'God spare Darcy, he'd always look in here and he passing up or passing down, and it's very lonesome I was after him a long while […], and then I got happy again […] for I got used to being lonesome.' (p.30) Immediately preceding an enquiry about her young lover Michael Dara, Nora's is a highly ambiguous statement, challenging any audience in its received interpretation of marital fidelity. A sexual implication is unavoidable, but no less so is the portrayal of Nora's loneliness in this travesty of a marriage. Indeed, her remark about Patch Darcy 'passing up and passing down' is later echoed by the most parodied lines in the play, where what Nora beholds when she looks out the door is the omnipresent evidence of the mist, an echo suggesting the extent to which a human face might alleviate the emptiness of her daily existence.

The remark about Patch Darcy 'looking in' on Nora is repeated by Michael Dara as an item of gossip in the neighbourhood; here its connotations are exclusively sexual. Nora Burke does not deny the physical aspect of the attraction. Rather she expands it to cover talking and looking, confirming that she has had many suitors and is a woman of exacting standards: 'it's a hard woman I am to please this day, Michael Dara …' (p.49) The central question posed by the play, why such an independent and fiery young woman should have settled for an old man as husband, is answered by Nora as another question, clarifying the stark choices facing women in Irish society at the turn of the century: 'What way would I live, and I an old woman, if I didn't marry a man with a bit of a farm […]?'(p.49) If she takes comfort from the men passing on the roads, she recognizes her own lost opportunities, the rights she appears to have forfeited by her match: to have two or three children like her friend Mary Brien, to have the right to wander where she pleases and to talk with whom she pleases.

The ending of Synge's play marks the most significant revision. In this household that may appear rustic and remote, its bourgeois origins are manifested in the punishment which the husband visits upon his wife: showing her the door in the

recognizably Victorian pose of the affronted patriarch banishing the fallen woman from the home. With the recognition that
the supposedly dead husband is still very much alive and that
there is accordingly no inheritance to marry into, Michael reveals his callow and callous nature when he rejects Nora and
suggests that she go off to the workhouse. The ground by
which the Tramp steps in and is prepared to make his offer,
that Nora accompany him to a life of greater freedom on the
open roads, has been prepared for earlier, as we have seen,
through their discussion of Patch Darcy. And Nora accepts
with her well-known line: 'you've a fine bit of talk, stranger, and
it's with yourself I'll go.' (p.57) The essentially verbal and fictive
nature of the reality the Tramp presents to Nora has long been
recognized and is of a piece with the more complex storytelling
procedures of Martin Doul in *The Well of the Saints* and Christy
Mahon in *The Playboy of the Western World*. When the scene is
viewed without the language and its seductions, however, the
resolution of the play becomes more suspect. Iconically, the
woman is seen to be passed from one male figure who has
definitively rejected her to another who now relinquishes his
claim until a third steps in and takes her on. Nowhere is Synge's
modification of Ibsen's *A Doll's House* more apparent than
when he has his Nora shrink from or never appear to consider
the possibility of going through the door on her own. Renewed
attention to the language of Synge's conclusion shows the
extent to which the Tramp's language takes over, telling Nora
over and over what she'll be saying and what she'll be hearing.
The current of the final scene is a virtual monologue to which
she ultimately accedes. Nora's own powerful speech has reas-
serted itself in one final turn of sympathy for the husband she is
leaving. But for the most part she is silenced as, in Synge's later
works, Mary Doul and the Widow Quin will be as their plays
draw to their denouement.

What Teresa Deevy recognizes in Synge's *The Shadow of the
Glen* is the all-pervasiveness of the patriarchy. It extends beyond
the alliance in the play's sardonic closing image of the husband
and the lover, having banished the woman, sitting down together to occupy the house and to share a drink. She sees

clearly that this patriarchal hegemony is *not* transcended by Nora's decision to leave with the Tramp but rather that it is continued and extended; Nora leaves at his suggestion and on his terms. At a key moment in each of her play's three acts, Teresa Deevy brings the Syngean figure of the Tramp into *Katie Roche*. The Tramp who appears in the Gregg cottage is looked to by the young wife as a wise man, a Christian ascetic who yet retains his pagan sympathies through continued intimacy with the natural world. Yet *he* is the one who brings the stick crashing down on her back for not observing the strict letter of her marriage with Stanislaus Gregg. The play's most important disclosure, scarcely credible on the level of probability but absolutely accurate in terms of the play's symbolic and social values, is that Reuben the Tramp is the orphan Katie Roche's natural father:

> **KATIE**: A man off the road to talk like that!
> **REUBEN**: (*Gentle*): Yes, – I'm a man off the road – and your father. (p.60)

Reuben's gentleness does not last long. Where Katie claims the same licence that her father has asserted in his actions and declares that she will 'make [her] own goodness', he urges her in wrathful Old Testament terms to be 'a good wife' (p.60). In Act Three he returns to pass on this advice directly to Stanislaus, arguing repeated applications of the stick we have earlier seen him wield with such force:

> **REUBEN**: I'd give her a flogging. She'll make her own goodness. What does that mean? She won't be punished. […] What she needs is humiliation, – if she was thoroughly humbled she might begin to learn. (p.105)

The complicity between the Tramp and the husband is briefly acknowledged at this point. When it is revealed that Reuben is Katie's natural father, Stan is obliged to show him a certain deference. His more habitual response to the arrival of the Tramp has been to indicate by a frozen formality that he wants him gone and to express bourgeois disapproval that this wild man of the roads has been let into the house by his wayward wife. He responds with '*surprise*' to Reuben's suggestion that he should beat his wife. Stan has his own more civilized methods of maintaining control: the weapons of speech and silence have now fully taken over from the big stick.

The other central feature of Synge's play that Deevy develops and explores across three acts is the dramatic situation of marriage between an older man and a younger woman. *Katie Roche* is quite explicit in its details about the gap of age and experience separating Katie from Stan. Stanislaus Gregg is introduced as '*a short stoutish man of about forty-five*' (p.7). He comes slowly into his sister's cottage as the play opens, moving to stand in the sunlight that is streaming through the window. Katie, who then enters bearing a teatray, is described as '*not yet twenty*' (p.8) and, in the one additional piece of information that Deevy supplies about her, is distinguished by '*a sort of inward glow, which she continually tries to smother and which breaks out in delight or desperation according to circumstances*'. In the Peacock production, director Judy Friel beautifully conveyed Katie Roche's inward glow of youthful possibility by starting the play with Katie already on, standing at the window in the afternoon sun and basking in its light. As a result of this, Stan's muted entrance was all of a piece, the first inevitable clouding or, to use Deevy's term, smothering.

Any possible equality that might exist between this man and this woman is heavily undercut in the play's clear representation of the givens of the social, economic and symbolic relations between them all the more relevant in that he has come expressly to ask her to marry him. The economic conditions are not equal. Katie, as we all too readily see from her entrance, is employed as a domestic in the Gregg household and is always on the watch for the return of her employer, Stan's older sister Amelia. But Stan's relationship to Katie is more exactly that of her employer, since it later emerges that he is the one who provides his sister with a subsistence on which she lives and that Amelia defers to her brother's every wish and opinion. Stan economically controls the lives of both the women in the play, and this contributes to the ways in which the Amelia plot is a parodic double of Stan's courtship and marriage of Katie Roche. That the proposal of marriage to her by her ostensible employer's brother alters very little of the power relations governing Katie Roche's existence is borne out in the early months of their married life in Act Two, where Katie reacts to the return of Amelia by rushing to prepare her tea.

The romantic fixation by which Stan has long determined that he will make Katie Roche his wife is not only put in question by our realization that he has had her in mind as a sexual partner since she was a child but by his insistence as employer that his demands must be acceded to. Although Stan has declared more than once that she is free to do as she wishes, and although Katie has at first responded to his proposal in the negative, he withdraws and bides his time. Amelia is deployed as the appropriate medium to convey his wishes:

> **AMELIA**: Katie, Mr. Gregg said to tell you, I mean Stan said to tell you –
> **KATIE**: What? (*Apprehensive.*)
> **AMELIA**: He's in the little room, if you care to go to him.
> **KATIE** (*Rises, alarmed.*): Must I go now?
> **AMELIA**: Do whatever you wish, dear. He said not to try to influence you. Do whatever you wish… (*Withdraws.*) (p.42).

In the brief interim she was alone on stage, Derbhle Crotty physically conveyed this most wrenching moment of the play's first act by twisting and turning her body on the rack of indecision – or rather in the constrained space of the lack of any real alternative. The dramatic and social situations directly contradict the reiterated verbal assertion that she is absolutely free to do what she wishes.

Stan steps back into the room to draw Katie into his arms and into the agreement that she will marry him. He compliments her on her decision as 'a good girl' (p.42). Throughout the remaining two acts, Katie is to grow increasingly irked by her husband's references to her as a little girl. They suggest, of course, that he is not taking her seriously as an equal partner in the marriage, that she is being treated rather like Nora in *A Doll's House*. But the term also brings out the extent to which Stan is old enough to be Katie's father and that as a result there is something profoundly wrong about their entering into mar-

riage. What gives the suggestion strength is the elaborate confession Stan makes during his proposal by which it emerges that
he could indeed have been her father, not just symbolically but
literally. He reveals that as a young man he was in love with
Katie's natural mother:

> **STAN**: Katie, your mother, Mary Halnan, was a wonderful
> woman. She was beautiful and all that. A crowd of them,
> long ago, were in love with her. I loved her; I could have
> knocked down the world for her. But – she said I was too
> young. (p.14)

This revelation immediately precedes his proposal. Katie,
confused by this doubling of her own identity with the ghost of
her dead mother, can only respond: 'Now is it ... or ... or
then?' (p.15) She is not taken seriously in her desires and expressions by this older man not only because she is a woman
and extremely young but because by doubling for her absent
mother she is a substitute for a beautiful romantic icon.

Katie Roche, it might be argued, has her own romantic
yearnings: to come from an aristocratic line, to enter a convent.
She certainly has her illusions about what married life with
Stanislaus will be like. But her romantic dreams must be seen in
the context provided by Stan's *idée fixe* about her. His romantic
obsession ('a long time ago I made up my mind that I'd marry
Katie', (p.39)), proceeds from the fact of his economic empow-
erment, as her employer and therefore a man able to be master-
ful; his desires may be enforced because they are underwritten
by the society and his secure place within it:

> **STAN**: Now I don't suppose you know why I'm here – because
> how could you?
> **KATIE**: Sure I couldn't. Unless you were short of the money
> and to stop here while you'll make more.
> **STAN**: I was not short of money. I'm thinking of buying this
> place.
> **KATIE**: And what would become of me? (p.13)

Katie's romantic yearnings, by contrast, proceed from and
are fuelled by her powerlessness. She announces early on that
she intends to be a nun. The proposal is scoffed at and even the

audience can see that this wildly impulsive young woman is not about to go quietly into a convent. The idea was formed early in life by her reading of the *Spiritual Maxims* and of the lives of women saints – almost the only female role models that would have been available to her in anything but romantic fiction. Katie's reservations about the convent as a means to sainthood derive from personal experience. For working at Miss Gregg's, as she says herself, is preferable to 'minding the kids at the convent beyond … When you'd be working for nuns you'd never be finished. *(Moves about her work.)* In at half-eight every night. But they had a grand library.' (p.12) Her experience of the nuns would derive from the long-prevalent practice in Ireland of farming out illegitimate young women to work as unpaid labour in convents. She has been rescued from this fate, first through adoption by the Mrs Roche who seems to have given her little but a distinguished name, then by working for the relatively benign Amelia. The stigma of illegitimacy can be erased in only a few instances: entering a convent she imagines to be one of them.

In the matter of forming relations in the secular world, Katie fears that her lack of a name will militate against her chance of a good match. In particular, she worries that her affair with the young Michael will founder on that rock of respectability. The Michael of *Katie Roche* is just like his namesake in the Synge play, proving as spineless before Stan Gregg as Nora's lover did before old Dan Burke. When Stan asks Michael if he has any intentions towards Katie, he denies those we have already heard him promise her with the man-to-man remark:

> What chance has she? Sure there's no one round here would think of her for want of a name. […] My mother would die if I were to bring her in the door. (pp.36-7)

In the face of a social reality which denies her any proper place, Katie instead is prone to romanticize her origins. She does so by imagining that she comes from an aristocratic background. When her father reveals himself to her, he does so with the avowed aim of beating such pride out of her. But his revelation confirms that behind the fictional persona of the Tramp

Reuben lies Fitzsimon of Kylebeg, just as behind the letters to
the actress Molly Allgood signed 'Your Old Tramp' lay John
Millington Synge, a scion of the landed ascendancy class. Where
Synge disguised his landed status in the guise of an unaccom-
modated Tramp, Reuben is revealed not as a Tramp but as an
errant member of the ascendancy class. The notions of nobility
that Katie asserts ('I'll be a great woman. I'll make my own
goodness', (p.60)) are less those of aspiration to a decaying
social order than a Yeatsian aristocracy of the individual. Katie
Roche's exercise in personal style and self-invention works
against the shortcomings and fragmentations of the society in
which she has been raised. The more general question that
emerges for her is: what am I to do, what course of action to
pursue to lead a meaningful life? The feminist dimension of the
question is expressed through the mirroring of Katie's plight in
the subplot involving Amelia Gregg, herself the recipient of an
unexpected marriage proposal from a long-time suitor. The
degree of sisterly feeling that develops between Katie and
Amelia leads the latter in Act Three to a most uncharacteristic
challenging of her brother's decision to punish Katie by taking
her away:

> **AMELIA**: Stan, Katie is very good.
> **STAN**: Thank you, Amelia.
> **AMELIA**: No, – but I mean, she does her best. She's a brave
> little soul. I think you're not quite fair to her, Stan! I came back
> to say that. (*Puts her hands on **STANISLAUS**'s shoulders. He does
> not move. She withdraws*). (pp.107-8)

The most romantic conception of herself that Katie Roche
owns, which she brings with her into the marriage with Stan, is
one that is intimately related to Teresa Deevy as a woman
playwright working within the inherited patriarchal structures of
Irish, as indeed of most, theatre. For this heroine conceives of
her life as inherently theatrical and of her identity as a restless
search for the role that will most fulfil her desires. What the
experience of married life teaches Katie is that her view of what
is acceptably dramatic does not accord with her husband's. This
is confirmed by what Stan says in responding to one of Katie's

gestures: 'Very romantic. You're not taking part in theatricals now.' (p.63) What has prompted her to go ahead and marry Stan is the possibility he holds out that she might help him in his work. There is much in Deevy's approach that recalls the drama of Ibsen; I have already mentioned Nora's plight in *A Doll's House* in relation to both the Synge and Deevy plays. The ironic, tragic gap between the heightened expectations with which Katie approaches life and the banal, humdrum routine embraced by her husband recalls the marriage in *Hedda Gabler*. Both the Ibsen and the Deevy convey a sense of the heroine operating at one level of theatrical reality while the play in which she finds herself trapped insists on operating at another. The cramped theatrical environment in which Hedda Gabler and Katie Roche must live seems determined to frustrate their ever-altering desires, to allow them no adequate expression. The fact that Stanislaus Gregg is an architect, and in particular the scene at the opening of Act Two, argue that Deevy is also re-working Ibsen's *Master Builder*. There, the ageing architect Solness is rescued from his soured marriage and his compromised artistic ideals by the arrival of a young woman who remembers him at his most inspired. This resembles the role Katie sees for herself in marrying her architect husband, that she will inspire him to create his romantic structures. In describing Stan's drawings to Amelia, Katie's account echoes *The Master Builder*:

> Can you see it all now like it was built there before you? The spire – can you see it? With maybe the sun shining on it? (pp.46-7)

Stan does not respond to Katie as Solness does to Hilde Wangel but rather as the Master Builder does to his wife, re-garding her as an encumbrance and a reproach. By combining the two figures of the wife and the young woman that Ibsen keeps apart and polarizes, Teresa Deevy shifts the focus away from the demanding sexual egotism of the male artist towards the denial of those women whose lives are subject to his every whim.

Katie's response to Stan's anal retentiveness, his withholding of any real exchange about his architectural designs to her, is to turn once more to the outside world, to assert her independence by going out the door. The consequences are more grave in Act Two than they were in Act One, since she is now a married woman. This move in turn brings us back to Synge and what he, rather than Ibsen, had represented on and for the Irish stage. As with *The Shadow of the Glen* and those early Abbey plays the setting of *Katie Roche* is within a rural cottage, now extended across three acts rather than one. And Katie Roche is a more liminal character than Nora Burke, whose legitimacy is not in question. Katie is marginal to the Gregg household and to the society of the play because of the clouded, indeterminate nature of her origins. She has two father figures, a man of the roads who betrays an aristocratic background and a respectable bourgeois who signals the consolidation of the Catholic middle-classes in the professions. She has two mothers, her natural mother Mary Halnan whom she knows only by romantic report and the Mrs Roche who helped to raise her. She has two employers, ostensibly Amelia Gregg, actually Stanislaus. And there are two milieus in the play with which she is associated and to which she is attracted, the outside world of music, dancing and walks across the hills and the inside world of an economic comfort and social respectability she has all along been denied.

The conflict in Act One centres on Katie's desire to go to a dance, to celebrate the annual regatta. The time is August and the season connects the dance with the idea of a harvest festival. In the design at the Peacock, a cornfield was visible outside the door, recalling as it must the setting and action of Friel's *Dancing at Lughnasa*. Friel's play is set in the same period as Deevy's and the lives of his women bear on hers. The nineteen thirties was the period in Ireland when opposition to dancing of both the foreign ('jazz') and native ('crossroads') variety was mounting; by the time Eamon de Valera came to apotheosize those comely maidens dancing at the crossroads in 1943, they had ceased as a social reality and become entirely symbolic. Amelia opposes Katie going to the dance on the grounds that dancing is neither 'nice' nor respectable and that she would not wish it for herself. Despite Katie's plea to Stan that he intervene on her behalf, he backs up his sister in her disapproval, not wanting to see the young woman he is romanticizing make herself cheap, or move outside the strict control of his gaze. Katie's failure to go to the dance lingers over the Deevy play as that of the Mundy sisters does over Friel's.

Katie's behaviour as a married woman in asking Michael into the house and sharing a drink with him is bound to be misunderstood. From Stan's point of view he must read it as a betrayal of the absolute hold he thinks marriage has conferred upon him. But Michael is no less cocky on this score, seeing himself as the romantic male chosen by the disappointed wife. He reads a great deal into her asking him in while she bridles against the assumption that the choices implied by her behaviour amount to no more than a choice between men:

> **MICHAEL**: What a great fool you were, Katie.
> **KATIE**: (*Steps back from him*): Michael Maguire, do you think I regret the thing I done?
> **MICHAEL**: So what made you call me to come in an' I passing? [...]
> **KATIE**: I had ever a great love for your music. (p.54)

In reaction to this, Stan's first move is to remove himself from the house and return to the bachelor life he has enjoyed all his days. When he returns in Act Three to tell Katie that he has decided to live with her again, his discovery that Michael has been in the house leads him to take her away for good. Throughout Act Three Stan keeps entering when Reuben is expected or announced and vice-versa. The act of substitution or doubling between the older husband and the Tramp has never been more apparent. It is finally Stan who enters in Reuben's place and tells Katie that he is taking her away, not away with the fairies but to a life that is the virtual extinction of her person. Deevy's ending resists the romantic allure of 'away' in the plays of Yeats and Synge. What Katie longs for instead is a life that could be lived in her own native place. There, the elements that have been at war within her, the forces to which she has been subjected by her liminality as a woman in Ireland of the nineteen thirties, might be integrated. Katie Roche's final cry before being led offstage is for a home – a place, a country, a dwelling – in which she could live and be herself:

> **STAN**: Go and get ready. We're going at once. We're not com-
> ing back… Get all your things…
> **KATIE**: Is it … for always? (*Silence.* ***STAN*** *goes to the window,
> stands with his back to her.*) I'd like to come back. (*Pause.*) I'd like to
> live my life here. (*Silence.*) I'd like the two of us to live here…. I
> think we're meant for this place. (pp.100-1)

In Marina Carr's *The Mai,* as with the two plays so far considered, the troubled relationship between a married couple is
central. The greater equality that now exists between men and
women is signalled by no detail more forcefully than by the
relative equality of their ages: the Mai is forty, Robert is in his
early forties. They have been married for seventeen years and
have four children, though the only one we get to see is the
eldest, their sixteen-year-old daughter, Millie. But what persists
so forcefully in the almost sixty-year transition from Deevy's
Katie Roche to the present is the pattern of withdrawals by which
the husband seeks to assert his relative independence and simultaneously to keep the wife in her place at home. The first
act of the play signals the Mai's joyous reception of her errant
husband's return after five years. Two of the characters, specu-
lating as to where he has been, suggest America, like his father
before him. In defending the male family line, Robert asserts
that his father went away to the USA to earn a living for his
wife and family back in Ireland. The Mai's grandmother retorts
that he should either have stayed at home or brought his family
with him. In the Deevy play Stan's return in Act Two causes
Katie no less delight but turns out to be as provisional and
qualified as Robert's. Both husbands declare at one point that
they need more time on their own, preferring their own company or that of other people to the at-home demands of the
women they have married.

What is less overtly dramatic than the big entrances and exits
by the men every few months or years is the pattern of internal
withdrawal they practise while remaining physically present
within the house. Robert concentrates on playing his cello as he

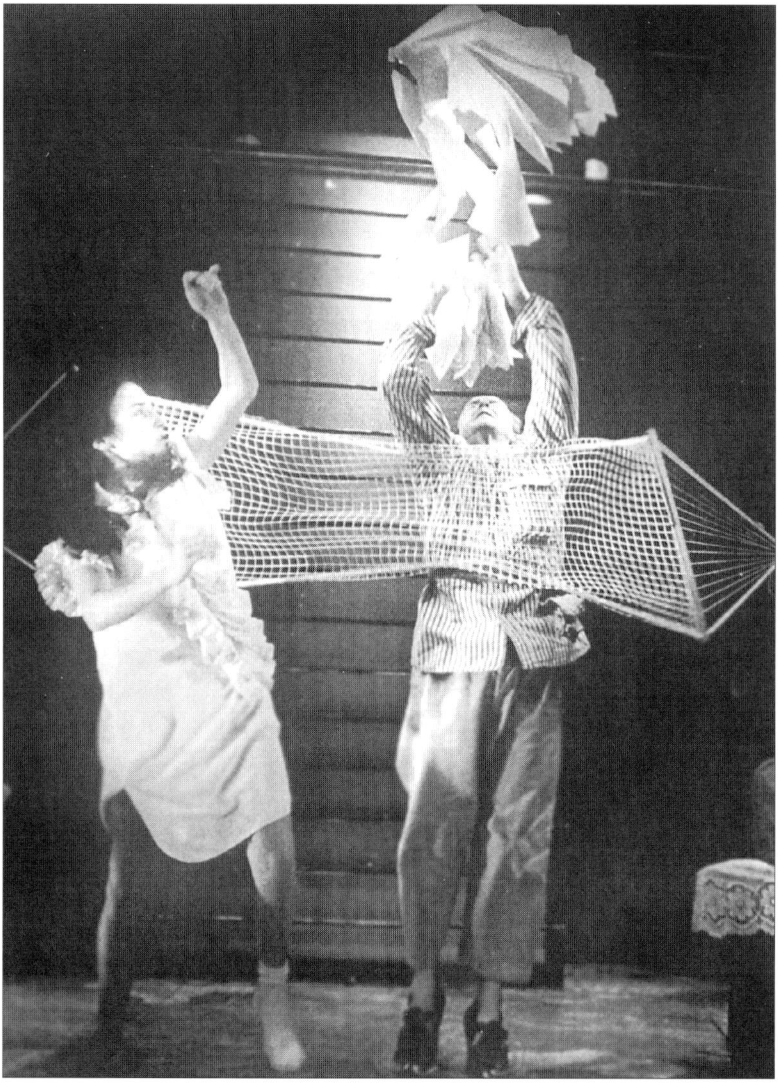

Photo by Fergus Bourke, courtesy of the Abbey Theatre Archive

Illustration 1
Olwen Fouéré (Tilly), *left,* and Mark Lambert (Tomred) in *Ullaloo* at the Peacock Theatre, Dublin (1991)

Illustration 2
From left to right: Joan O'Hara (Grandma Fraochlán), Derbhle Crotty (Millie) and Owen Roe (Robert) in *The Mai* at the Peacock Theatre, Dublin (1994)

Illustration 3
Olwen Fouéré (The Mai), *left,* and Owen Roe (Robert) in *The Mai* at the Peacock Theatre, Dublin (1994)

Illustration 4
Owen Roe (Robert), *left,* and Olwen Fouéré (The Mai) in *The Mai* at the
Peacock Theatre (1994)

Illustration 5
Owen Roe (Robert), and Olwen Fouéré (The Mai), *left*, and Derbhle
Crotty in *The Mai* at the Peacock Theatre, Dublin (1994)

pursues his romantic dream of being a great musician. The psychological transference was expressed in Brian Brady's production of *The Mai* in a surreal moment when Olwen Fouéré as the Mai was substituted for the cello. The idea for this visual substitution is contained in a scene where the Mai plucks at herself as if she *were* a cello. Robert is always buying her presents, returning from another brief absence with chocolates and copies of *Cosmopolitan* magazine as alibis. He pours himself drinks without offering her one and sits reading his newspaper on Christmas Day. Where the husband in the folktale of the *Unfaithful Wife* asserted his authority with a stick, the twentieth century version does so by means of silence and physical withdrawal. Synge has already developed this more modern interpretation in *Shadow*. Dan Burke, while remaining physically present and in a dominant position, has withdrawn to such an extent that he appears dead and has given his wife an explicit injunction that his body is not to be touched. In *Katie Roche*, '*silence*' is repeatedly inscribed as a stage direction as the ultimate sign of non-communication between husband and wife.

Nora Burke turns to the Tramp when her husband and lover reject her. Katie Roche has nowhere to turn: Amelia Gregg is too wedded to her brother to offer more than fleeting sympathy; Michael misunderstands her appeal; Reuben rejects her. To offset the Mai's isolation Marina Carr has filled the stage of her drama with an ensemble support system of female energy: two sisters, two aunts, a daughter and a hundred-year-old grandmother. When Grandma Fraochlán makes her memorable entrance, she does so bearing a big colourful stick, not one with which to berate her granddaughter but an oar which she is determined to intrude and which is the flamboyant sign of her unorthodox and romantic life with her husband, the nine-fingered fisherman. She even, one character remarks, takes the oar to bed with her. The grandmother bears in her first name an archetypal female status and in her second the name of the island on which she reared the Mai when the natural mother, her daughter Ellen, died young. What Grandma Fraochlán has to offer is stories, drawn from her 'ancient and fantastical memory'. As her great-granddaughter Millie recalls:

> The name alone evoked a thousand memories in me. She was known as the Spanish beauty though she was born and bred on Inis Fraochlán, north of Boffin. She was the result of a brief tryst between an ageing island spinster and a Spanish or Moroccan sailor, no one is quite sure, who was never heard of or seen since the night of her conception. [...] Whoever he was, he left Grandma Fraochlán his dark skin and a yearning for all that was exotic and unattainable.[10]

Grandma Fraochlán is the Tramp in the play, enlarging the scope of the environment with her exotic presence and her fund of storytelling, its connection to the world of myth and legend. The figure of the Tramp has changed gender and now offers a matrilineal line of support and continuity rather than a substitute patriarchy. Grandma Fraochlán's presence and the tales she tells do not induce a split in the consciousness of either Millie or the Mai. For she is the woman from whom they both claim their descent, the one whose stories can supply them with a personal history of Ellen and the other women in their past. She connects them more fully to a sense of their own identity as something they carry with them rather than something that is dependent on a particular place.

This legacy has borne fruit in Millie, who occupies a crucial dual role in Marina Carr's play. She is the daughter who bears the brunt of the tensions between Robert and the Mai. But as she talks, we gradually realize that Millie is not merely responding to what is occurring onstage but is narrating to the audience an entire drama that has occurred many years in the past. The first monologue to convey this is one in which she describes how, when she now meets her father, 'we shout and roar till we're exhausted or in tears or both, and then crawl away to lick our wounds already gathering venom for the next bout' (p.128). This speech not only establishes Millie as the play's storyteller

---

[10] Marina Carr, *The Mai* in *Plays 1* (London: Faber, 1999), pp.101-186 (pp.115-116). All subsequent quotations from *The Mai* are from this edition and will be incorporated in the text.

but shows that, far from being aligned with the words and deeds of her father, the Mai's husband, she is battling him verbally for control of the Mai's narrative.

Marina Carr is among those who have restored the storyteller's perspective to the drama. When Synge delegated the storytelling function to the figure of the Tramp in his plays, he made it the sole possession of only one character among many, even in as highly developed an examplar as Christy Mahon. The Tramp was no longer telling anyone's story but his own; and when the women in his plays looked for ratification of their own life narratives, there was no one to be found. (This is part of the loss that Pegeen Mike laments at the close of *The Playboy*.) The Tramp in *Katie Roche* seemed to offer the heroine greater access to her own personal history and identity when he revealed himself as her father; but the paternity was one he was not able or willing to own in anything other than the strictest and most impersonal terms. When Katie cried out for acknowledgement by her father, she was met with harsh words of reproof and chastisement. Grandma Fraochlán strengthens the link with her granddaughter by acting as a living conduit to the dead. But Grandma Fraochlán can only do so much; and her other granddaughters argue that she may not have been the best of mothers, since her husband had all her love. She herself, however larger than life and dramatically energizing she may be, remains a character within the play.

The figure who takes responsibility for bringing the story of the Mai into the dramatic present is Millie, now aged thirty and with a five-year-old son of her own. Such a move is not without precedent in the recent history of contemporary Irish drama. In watching Derbhle Crotty as Millie in *The Mai*, one cannot help but recall the narrator Michael in Friel's *Dancing at Lughnasa* directly addressing the audience in order to conjure up his five aunts from the nineteen thirties. When Millie reveals before the play is half over that the Mai took her own life, the effect resembles that moment when Friel's Michael discloses the squalid death of one of the women we see so vibrantly alive before us. Although Carr's Millie and Friel's Michael occupy the sidelines of their respective plays, they are central to the construction of the drama, since they are the ones actively remembering all the other characters into existence. As I have argued elsewhere, Michael's ambivalent position could be read as Friel's acknowledgement that, for all of *Lughnasa*'s emphasis on women, it is being authored by a man.[11] Similarly, the presence of a young woman narrator in *The Mai* is an acknowledgment that the play is being authored by a woman. Millie and Grandma Fraochlán reintroduce and re-orientate the key roles of the storyteller and the Tramp that this article has examined, establishing less a line of continuity than a multiple embrace of the three women across chronological time in the recurring present of the play.

The final image is of the Mai, standing alone at the window of the house. This is the dream house she has constructed from her teacher's salary, from the cleaning jobs she has taken, and from getting the builder to let her have it for a song. It has been built according to her specifications, to house herself and her four children and to prepare a place for the long-desired return of her husband. Its central feature in terms of the staging and Kathy Strachan's design (for the Peacock) is a huge window centre stage which gives out on to Owl Lake, the pattern of the lake reflected around the stage. When characters appear up the steps, it would seem more natural for them to step through than to go round to the door. The Mai is most often to be found standing in that window, as much looking in as looking out, not fully contained by the house she has built. Millie the storyteller brings Act One and the first half of the play to a close by telling us the legend of Owl Lake:

> Owl comes from the Irish, Loch Cailleach Oíche, Lake of the Night Hag or Pool of the Dark Witch. The legend goes that Coillte, daughter of the Mountain God Bloom, fell in love with Bláth, Lord of all the flowers, so away she bounded like a young deer [...] over the dark witch's boglands 'till she came to Bláth's domain. There he lay, under an oak tree [...] and so they lived freely through the spring and summer [...] One evening, approaching autumn

[11] Anthony Roche, *Contemporary Irish Drama, From Beckett to McGuinness* (Dublin: Gill and Macmillan, 1994), p.285.

Bláth told Coillte that soon he must go and live with the dark witch of the bog, that he would return in the spring and the next morning he was gone. Coillte followed him and found him ensconced in the dark witch's lair. He would not speak to her, look at her, touch her, and heartbroken Coillte lay down outside the dark witch's lair and cried a lake of tears that stretched for miles around. One night, seizing a long awaited opportunity, the dark witch pushed Coillte into her lake of tears. When spring came around again Bláth was released from the dark witch's spell and he went in search of Coillte only to be told that she had dissolved in a lake of tears. Sam Brady told me that when the geese are restless or the swans suddenly take flight, it's because they hear Bláth's pipes among the reeds, still playing for Coillte. (p.147)

This mythic narrative is acoustically echoed at the play's close when 'sounds of swans and geese taking flight' accompany the image of the Mai at her window. We are never directly given the Mai's death; it would be unnecessary and untrue to the way in which her story is told. Her search is like that of the old woman in Beckett's Rockaby, looking 'for another/ at her window/ another like herself/ a little like'.[12]

In choosing to build her house at Owl Lake, the Mai has according to her daughter been 'looking for that magic thread that would stitch us together again.' It is not to be found there, as the play poignantly demonstrates. The magic thread stitching the women's lives together is the act of shared memory which is the play itself, the thread of affiliation which binds Grandma Fraochlán, the Mai and Millie together across time, space and the absence of death. Grandma Fraochlán is as old as the century and Synge's drama; she resembles his characters in the closeness of her speech to Gaelic, her Rabelaisian humour and her myth-making capacities. The Mai is caught in the same in-between space as Deevy's Katie Roche; both are poised on the threshold between an inner security never experienced and an outer freedom never fully within reach. Millie is of the present

---

[12] Samuel Beckett, *Rockaby* in *The Complete Dramatic Works* (London: Faber and Faber, 1986), pp.431-442 (p.437).

and the future, like Marina Carr herself, expressing uncertainty and openness in the telling of a story and the making of a play. Through the hundred year span covered by Synge's *The Shadow of the Glen,* Deevy's *Katie Roche* and Carr's *The Mai* there runs a magic thread which this article has sought to elucidate.

3 | Authentic Reproductions:
Marina Carr and the Inevitable

Clare Wallace

Responses to Marina Carr's plays since *The Mai* have seldom been lukewarm, and are regularly hyperbolic. The strength of her work is often attributed to its engagement with eternal and essential dilemmas. The notion of destiny, allusion to myth, folktale and a harsh version of midland speech permeate Carr's writing to such a degree that in many respects it hardly seems of the contemporary world. Nevertheless, it is important to re-member that Carr and her drama are still products of the late twentieth and early twenty-first century. In particular, her public image and her work need to be examined in terms of their relation to a discourse of authenticity in a postmodern context both in Ireland and elsewhere. This essay proposes to explore these issues in three ways: firstly by looking at an example of a recent non-Irish production of *The Mai*, then by turning to the public versions of Marina Carr the playwright, and finally through an analysis of several pertinent aspects of her drama, focusing on the ways in which Carr's plays problematize the very issues of authenticity that her image invokes.

The Mai in Liberec

Frank McGuinness has claimed that, '[t]here is no knowing what is going to happen in any play by Marina Carr except the inevitable.'[1] The first Czech production of a Marina Carr play, which premiered on the 23rd November 2001, proved (unintentionally and humorously) McGuinness's dictum to be both true and false. The Mai was translated as Maja by Jan Hancil of the Czech National Theatre, directed by Lida Engelová, and performed in part of the F.X. Salda Theatre in Liberec in Northern Bohemia. Between the midlands of Ireland and the heartlands of Europe the transformation of The Mai to Maja produced some rather surprising and some perhaps inevitable results, which indirectly lead to a constellation of issues around the inevitable and the authentic.

The production stressed the 'Irishness' of the play in a number of ways. The first sign of 'Irishness' referred to place, and unravelled an opposition between the interior and modern scene of the play and the exterior and ancient landscape of Ireland. The anonymous modernity of the stage design, a living room with all the blank emptiness of a television soap opera set, stood in stark contrast with the programme design. As if to supplement the lack of 'Irishness' in the spectacle of the play, the programme consisted primarily of a series of striking photographic images of typical Irish landscapes and icons – the Burren, seascapes, a dolmen, a menhir, a whitewashed cottage, the Cliffs of Moher, a Celtic cross. The fact that these images were without the intrusion of people or animals facilitated a fetishization of a landscape, (a practice familiar to many through John Hinde postcard/calendar photography and Bord Fáilte advertising) marked most dramatically by the ruins of diverse periods, from megalithic pre-history through to more recent pre-industrial rurality. These ruins have various connotations, not least of which is the sense of the ruin as an enduring

---

[1] Frank McGuinness, http.//www.sjrep.com/plays/studyguides/-
    bogofcats_studyguide1.shtml/

remnant 'which outlasts human intentions and becomes an historical sign, a sign of an inaccessible past, of something that is strange, incomprehensible, threatening […] a monument of an alien culture or of the past as a different age.'[2] However, these 'authentic' and stereotypical images of scenic Ireland (ironically enough, none of them seem to be of the midlands) bore the slight, but noticeable, marks of computer enhancement – the colours had been altered and the pictures overlaid with a water marked pattern, obviously an allusion to another well-known aspect of 'real' Ireland. The result was the impression that one was looking at the landscapes through a tainted rain-dashed glass or window. Ironically, these touches lent a degree of technological surreality to the eulogizing of the ancient topography.

Similarly, the programme cover image – of a young woman wearing a strapless white dress with tousled fair hair, her back to the camera – seemed to amend the lack of youthful, lyrical femininity in the play itself. In addition to the series of picturesque images and superimposed upon them was a portion of Eileen Battersby's *Irish Times* interview with Carr, 'Marina of the Midlands,'[3] which began and ended with photos of Carr herself. Thus, in a highly visual manner, Carr was mapped onto the simulated landscape of a 'real' Ireland – dramatic, lonely, isolated, natural, beautiful, perhaps, feminine – before the performance of *The Mai/Maja* even began. The themes of destiny in the play were therefore prefigured obliquely in the assemblage of the programme as if Carr and her work were in some way the inevitable products of this dramatic and foreboding landscape and the culture it implies.

The performance, too, was supplemented by the citation of certain signs of 'Irishness'. These, being intended for a non-Irish and non-English speaking audience presumably largely unfamiliar with Irish drama, tended to be more overt than those

---

[2] Aleida Assmann and Martin Procházka, 'Introduction: Reading in Ruins', *Litteraria Pragensia* 8:15 (1998), 3.

[3] Eileen Battersby, 'Marina of the Midlands', *Irish Times* 4 May 2000, 15.

the play already contains. In general, the dramatization of the characters seemed somewhat extreme (reminiscent of the extreme landscapes of the programme) and explicitly passionate, maudlin and violent (reminiscent perhaps of many rather familiar racial stereotypes). The characters of Julie and Agnes, for instance, were reduced to comic caricatures, who rolled on the Persian rug on their first visit to the Mai's new house.[4] Nevertheless, while the 'Celtic' music, the liberal consumption of whiskey, and the Irish dancing (added in Act II after The Mai, Connie and Beck sing together), which punctuate *Maja* might be dismissed as mere misunderstandings or distortions, the intention was, clearly, to ameliorate the 'authenticity' of the play by citing signs of 'Irishness' for the benefit of the audience (who, on the night of the premiere, responded extremely positively). Moreover, these signs follow a tendency within the play itself to employ other signs of 'Irishness' – especially folklore and dialect – to authenticate its tale. *Maja*, in its efforts to be an authentic reproduction of Carr's play, drew attention to the ways in which these signs can be overdetermined to the detriment of the other facets of the drama.

'Authentic Irishness' and Irish theatre

The significance attributed to the 'Irishness' of Carr's work is far from accidental and may be seen as symptomatic of wider concerns regarding theatre in and from Ireland. Ireland's realities (and unrealities) have radically changed in the last decade to the extent that now the nation's post-coloniality appears to be overlaid, or at least interwoven, with a kind of postmodernity. The narratives of progress, success and inflation which, apparently, have been structuring a 'New Ireland' are powerful but equivocal. With regard to theatre, Eamonn Jordan in the introduction to *Theatre Stuff: Critical Essays on Contemporary Irish Theatre*, draws attention to the fact that 'Irish theatre has never been so successful' yet, simultaneously 'never in more need of rigor-

---

[4]Marina Carr, *The Mai* (Meath: The Gallery Press, 1995), p.32.

ous evaluation.'[5] If globalization has brought to Ireland the inescapability of information technology, consumer culture and a species of Americanization and Europeanization, accompanied by the disintegration of the familiar narratives of identity, then how is contemporary theatre responding to these realities? Jordan's essay poses some salient questions about today's dramatic practice – he asks 'what are our playwrights peddling?', 'what is the standing of contemporary writing practice?' and, perhaps most importantly, what is the truth of 'the huge success of Irish drama of late?' He concludes with a pertinent, if unanswerable, question – 'How do you write about the present?'[6] Each of these enquiries has provocative implications; playwrights as part of consumer culture must have something to sell and products are marketed. If, on one hand, a 'Buy Irish' spin is put on some of the work competing for attention in London and elsewhere, on the other, these products are often (over)interpreted as being representative of 'Irishness'. However, they are also being evaluated by audiences and readers who, given the fragmentation of postmodern culture in the developed world, may well understand the product or, indeed, the us Jordan's enquiries assume, in an unforeseen manner. The familiar elements of 'real' Irish theatre – the sovereignty of language, storytelling, frequent recourse to myth and folklore – have brought considerable international success to a number of Irish playwrights since the 1990s, but also generate some frustration. Playwright and director Declan Hughes voices this frustration forcefully:

> Too often when I go to the theatre, I feel like I've stepped into a time capsule: even plays supposed to be set in the present seem burdened by the compulsion to… well, in the narrowest sense, be Irish […]. Irish drama needs to show more guts: the guts to stop flaunting its ancestry, to understand

---

[5]Eamonn Jordan, ed. and intro., *Theatre Stuff: Critical Essays on Contemporary Irish Theatre* (Dublin: Carysfort Press, 2000), p.xi.
[6]Jordan, pp.xiii-xiv, xlviii.

that the relentless dependence on tradition collapses inevitably into cannibalism. The village will eat itself.[7]

What Hughes decries, to some degree, is Irish theatre's tendency towards self-citation and a kind of nostalgia, which he envisions as ultimately cannibalistic. This is not necessarily a 'new' response – see for example Tom Murphy's memories of how Noel O'Donoghue and he collaborated on their first play, *On The Outside*, in 1962.[8] Contemporarily however, an undertow of discontent is evident in many of the essays by theatre practitioners and critics in *Theatre Stuff*. The issue, for Hughes, is not 'that people don't live in the country any more, or that rural life isn't 'valuable'; it's that culturally, it's played out. It no longer signifies. [...C]ulturally we persist in defining ourselves by the ethnic, the pastoral (and that qualified form, the tragic pastoral).' (*Theatre Stuff*, p.12) While rural life's failure to signify is debatable, the tendency to privilege certain cultural definitions and the formal reliance upon particular dramatic traditions, is ongoing, and is in striking contrast not only with the changes in Irish society in the last thirty years, but also with many of the experiments, innovations and trends in theatre and performance in the last sixty. In order to explore why this is the case and, by implication, what role Marina Carr might play in this scene, one first needs to interrogate some of the meanings inherent to a concept of 'Irishness' and how they are entangled with notions of value and authenticity.

---

[7] Declan Hughes, 'Who The Hell Do We Think We Still Are? Reflections on Irish Theatre and Identity', in *Theatre Stuff*, ed. Eamonn Jordan (Dublin: Carysfort Press, 2000), p.13.

[8] Murphy recalls an exchange with O'Donoghue, the tone of which is replicated in Hughes and others: 'O'Donoghue said to me, 'Why don't you write a play?' I said, 'What would we write about?' And he said, 'one thing is fucking sure, it's not going to be set in a kitchen.' That was the most progressive thing anybody had ever said to me.' in David Murphy, ed. *Education and the Arts: A Research Report* (Dublin: Department of Higher Education and Educational Research, Trinity College, 1987), p.173.

In *Deconstructing Ireland* Colin Graham traces some of the dynamics of concepts of authenticity both in general and as they pertain to Ireland. He remarks how, in many respects, as colonial domination was displaced, the definition of the authentically Irish became central to claims for value.[9] As the Czech production of *The Mai* demonstrates, 'Irishness' is still, in multiple, sometimes contradictory ways, conceived of as what might be called a 'marketable sign of value,' but one which also needs supplementary commentary.[10] Unlike Martin McDonagh's *Leenane Trilogy* which deploys 'Irishness' in an ironic, comic fashion, the 'Irishness' of Carr's work is essentially serious. Nevertheless, the stereotypes which tend to be satirized by McDonagh, and those which are commented upon in Carr's plays demand from the reader/audience at least some knowledge of a particular language of in/authentic identity in an Irish context.

As has often been noted the language of authenticity inevitably involves the privileging of certain qualities and, explicitly or implicitly, excluding others.[11] Authenticity, and with it, authentic 'Irishness', attempt to authorize themselves through the citation of origins, although, as Graham observes, this relationship is ambiguous since it relies upon antiquity to guarantee its value but at the same time mystifies/mythologizes that history.[12] These 'origins' can never be definitively located or dissected, in the same manner as authenticity itself eludes absolute definition. This coupling of the drive toward self-legitimating referentiality with the mystification of sources is integral to the machinations of authenticity and is evident not only in much of Carr's drama, but also in how her image has been constructed.

---

[9]Colin Graham, *Deconstructing Ireland: Identity, Theory, Culture* (Edinburgh: Edinburgh University Press, 2001), p.132.

[10]For further discussion of how essence and the authentic require explication see Graham p.133.

[11]One might refer here to Theodor Adorno's conceptualization of authenticity as a jargonized system, see Theodor Adorno, *The Jargon of Authenticity* (London: Routlege, 1986, 1964), p.5.

[12]Graham p.137.

Another unavoidable dimension to authenticity is nostalgia. In the midst of postmodern insecurity, proliferation of information and apparent amnesia, authenticity may no longer be the measure of value but reveals a need for value, which it then fulfils. As Jean Baudrillard argues, in this context authenticity might be thought to simulate what is lacking or lay claim to legitimacy through 'retro' and simulacra. It (re)produces origins and in a circular movement (re)produces itself, thus:

> When the real is no longer what it used to be, nostalgia assumes its full meaning. There is a proliferation of myths of origin and signs of reality; of second-hand truth, objectivity and authenticity.[13]

Nostalgic modes proliferate at all levels of contemporary culture to the extent that, oxymoronically, it seems that nostalgia is the future. Evidently this transforms cultural practices and products – one striking example being the popularity of the remake.[14] Theatre in Ireland has adopted the remake, more respectfully referred to as the adaptation, with gusto. Marianne McDonald offers an impressive list of over thirty adaptations of Greek tragedy since 1984 produced by some of Ireland's best known writers. While McDonald argues that this phenomenon is a result of colonial oppression and that Greek tragedy, being the 'epitome of civilization', is a suitable vehicle for a 'literature of protest,'[15] such a diagnosis fails to engage with the aesthetic implications of such referencing practices.

Indeed, this may be another dimension to Hughes's provocative indictment. The 'time capsule' of Irish drama is

---

[13]Jean Baudrillard, *Simulations* trans. Paul Foss, Paul Patton and Philip Beitchman, (New York: Semiotext(e), 1983) pp.12-13.

[14]For a discussion of the significance of the remake to reading/viewing practices see Fredric Jameson, *Postmodernism, or the Cultural Logic of Late Capitalism*, in Thomas Docherty, ed. and intro., *Postmodernism: A Reader* (New York: Harvester Wheatsheaf, 1993), p.76.

[15]Marianne McDonald 'Classics as Celtic Firebrand: Greek Tragedy, Irish Playwrights and Colonialism', *Theatre Stuff* ed. Eamonn Jordan (Dublin: Carysfort Press, 2000), pp.16, 17.

(re)produced through the citation of signs of 'ancestry' and these are not restricted to Irish traditions alone. Nostalgia and simulacra interact to produce a kind of neo-primitivist reflex action which gives weight and meaning to their products. Undoubtedly, Hughes's comments are not applicable to all theatre in Ireland; certainly he has his own agenda which involves producing a more 'real' and contemporary theatre. Nevertheless the criticism and the agenda still lead us back to the core issue of authenticity and its operations in a postmodern context.

Authenticity Performed

In the following sections of this paper I would like to unpack some of these theoretical issues in relation to Carr and her work. The role played by commodification in the making of a successful dramatist is one which has seldom been explored and yet is especially relevant in the Irish context where firstly, play writing still appears to have some kudos, and secondly, very few women playwrights since Lady Gregory have had such a public profile. For these reasons it is worth analysing not only the plays, but also how Carr's public persona has developed through interviews and speeches, as well as how she is represented. While these aspects of Carr as a dramatist might seem liminal or trivial, they nevertheless inform how we 'read' and interpret her work.

Accessible, printed interviews with Carr are few. However, her statements on writing, on theatre and on her beliefs are revealing. In a remarkable lecture given at the Peacock Theatre in 1997 entitled 'Dealing with the Dead,'[16] subsequently printed in *Irish University Review*, Carr relates some of her attitudes about creativity, in the form of reverent speculations on 'great dead writers.' In this piece Carr's approach relies quite explicitly upon strategies of glorification and mystification of 'genius'. The writers she discusses (Homer, Keats, Dickenson, Ibsen, and Shakespeare) take on a heroically untouchable status; 'They

---

[16]Marina Carr, 'Dealing With the Dead', *Irish University Review* 28:1 (1998), pp.190-196.

are the poet god's children, Apollo's favourites, Apollo's golden offspring', 'Apollo's darlings', 'Apollo's royals'.[17] She asserts that,

> there are the royal writers and then the rest of us who write. The royal writers – their ink is supplied from the blue veins of God, from the lyre strings of Orpheus, from the well spring of another world. The rest of us are not aware of that inkwell or are dimly aware or are struggling very hard to hear those sounds. (p.190)

What is in evidence in these statements is peculiarly anachronistic; an almost Kantian notion of genius, that is the genius as 'no product of history [but] a gift of nature.'[18] There is a double movement in the logic of creativity here, which on the one hand attempts (however hesitantly or humbly) to claim a literary heritage – the writer struggles hard to hear the 'lyre strings of Orpheus' – while on the other, depicts it as unattainable – the 'well spring of another world' is one which most writers may not draw from, or in the wake of Shakespeare's genius, may only pick among the leftovers (*DWTD*: p.195, p.196). As an aesthetic stance, Carr distances herself from most of the twentieth century, and expresses a desire 'to return to an old and simple division, that of prose and poetry.' (*DWTD*: pp.194-5) Interestingly, coming from a dramatist, this reversion erases theatre writing from the equation entirely.

In an essay on *By the Bog of Cats...*, Melissa Sihra cites how, 'as information technology, global systems and genetic manipulation rapidly transform contemporary reality Carr ponders over "...this anti-heroic age [... where...] the all consuming intellectual pursuit seems to be that of de-mystification"'.[19] The contradiction inherent in the stress upon 'old and simple' and the

---

[17]Carr, 'Dealing With the Dead', pp.190, 194.

[18]David Cook 'The Last Days of Liberalism', *Postmodernism: A Reader* ed. Thomas Docherty (New York: Harvester Wheatsheaf, 1993), p.124.

[19]Melissa Sihra, 'A Cautionary Tale: Marina Carr's *By the Bog of Cats...*' *Theatre Stuff*, ed. Eamonn Jordan (Dublin: Carysfort Press, 2000), p.265.

desire for the complexity of mystification, stands as a nostalgic sleight of hand which refuses resolution, and is part of the structure of the concept of the authentic at work here. The repeated invocation of Apollo suggests a compulsion, if not to return to a point of origin – the myth cradle of Western civilization – then to reproduce and thus repossess it. If Apollo, as an authentic source, authorizes genuine creative talent to his 'favourites' then, according to the exclusionary logic which sustains authenticity, those not in favour must be labouring under a delusive and inauthentic creativity.

When speaking specifically on theatre we find that Carr emphasizes her belief that plays are primarily texts, and should be read and treated as such.[20] Her favoured dramatists are those whom she locates on Apollo's side of the 'old and simple division':

> In the theatre too there are poets…and there are prose writers […] The ones who interest me are the poets of the theatre: Chekhov, Ibsen, Tennessee Williams, Wilde, Beckett and of course the king himself – Mr Shakespeare. (*DWTD*: p.194, p.195)

She regretfully remarks in 'Dealing with the Dead' how 'theatre seems to have been demoted to the scum end of literature. Plays are not read anymore and hardly ever reviewed. Performances are, of course, but that is an entirely different discipline to that of the art of playwriting.' (*DWTD*: p.194) Carr's advocacy of plays as text ironically diminishes the role of performance in play making, a gesture which it may be argued, is a considerable element of what defines theatre as theatre. More recently in the RTÉ interview series *Reading the Future*, she speaks of theatre with continuing pessimism:

> People don't believe in things anymore. They go to the theatre and they want two episodes of a soap opera. They don't want to be told about a ghost. […] The worst thing they can say about you is that it's not believable. But the yardstick is frighteningly limited, and to work within those parameters is

---

[20]See Eileen Battersby interview and 'Dealing with the Dead'.

impossible for any writer who is on a journey, or who is trying to figure out what we're here for.[21]

These comments are worth quoting in full for they open onto another cluster of issues about what might be at stake for a young female playwright at the beginning of the twenty-first century. Firstly, theatre, drama and playwright are conflated and viewed nostalgically as a single dying art which is being suffocated, in part, by technology. Carr's stress upon a textual base is not surprising given Ireland's theatre traditions. As Anna McMullan describes in an essay in The State of Play: Irish Theatre in the Nineties:

> [w]hat is striking about the Irish theatre tradition of the last hundred years, as it is usually perceived, is its almost total reliance on text, and its avoidance or insulation from the performative experiments of twentieth century theatre.[22]

Similarly, Caoimhe McAvinchey points out the incongruences between the 'high level of visceral stimulation'[23] that audiences expect from other media such as the internet, television and film, and the techniques and structures of most contemporary theatre produced in Ireland, which have remained largely static. McAvinchey notes that while 'directors like Peter Brook, Robert Wilson and Elizabeth le Compte have shattered the mould of audience expectations', in Ireland their methods are 'rarely seen [...] as a possible alternative, exciting and successful approach'.[24] Although Carr opposes what she seems to posit as an audience demand for realism – soap opera – to the fantastical – a ghost – as the above writers/directors/dramatists suggest, there are many other ways of telling in the theatre which this opposition elides.

---

[21]'Reading the Future: Irish Writers in Conversation with Mike Murphy' http://www.rte.ie/radio/readingthefuture/carr.html.

[22]Anna McMullan, 'Reclaiming Performance: The Contemporary Irish Independent Theatre Sector', The State of Play: Irish Theatre in the 'Nineties ed. Eberhard Bort (Trier: WVT, 1996), p.30.

[23]McAvinchey, Caoimhe. 'Theatre – Act or Place?' Theatre Stuff ed. Eamonn Jordan (Dublin: Carysfort Press, 2000), p.85.

[24]McAvinchey p.85.

The other issue which emerges with clarity is how Carr sees her role as a writer. In a statement ripe with (I believe unintended) ambivalence, Frank McGuinness has described Carr as 'a writer haunted by memories she could not possibly possess.'[25] Eminent in her statements in the various pieces quoted here, is a belief in the supernatural and to some extent the inevitable – creativity and inspiration are other-worldly, theatre has been in her blood since she was a child and she claims to believe, in some sense, in angels, ghosts and banshees. Ghosts, like the art of playwriting, are remnants of a cultural heritage which is waning:

> The culture believes in ghosts, certainly in the country. The banshee was a huge thing [...] In the city everything is forgotten now, everything is homogenized, and all of this seems so remote, but to me it's not remote, it's entirely natural. I'm a great believer in the whole angel thing, I don't know what I believe in, but I do believe in something.[26]

The author's role in 'trying to figure out what we're here for' introduces an important ontological dimension. Ghosts, banshees, angels are seen to be part of a culture of belief which is non-urban, non-modern and, above all, natural to the writer. These beliefs which have largely been dismissed or forgotten in the modern age are reinstated by Carr as valuable to an understanding of identity and furnish the severe alternative world of her drama.

The relation of identity with origins and ontology may also be seen at work in the images of Carr generated by these interviews and articles and, to a lesser extent, in photographs which construct her (again perhaps inevitably) as implicitly and explicitly rooted in a particular landscape. Battersby's article is a significant example of this overdetermination of context. Even its title, 'Marina of the Midlands' suggests, with rather quaint syntax, Carr to be not merely a product of that region, but also

---

[25]Frank McGuinness, ed. and intro., *The Dazzling Dark: New Irish Plays* (London: Faber and Faber, 1996),p.ix.

[26]'Reading the Future: Irish Writers in Conversation with Mike Murphy' http://www.rte.ie/radio/readingthefuture/carr.html.

perhaps, a representative native, despite the fact that she lives in Dublin and has not lived in the Midlands since the age of seventeen. In the article, which is dominated by a large photo of the playwright (posed thoughtfully gazing away from the camera), Battersby devotes over two paragraphs to a detailed description of Carr:

> A shrewd, deliberate individual, she possesses an unusual poise; she is friendly, wary, very funny and highly intelligent rather than clever. There is a naturalness about her which can be disarming. Also, she conveys a strong sense of having another, extremely normal life, well removed from the solitary hours writing in a spartan office.
>
> Her broad dreamy girl's face, long hair and student aura, make her seem younger than she is. Her voice is low and easy, while her accent, which remains of the midlands, is further diluted by traces of the west. [...] Although obviously confident of her work, Carr does not offer easy pronouncements about writing. Nor is she random, or casual, giving the impression that it's all due to inspiration.[27]

This journalistic setting of the scene builds the character performed in the interview. Carr is represented as intuitive, thoughtful, feminine, canny and rural. She is natural on a number of levels: she is feminine in a wholesome, youthful, unthreatening manner (as the publicity photo affirms); her speech is both unaffected and an amalgamation of West of Ireland accents (placing her in close proximity with the essence of Irishness wafting in from the West); she is, seemingly, naturally inspired. As an artist known for producing horrendously traumatic stories of obsession, incest, suicide and murder, she is comfortingly sane and, thankfully, normal. In all these ways Carr is the opposite of artifice, artistry and affectation, and these familiar signs (and 'real' femininity) of authenticity underwrite her authority as a playwright.

Another particularly interesting image of Carr which might be said to visually duplicate these aspects of her public persona is a photograph by Patrick Redmond which is to be found on

---

[27]Battersby p.15.

the website for the *Reading the Future* series, and in the accompanying book published by the Lilliput Press.[28] Predictably, Redmond photographed Carr on Pullagh bog in Co. Offaly. Again, we are confronted with the playwright, and by inference her work, mapped in the midland landscape. The strategically framed shot shows Carr in the foreground looking directly at the camera, with a benevolent enigmatic half smile, holding her son. She wears a simple woolly jumper and little or no make-up. The baby's bald head and closed eyes are just within the frame of the photo. The background, though blurred, is a flat country terrain.

The combined force of these images and Carr's own explicit and implicit appeals to tradition, the supernatural, and the natural, are evidently enmeshed in a web of connotation. Stereotype is an important aspect of this. Tom Kilroy notes the persistence of stereotypes of the Irish writer – usually as outspoken, alcoholic, male, inspired rather than intelligent. Carr's public image seems to be caught up in particular with the last he mentions – the writer as 'un-tutored, natural genius and Irish writing as a pure natural flow of words', although, as revealed above, Carr is fortunate enough also to be credited with intelligence.[29] Carr herself is partly responsible for the doggedness of such stereotypes, for instance in her descriptions of poetic or lyrical writing as typically Irish: 'how we tell a story is so important. It is not the facts we are looking for, it is the details, the embellishments. I think that most Irish people know how to tell a story instinctively and to tell it well.'[30] Inevitably the web of connotation is extensive and complicated, however the processes of commodification and credibility involved in promoting

---

[28]'Reading the Future'
http://www.rte.ie/radio/readingthefuture/carr.html and *Reading the Future* ed. Cliodhna Ni Anluain (Dublin: Lilliput, 2000).

[29]Tom Kilroy, 'A Generation of Playwrights' *Theatre Stuff* ed. Eamonn Jordan (Dublin: Carysfort Press, 2000), p.7.

[30]Cited in Sihra page 265 from *Rage and Reason* (London: Methuen, 1997), p.149.

and distributing 'Marina Carr the playwright' are certainly important parts of its structure.

Ontological Uncertainty and The Simulation Of Tragedy

Carr's drama is notable for the ways in which she draws upon certain sources. If in her earlier plays the influence of Beckett, theatrical experimentalism, the absurd and feminism dominated, then from *The Mai*, *Portia Coughlan* and *By the Bog of Cats...*,[31] (plays in which Carr seems to have 'found her voice' as a dramatist) we can see her shaping her art using other inspirations. The tendency towards citation in her drama as a means of authentification, discussed in the previous sections, has far reaching implications. As she says herself with respect to Shakespeare:

> He took from everywhere, but what he did with his plunder! And this points up something else about all these great dead writers. It seems that you are allowed to steal what you need while learning the craft and that there is no crime in that. The crime would be to diminish or desecrate what you have stolen. (*DWTD*: p.196)

Citation creeps in here as inevitable but it is also a duplicitous process which fails to preserve pristine original signs. Though Carr's ideas on 'great dead writers' and genius/genesis seem to privilege fixed meanings and stable identities, in her writing the slippery nature of origins is constantly present.

Citations and simulations have occurred in Carr's drama in a number of ways. Formally the three plays mentioned above

---

[31]Marina Carr, *The Mai* (Meath: The Gallery Press, 1995). *Portia Coughlan* in *The Dazzling Dark: New Irish Plays* ed. Frank McGuinness (London: Faber and Faber, 1996) and published separately by The Gallery Press, 1998. I will refer to the latter. Marina Carr, *By the Bog of Cats...* (Meath: The Gallery Press, 1998).

reveal Carr's inflection of particular generic aspects of tragedy.[32] Her interest in 'the Greek idea of destiny and fate and little escape'[33] has taken shape in these plays through an intertextual process. At the outset, the term 'tragedy' needs to be understood as both hybrid and heterogeneous. Carr's plays do not adhere to any single definition nor do they replicate Classical or Elizabethan tragic drama. Rather her recent work incorporates fragments of different formulations and (mis)understandings of tragedy and the tragic, assembled from various sources. Her use of tragedy, therefore, is complex, simultaneously drawing upon retrospective elements as well as highly contemporary ones ranging from Aristotle to Raymond Williams. One might remark upon how the plays incorporate the Aristotelian elements of *hamartia* and *catharsis*, draw upon the heritage of Shakespearean tragic heroes, as well as sharing a family resemblance, however slight, to the drama of Ibsen, Strindberg and O'Neill. As Williams has noted, the discourse concerning tragedy tends to assume a tradition which is conceived of as continuous but has in fact been continuously chameleonic. Twentieth century readings of Greek tragedy tend to psychologize a form in which an individualized 'tragic hero' clearly did not exist and the desire to unify tradition has lead to 'the assumption of a common Graeco-Christian tradition which has shaped Western civilization.'[34] This desire for cultural continuity is powerful, and the illusion of 'Hellenes and Christians, in a common activity'[35] is particularly attractive, as has been evidenced perhaps most strikingly in contemporary Irish theatre by Brian Friel's *Translations*. To a degree it would appear that this is the illusion on which Carr's engagement with tragedy is founded. 'The Greek

---

[32]For more detailed analysis of Carr's work and tragedy see Clare Wallace 'A Crossroads Between Worlds': Marina Carr and the Use of Tragedy', *Litteraria Pragensia* 10:20 (2000), 76-89.

[33]James F. Clarity, 'A Playwright's Post-Beckett Period', *New York Times* 3 Nov 1994, C23.

[34]Raymond Williams, *Modern Tragedy* (London: Chatto & Windus, 1966), p.16.

[35]Williams, pp.15-16.

idea of destiny and fate and little escape' is fascinating, not because we share a Greek sense of the meaning of Fate, but because of the evocation of origin. The spectre of *Medea*, which haunts *By the Bog of Cats…* bears witness to what Bruce Stewart refers to as an atavistic urge.[36] This urge is directed toward a legitimizing connection with moral values and dilemmas under-stood as part of a tradition of tragic drama. Contemporary reproductions of 'tragic drama' might be thought of as simula-cra which fulfil, among other things, a desire for age-old stories and narrative closure.

A similar authenticity is supplied by Carr's attention to ac-cent and use of location. Each play from *The Mai* to *By the Bog of Cats…* and latterly *On Raftery's Hill*, is set in the Midlands and all draw upon that regional diction. The area has become as she says, 'a metaphor for a crossroads between worlds'[37] and she treats landscape as 'another character', which needn't 'be overly symbolic and self-conscious' but needs 'to be present, to have presence.'[38] However, it is the richness of the engagement with origins and ontology in the structures of each play which is noteworthy. Carr's exploration of the ambivalences of identity is powerfully communicated within the structures she has chosen. Destiny is articulated and implied on multiple levels, through naming, genealogy, memory and storytelling.[39]

Carr's use of names becomes increasingly deliberate and meaningful from *The Mai* to *By the Bog of Cats….* As in folkloric narrative traditions, names indicate character and bear multiple significances as stigma or stigmata. Characters then inhabit the

---

[36]'Bruce Stewart, "A Fatal Excess' at the Heart of Irish Atavism', *IASIL Newsletter*, 5:1 (1999), 1. Victor Merriman carries the notion of atavism still further in 'Decolonisation Postponed: The Theatre of Tiger Trash', *Irish University Review*, 29:2 (1999), 305-7.

[37]*The Dazzling Dark: New Irish Plays* ed. Frank McGuinness (London: Faber and Faber, 1996), pp.310-11.

[38]Battersby p.15.

[39]See Clare Wallace 'Tragic Destiny and Abjection in Marina Carr's *The Mai, Portia Coughlan* and *By the Bog of Cats…*' *Irish University Re-view* 31:2 Autumn/Winter 2000, 431-449 for an extended examina-tion of the three plays.

role invoked by their names. For instance, Grandma Fraochlán's name emerges as a cipher to a whole family's intricate and unfortunate history of (self) deception. The name is equivocal, functioning to anchor her amid all her flights of fancy to a place of origin and as an implicit reminder of the social stigma of her illegitimacy. '[T]ha on'y bastard on Fraochlán in livin' memory' (60) is given the island's name in place of a father's name as a means to maintain a façade of respectability or legitimacy. In this manner, the name also facilitates a symbolic contraction rendering grandmother and island synonymous, both sites of origin, mapping the fertility of the woman (the *über* mother of the play) onto the land. This name with its various resonances encodes a history that mars the future generations of women in the play while men continue to be absent.

Similarly, Carr invests heavily in the names of characters in *Portia Coughlan* and *By the Bog of Cats*.... Hester Swane's destiny, in the latter play, seems largely dictated by her name which yokes her life span with that of a black swan which also lives by the bog – 'swane means swan' (p.22). Moreover, the name inevitably alludes intertextually to Hawthorne's Hester Prynne of *The Scarlet Letter*, another 'fallen' woman with an illegitimate child. Hester's scarlet letter will ultimately take the shape of her own heart, cut out of her chest in the play's final scene. Questions of legitimacy and naming also arise in regard to her daughter Josie. Josie is named after Hester's mother but her surname is contested by her paternal grandmother. Young Josie straddles both identities and lineages, maternal and paternal, as both a Kilbride and a Swane.

A concern for genealogy and the notion of heredity as destiny is foregrounded in narrative terms by the testimonies of different generations of characters in the plays. In each the present is haunted by the past and seems determined by its spectral legacy. In *The Mai*, a span of four generations of women is represented. The oldest, Grandma Fraochlán, provides an imaginative archive of fantasies and far-fetched stories, passed on to her by her mother 'The Duchess', many of which hinge upon her father's identity; an exotic, mysterious Spanish/Moroccan/Tunisian sailor. Grandma Fraochlán's difference is underlined by the language she uses, which is a curious mixture of heavily accented Connemara English tempered with the sentiments of popular romance. In addition, her frequent use of the word 'sublime' is replete with associations with English Romanticism, and coupled with her opium habit, serves to align her with escapism and the imagination. This proliferation of myths of origin to supplement 'reality' is crucial to the course of the play.

Portia Coughlan also delineates a territory of corrupted relationships in which an atmosphere of foreclosure is conjured through genealogy. Again, generations of characters appear on stage. Portia is the last in a three-generation line of poisoned marriages and her parents' hidden and inadvertent incest resurfaces like a hereditary disease. Portia associates her dead twin with her essence/origin. As proof she relates a fantasy memory of how they were 'lovers' in their mother's womb and how they came into the world holding hands. Significantly, her mother's memory is more sinister – Gabriel '[c]ame out of the womb clutchin' [Portia's] leg and he's still clutchin' it from wherever he is' (p.62). The echoes of the legend of Romulus and Remus, where twinship involves a struggle for dominance and ultimately survival, cast into doubt the authenticity of Portia's version of events.

Carr continues to explore questions of identity and ontology through her use of stories within the plays. The tales of Owl Lake (*The Mai*) and the Belmont River (*Portia Coughlan*) facilitate a metonymic shift where the protagonists are doubled in other 'fictions'. In contrast, *By the Bog of Cats...* follows Hester's quest for the 'story' of her mother, which is revealed only in fragments. She cannot wholly recall this narrative alone, but desperately needs it to define her own identity. Snatches are supplied by different characters, but Hester wishes to tailor their unsatisfactory versions to her own needs. The idealization she desires is undermined since 'what [she can] remember doesn't add up' (p.21). The Josie Swane she wants to remember – who '[made] up songs for every occasion', who was invited everywhere to sing at funerals, weddings, harvests, who took her daughter with her on those 'singin' sprees' (p.65) – cannot be reconciled with the mother who abandoned her. Throughout the play, Hester's ideal Josie is continually dismantled and destroyed by the fragmentary stories told by other characters. As Monica warns her toward the end of the play, 'she's not comin' back [...] This waitin' is only a fancy of yours [...] You up on forty, Hester, and still dreamin' of storybook endin's, still whingin' for your Mam' (p.65). Similar to Portia Coughlan, Hester's memory betrays her, and ontological wholeness, in which the separation between her self and her mother/origin would no longer exist, is revealed as illusory.

In each of the plays it is evident that origins are supposed to determine destiny and yet in each play the problematic nature of origins is stressed. Carr's multiple strategies of developing the notion of destiny and the inevitable, all have some ontological dimension, and in every case reveal a lack which is amended through simulation – illusion, fantasy, false memory, story. Although the dramas achieve a 'destined closure' more powerful is the traumatic unstable space of subjectivity they open.

To conclude, issues around notions of authenticity can be seen to permeate both Carr's work and her image in myriad and often conflicting ways. With regard to her public persona, some of the authenticating or authorizing gestures are her own, while some are produced by her commentators and critics. With regard to the plays especially since *The Mai*, the term 'authentic reproduction' though ripe with paradox seems particularly appropriate to the ways in which Carr draws upon different traditions and stereotypes.[40] The replication of aspects of various dramatic traditions provides a legitimizing connection with moral values and dilemmas, which might be understood as inevitable and authentic. These reproductions can be understood as simulacral, fulfilling a yearning for timeless stories and narrative closure at a time 'when the real is no longer what it

---

[40]Graham p.132.

used to be.'[41] Within the plays, however, the duplicities of nostalgia are critically present and identity, amidst a plethora of fantasy and false memory, is structured by the failure to locate any ontological plenitude.

---

[41]Baudrillard, pp.12-13.

4 | Playing the Story:
Narrative Techniques in *The Mai*

Eilis Ní Dhuibhne

Marina Carr's greatest gift is her facility with language. Her ability to select and reproduce the richest aspects of dialects and idiolects, to exploit phrases, sentences, and proverbial expressions for their humour or beauty, and her skill in selecting words which can, on occasion, convey elemental passion or the mystical attachment of people to their natural environment, are the most impressive aspects of her particular genius. In her love affair with her own language, literary English, and with the versions of oral English used in the part of rural Ireland she comes from and writes about, she has more in common with the novelist Edna O'Brien than with most contemporary Irish playwrights. There are other aspects of her imagination which support this comparison: like many of O'Brien's later novels, Carr's plays are set in country places in rural Ireland which combine great beauty with inescapable threat[1]. Owl Lake, the bog in *By the Bog of Cats...*, Raftery's Hill, mirror the sort of

---

[1] Examples of the use of landscape in this way in O'Brien's work are Cluais Wood, in Edna O'Brien, *In the Forest* (London: Weidenfeld and Nicholson, 2002), *passim*; the image of the bog, op.cit., and in Edna O'Brien, *Wild Decembers* (London: Weidenfeld and Nicholson, 2000).

highly-charged settings characteristic of Edna O'Brien's work.[2] Both writers frequently chart the tragic histories of sensitive, sometimes artistic or aesthetically discriminating women or girls who do not fit in to the physically charming but socially brutal environments in which they find themselves.[3] But one can also say that, like Edna O'Brien, Marina Carr is a storyteller, and, also like O'Brien, a storyteller with a lyrical bent whose work combines poetic and narrative qualities.[4]

Unfortunately, the word storyteller seems almost meaningless to me as I write it, since it is the fashion of the day to attribute to every writer, and also every public speaker, every politician, every historian, everyone, in fact, the skills of the storyteller. It is undeniable that in a certain sense all anecdotes, all reports of personal experiences, are 'stories', with characters, setting and some sort of plot. But if everyone is a storyteller, the word loses its force. I will therefore try to define what I mean by storyteller.

A storyteller, in the context of drama, is someone who narrates rather than acts out an epic event. A storyteller is someone who understands how to affect an audience's emotions by the judicious selection of images, ideas, and words. Whereas a dramatist relies on the tensions between characters for the

---

[2] In *In the Forest*, the heroine, Eily, cannot control the marshy field that surrounds her house. The place she has chosen as her home rejects her, not by throwing her out but by sucking her in. She is murdered and buried in the pleasant soft leaves of Cluais Wood. The indigenous people of the area collude with the landscape to destroy the intruder.

[3] Mary, the victim of paternal sexual abuse in *Down by the River* (London: Weidenfeld and Nicholson, 1997), has obvious parallels with the daughters of Raftery in *On Raftery's Hill*. Eily, in *In the Forest*, a beautiful young artist, shares certain qualities with heroines like Portia Coughlan or The Mai. A close examination would reveal, I think, that O'Brien's female heroines are victims of community in its setting, whereas Carr's are victims of family, often isolated from the community, in its setting.

[4] My guess is that the parallels between these two writers are not the effect of intertextuality or direct influence.

creation or suggestion of meaning to the audience, a storyteller relies more on the effects of language and the constructs of language to convey meaning, emotion, even catharsis. Marina Carr is a dramatist as well as a storyteller, and as such of course reveals dramatic tensions between characters. She relies a good deal, however, on the power of the narrated rather than the acted story.

This is particularly evident in *The Mai*, the first play to bring Marina Carr to national and international attention. It is her lightest, most humorous, and, within the limits of its tragedy, her happiest play. It is also the work which most clearly exploits overt narrative techniques.

The Mai focuses on the eponymous heroine, a middle-aged mother and school-teacher who suffers, for years, from the infidelity of her husband, Robert. A sort of cross between a pagan goddess and the Blessed Virgin, The Mai, dressed in the pale blue of summer skies and May altars, is the epitome of romantic marital purity. Monogamous to the core – almost – she devotes her life to her doomed love for Robert, regardless of the effect of her unhappiness on her family. She is a sort of Chekhovian heroine, brave, intelligent, beautiful, but hopelessly in love and unable to pull herself out of her delusion that the love of Robert is the most important part of her life. Surrounded by her own family of origin – her mother, Grandma Fraochlán, her aunts, her sister Beck, all of whom share in different ways her romantic yearnings for the one right man – she is, to put it bluntly, a dramatic personification of that stalwart of women's magazine agony aunt columns and stories, the woman who loves too much. (This is not such an irreverent accusation when one considers that Chekhov frequently deals with exactly the same sort of character, in his plays and even more so in his short stories.) It is thanks to Marina Carr's poetic, psychological and narrative skills that what is fairly commonplace, even banal material, is lifted into another artistic realm.

The Mai exploits narrative techniques in two ways. In the first place, it is actually told by a narrator, Millie, who sits on the side of the stage throughout most of the play, introducing, commentating, interpreting, and summing up. She is not an objective commentator, but, like the narrator in Brian Friel's *Dancing at Lughnasa*, the child of the heroine. The Mai's story is in fact Millie's story; as in *By the Bog of Cats...* or *On Raftery's Hill,* the story of a parent or parents is the legacy of their children. Marina Carr's principal theme in all her plays so far has been that the problems of parents impinge, permanently, on the lives of their offspring. The point of view which recurs in her plays is that of the wronged child.

At first Millie recounts the story of her parents in language and tone which seem dispassionate and objective. The use of the narrator's voice allows Marina Carr to highlight the difference between formal literary English and the informal oral language which her characters speak. One of her great contributions to Irish literature has been the presentation of dialect in her plays, and she becomes more confident about reproducing the dialect of the midlands as she writes more. In *The Mai*, there is less of it than in a later play such as *On Raftery's Hill*, and in the former play the difference between the narrator's language and that of most of the characters is one of formality versus informality, rather than of standard English versus dialect. But dialect intrudes to some extent in the language of Grandma Fraochlán:

> He didn't wanta go ouh an account a my impendin' delivery
> buh word cem tha salmon was leppin' an tha' Bofin side.[5]

The contrast of this style with that of Millie is dramatically extremely effective, and Carr exploits this type of contrast much more in her later plays. However she has already discovered this device in The Mai, principally thanks to using Millie as a narrator.

In addition to introducing and linking various episodes in the play, Millie narrates in a second way: she tells several short anecdotes or stories, as do some of the other characters, espe-

---

[5] Marina Carr, *The Mai* (Oldcastle: Gallery Press, 1995), p.69. In the Faber edition of *The Mai*, Grandma Fraochlán's use of dialect is re-written in more-or-less standard English, see *Plays 1*, p.181.

cially Grandma Fraochlán. The most striking example is the
legend of Bláth and Coillte, which is told by Millie at the close
of Act One. Underpinning a play with a folktale or myth is
characteristic of Marina Carr's technique and a practice which
recurs in later plays. *Portia Coughlan* alludes to Shakespearian
drama*, By the Bog of Cats...* and *On Raftery's Hill* to classical
myths. In the case of *The Mai*, its folkloristic parallel is not a
well-known story, but a local legend, and so it is essential for
the audience to hear the actual story to understand its place in
the play, since it can be presumed that they will not be familiar
with it in advance. Carr deals with the problem of an obscure
subtext in the most effective and direct way, by allowing Millie
to tell it. She narrates the legend of Bláth and Coillte, a love
story and a myth of seasonal death and resurrection: Bláth
leaves Coillte and goes to the cave of the dark witch for the
winter, promising to return in the spring. Coillte however
mourns so much that she turns into a lake of tears, which is
Owl Lake, where the family of The Mai lives. When Millie tells
the story, she explains its importance:

> A tremor runs through me when I recall the legend of Owl
> Lake. I knew that story as a child. So did The Mai and
> Robert. But we were unaffected by it and in our blindness
> moved along with it like sleepwalkers along a precipice and
> all around gods and mortals called out for us to change our
> course and, not listening, we walked on and on. (*TM*, p.148)

I am not quite sure what Millie's interpretation of the story
is: that Owl Lake is a dangerous place, that The Mai should
learn a lesson in patience from Coillte and not make her mistake, or that The Mai should leave Robert, who is fated to
abandon her periodically? The ending of the play suggests that
it is probably the latter. The dramatic significance of this narration, however, is that it injects the ordinary soap opera story of
the play with a mysteriousness and depth which it might otherwise lack; it provides an ancient history for the new house at
Owl Lake, and manages to link the events of the play with
forces which are as elemental and ancient as the lake itself. The
telling of this tale, combined with the extraordinary natural

beauty of the setting of the play – as described in the words of the players – are forces which are crucial in enhancing the play and rendering it memorable and impressive. These forces are the powers of myth, poetic powers which reside in nature, the eternal and the divine, rather than the essentially human dynamic of drama.

The telling of this mythical story at the centre of *The Mai* reflects Carr's attraction to mythology and folklore, an attraction which is persistent. In all her plays, she employs images and places which have a mythic resonance – the settings of the plays are similar to those which occur in fairytales: lakes, bogs, forests, hills. Even The Mai's house is a sort of fairytale palace on the side of Owl Lake. The names which Marina Carr gives her characters also reflect those used in fairytales, where proper names are either avoided totally, or tend to be either so commonplace that they have no specificity whatsoever, names such as John or Ivan; or utterly outlandish: Cinderella, Rapunzel, Rumpelstiltskin. Names which are seldom encountered in everyday life are frequent in Marina Carr's work: The Mai, Grandma Fraochlán in *The Mai*; Sorrel, Ded, Red, in *On Raftery's Hill*, Portia Coughlan in the play of that title. Like the elemental places she selects for her settings, these personal names resonate with mythical association.

Thematically, Carr's plays present certain parallels with the themes of great folktales. Like almost every *Märchen*, her plays deal with the children of unsupportive families. All fairytales concern the journey of the adolescent from the family of origin to the re-establishment of a new family – typically, the hero or heroine is abandoned by the family of origin, often owing to conflict with a figure such as an evil stepmother. Having passed a series of tests and overcome various obstacles, the hero/heroine succeeds in finding a suitable spouse and getting married, so re-establishing him or herself in a new and supportive family. The theme of every fairytale is the trauma of the adolescent striving to grow into independent adulthood, to escape from parental control and to deal successfully with the grief or guilt attendant on this necessary separation. This pattern is at the heart of *The Mai* and *On Raftery's Hill*, where it is subverted – the happy ending of the fairytale is lacking in both, and in *On Raftery's Hill* it is utterly reversed. In Marina Carr's plays, the child-heroes are so damaged by the flaws of their parents that they never achieve the independence which is the normal 'happy ending' of adolescence (symbolized in delightful weddings in fairytales and romantic novels). In *By the Bog of Cats…* the daughter in her white dress dies long before she reaches adulthood; Sorrel in *On Raftery's Hill* is denied her wedding. Millie, the most successful survivor of all Marina Carr's abused heroines, finds it impossible to settle into any semblance of a 'normal' stable life. Carr's fairytales end with an un-wedding, an acknowledgement that excessive emotional abuse of children (whether inflicted deliberately, as in *On Raftery's Hill*, or through carelessness, as in *The Mai*) allows no redemption.

The story of Bláth and Coillte is the narrative focal point of *The Mai*, but is not the only story that Millie tells. In the course of the rest of the play, she presents three more short anecdotes: one reporting on The Mai's experience as a hairdresser's assistant during a summer holiday, one about a neighbour, Sam Brady (and his cow, Billy the Black), a bizarre character who prefigures Red in *On Raftery's Hill*, and finally the story of her own (Millie's) experience of motherhood, when she gave birth to a son in New York.

The final anecdote is central to the play's theme, the way in which parents hand on legacies of pain to their children. It is a serious story, sombrely told. The others, however, are light-hearted and humorous, and, like the various tales told by Grandma Fraochlán, whose function is almost wholly comic, although she too has played her part in sculpting this unhappy family – a family of women who love men to excess and do not love their children enough. Whether mystical, like the legend of Owl Lake, comic, like the tale of Billy the Black, or of the nine-fingered fishermen told by Grandma Fraochlán, or surprising, like the tale of The Mai and the Arabian princess at the hair-dressers, all these stories serve more than one function in the unfolding drama. Most of them throw some light on character and theme, even the story of Billy the Black, which sits less easily in the play than the others. However, it reveals quite cleverly the effect Robert's behaviour is having on the neighbours in Owl Lake, and the shame which this brings to the family, heaped on the hurt already endured. But in addition to developing our understanding of the theme, these stories enhance the texture of the play. Instead of being a realistic drama about adultery, a women's magazine story, (albeit with the seriousness of its accusation against the adults in the play – that they are children, while their children are forced to play the role of adults), *The Mai* is lifted into the domain of folklore and myth; it is studded with humour, flights of fancy and imagination; it establishes links with elemental nature and with the otherworld. It would be a witty and interesting play anyway, thanks to Marina Carr's use of dialogue, but the injection of the play with these stories gives it a sparkling originality and a liveliness which a story such as The Mai's, however convincing, could not otherwise achieve.

The power of stories is well understood by Marina Carr. This is not so much evident in Millie's warning at the end of Act One, relating to the Owl Lake legend, as in what happens at the end of the second act. Towards the end of the final scenes, Millie makes her last speech, tells her last story, which is the tragic story of The Mai's children.

> None of The Mai and Robert's children are very strong. We teeter along the fringe of the world with halting gait, reeking of Owl Lake at every turn. I dream of water all the time [...] it goes on and on till I succumb and linger among them there in that dead silent world that tore our hearts out for a song. (TM, p.184)

At this point, Millie's narrative control is fractured completely. Her story stops and she slips back into the play as a character, finding her mother late at night, waiting for her father to come home. It is as if she cannot withstand the power of her own storytelling to revive the scenes of the past – she lives again an argument in which she tries to persuade her mother to leave her father. It is a quiet but terrible scene, revealing Millie as a child involved in matters from which she should be protected, a scene in which the daughter takes on the role of counsellor to her mother. The Mai has the last word, a plea for understanding of the inevitability of her fate. Love is everything, she is powerless to withstand it, and she must live her half-life, since nothing better is available. And this explanation is convincing enough as far as it goes. But the authority of the lover faithful to the betrayer, the relentless romantic, is seriously undermined by the ever-present daughter, Millie (*'Millie remains onstage throughout the play'* is the direction (p.107)). Millie never leaves the stage, and the story of her mother is therefore illuminated by her presence, and revealed as a very different story than it would be were the perspective of her child ignored.

It is at this juncture, when Millie ceases to be a storyteller and becomes a dramatic character, that the central dramatic struggle of *The Mai* is exposed. The conflict at the heart is not that between The Mai and her faithless husband, but that of The Mai and Millie her daughter. By projecting Millie suddenly into the play at this crucial late stage, by pulling her away from her superior druidic position as storyteller and revealing her as a vulnerable character on the stage, as real or unreal as The Mai or any of the other characters, Marina Carr gives us an insight into what storytelling can and cannot do. It may be that this moment, when the storyteller abandons her tale and falls into its drama, is the moment of psychological redemption for Millie, the only redemption she is likely to experience. It is also the moment when the playwright acknowledges simultaneously both the intense power and the ultimate impotence of story. Story strives to bring the dead to life, to make present of past. It allows the narrator to control the chaos of past experience and to achieve an understanding of it. But the cost of this control is distance. Drama depends on the opposite, total engagement. When Millie stops narrating she starts to be. For her, it is at this moment that drama, the mirror of life, takes over from narrative, its reporter.

5 | Aperçus

Where Your Treasure Is: *The Mai*
Programme Note: Peacock Theatre, 1994

Tom Mac Intyre

Marina Carr's *Low In The Dark* (Project Arts Centre 1989) gave evidence of an original voice – zany, enquiring, free-wheeling as regards structure, the focus on love and the sensual. In *Ullaloo* (Peacock, 1990) – three plays later – you could see her testing, with a kind of proper hesitancy, the languages available, testing, especially, the relationship between word and image. And if the theme was the same as in the earlier work, the zany note had been tempered. There were shadows, on the prowl. The piece was tense, brittle. The sense of a writer wondering what next was riskily close to the surface.

The Mai, it seems to me, decisively claims new ground. This playwright's distinctive voice is far more audible. Suddenly – and not at all suddenly – she has made vital contact with her West of Ireland inheritance. What is it? It's a poetry compounded of myth and folklore, dream and fantasy, the breeze from the sea, the currach on the shore. It's the stuff of romance, story-telling and a mode of survival, and also, story-telling as a mode of escape from demanding imperatives. A special *frisson* of Marina Carr's exploration of her gift here is the way in which it salutes the wild imaginings which help the walking wounded from one day to the next – while at the same time ruthlessly pointing the cost of failure to meet essential questions of our lives. All that is to say this piece has an *interior* not present in her work before. There's a lyric daring in her probing of pain which I find enormously exciting: a mother in distress sends her child to the butcher's for a needle and thread: a farmer shows his disapproval of a wayward husband by shooting the head off a cob feeding by the lake… 'swans keen their mates […] It's a sound you hope never to hear again and it's a sound you know you will': a daughter sings an elegy to her mother's relationship with an Arab child princess: 'Two of a kind, moving towards each other across deserts and fairy tales and years… Two little Princesses on the cusp of a dream, one five, the other forty…'

Wit and humour have always been part of this playwright's music. Here the wit is sharp as ever, the humour strikingly enhanced. The comedy of romantic yearning, the contortions of sibling rivalry, the opium-drenched meanderings of Grandma Fraochlán, all these are rendered with a deliciously ample warmth. Grandma Fraochlán, indeed, is an extraordinary creation. Kavanagh – who knew that tragedy is under-developed comedy – would have loved her. She comes towards us with her souvenir oar, her scars, her illusions, and she lets us know that tenderness is all, that people will travel long miles to see a 'missing finger' – missing arm – missing leg – because 'people never tire of great love stories.' You may call this Grandma Falstaffian. Generously, and to her own beat, she too lards the lean earth as she walks along.

And Marina Carr's energetic search for varieties of structure continues in this new play, rummages possibilities more compellingly than before. The hungry story-teller in her cuts loose here with tremendous verve, she takes the *chronicle* mode and studies it, plays with it, every which way. The pictorial isn't neglected. In counterpoint to the rip of story-telling, she sets a key image – a window, through which a lake is visible. Chronicle and pictorial fuse. That window opens onto the unconscious, the zone from which the treasure must be redeemed. Return with the treasure – and you've a story to tell, stories happen to you – in abundance. The window larger, the lake deeper? Yes.

There are writers, said Trumane Capote, *and there are typewriters.* No one will cross him on that. You could also say – *There are writers and there are quest-writers.* Marina Carr is a quest writer. She puts her life on the line. She must *know.* Daring, however, is never fatal – she has that large protection – and our sustained attention – as she fashions herself an exemplary road.

Masks: An Introduction to *Portia Coughlan*
from *The Dazzling Dark*[1]

Frank McGuinness

I'm writing this introduction as October comes to an end and we're nearing Hallowe'en. Since Celtic times we've celebrated this festival and recently, in a mad fit of sanity, the Irish government declared it a public holiday. All Soul's Night, Hallowe'en, is our Mardi Gras, a time for wearing masks and remembering the dead, as if by remembering them we resurrect them. And the mask is the outward sign that we are engaging in this ritual communication between the living and the dead.

Marina Carr is a writer haunted by memories she could not possibly possess, but they seem determined to possess her. This haunting is a violent one, intensified by the physical attack on the conventions of syntax, spelling and sounds of Standard English in the language of *Portia Coughlan*. It is a violence that avoids resolution to its conflict. Through the disruption of its narrative, Portia herself, like the ghosts of Japanese theatre, lives, dies, comes back to relive her suffering. By the play's end she stands by a river, a river that does not carry her to peace. The war goes on, the war of words where the weapons are the fighting talk of mother, father, son and daughter, sister, brother, wife and husband. The landscapes where they conduct their

---

[1] Ed. by Frank McGuinness (London and Boston: Faber and Faber, 1996) pp.ix-x.

campaigns begin by seeming to be familiar. Yet they, by the perverse logic of love and hatred, grow foreign through their very familiarity. The unhappy, unholy family is the only constant in this universe, and it is in the process of tearing itself to pieces. Tragedy is so often the consequence of a fatal lack of self-knowledge. Marina Carr rewrites the rule. Her characters die from a fatal excess of self-knowledge. Their truth kills them. And they have always known it would.

Portia Coughlan:
Programme Note: Peacock Theatre, 1996

Tom Mac Intyre

Marina Carr is an original. That means, among other things, it's hard to trace the source of her marvels. Nevertheless, William Faulkner – pipe smoking in the cotton fields of the beyond – was surely smiling as she penned *Portia Coughlan*. Carr's music of shameless comedy counterpointing Gothic despair, her implacably tender study of severe disturbance, and her recklessly inspired handling of Irish midland vernacular, posit Faulkner as a benign – albeit remote – ancestor.

Unquestionably, the comedy is what makes the dark of the piece bearable. It's a comedy which has a wide range, varying from the domestic zany to the blackest of black, and finding many tints between. It is – in the best Irish tradition – comedy fiercely rooted in joyful observation of the human, and – in equal measure – given resonance by a characteristically Irish sense of our helplessness (not quite total) in the hands of The Powers. Lake and river invite – and furnish – destruction. That granted, tomorrow is another day and not a bite out of it yet. This dicey equilibrium – pennants flying – is close to the centre of Carr's eloquence.

Another element sustaining the piece – as shadows bloat by the minute – is the lyric ripple across Portia's torment. There's a fresh boldness in Carr's pen here, one which enables her to explore with unfailing tact the sister-brother bond at the heart of the play. What carries the writer triumphantly through is her willingness to take on the challenge of the love-death theme – a bog where armies whole have vanished – and, the challenge once accepted, her discovery or resources, worlds, available to her that have been suggested but not fully realized in earlier work.

There's a tenderness in the writing around Portia which catches the breath, it's never tainted by the sentimental. With the lightest of touches – an extraordinary paradox since the composition is unabashedly Gothic – we are led into the dusk, and on into the night of this woman's extreme perturbation. A howl is made audible and believable, and the howl is of today. Carr has a wicked eye – because she's trained it. And her middle name is *immediacy*.

A lyric ripple. A tenderness. A vocabulary to contend with. A huge joy of Portia is the freedom of language Carr brings to the venture. The tatterdemalion promise of her frolic with words in *The Mai* (Peacock, 1994) is here abundantly in blossom. There are no rules because the writer has thrown them away and, as in all quality writing, she simply makes it up as she goes along or, better, she relies on the *it* factor to foster the magic. The writing throughout Portia is drenched by the unconscious. Accordingly, the sweep of articulation in the play is constantly – and unforecastably – seductive.

Grotesquerie is another potent ingredient, a grotesquerie that aspires to the mythic. We're in a world – the Irish sagas come to mind – where it's as near normal as makes no difference to have half a leg chopped off in the firm hope of massive compensation; where, an eye gouged out as part of some night's entertainment, the victim may merrily ring the changes of eye shade colour to meet the mutabilities of life; where sibling ghost sings from storied river – that soprano siren colliding with the dulcet tenor of John McCormack (O, the purity of the diction…) even as Grandma charges from her wheel-chair to wage war, and damned be him who cries *Hold, enough*!

One returns to Portia, surely a figure of mythic force: there's such valour in her self-destruction. Her targets are appropriate – she can recognize the gormless and the tyrannical. She looks about her and knows 'this place must be the dungeon a the fallen worldt'; her self knowledge, whatever its obscurities, can point her to 'a wolf tooth growin' in her heart', and identify the coffin smell for what it is, a smell 'atwane honeysuckle an new mown putrefaction'. All these things endear her to us, even as we watch and wait – for calamity. Perhaps what endears her most to us is the *search* energy in her, the quest compulsion, and its attendant verities. When a body goes looking for that which is lost, Marina Carr wisely tells us, everything becomes a sign.

Shooting from the Lip:
Review of *Portia Coughlan*, *Sunday Times*, 31 March, 1996

Medb Ruane

'I spent the first eighty years of me life holdin' me tongue, f***in' and blindin' into the pillow,' says Blaise Coughlan, and you know she's about to make up for it. There are more F-words in Portia Coughlan than outside the Belgard Inn at closing time. Curses fly across the Peacock stage like poisoned arrows, flaying the social skin remorselessly and with that picky devotion of carrion birds on a dying corpse. Here in the mid-lands of Marina Carr, quips are what get you laughs: pubs are called after TV programmes, people are named for angels but poetry signals a fissure which deals a mortal wound. None of the confessional, sentimental excesses of The Mai survive in Carr's new play. Portia Coughlan is a brutal and passionate drama of family relationships and personal disintegration, set on the day of Portia's thirtieth birthday over three, time-bending acts. Fifteen years earlier, Portia's twin brother Gabriel drowned in her beloved Belmont river; soon after that, she married Raphael Coughlan, a good catch but dull as ditchwater. He's safe and she's sorry, so for most of their marriage she's been screwing Damus Halion, though she also throws shapes at the barman in the High Chaparral, where she hangs out with her pal Stacia. She's got three kids but she can't stand them, parents she dreads and a granny from hell – the eff-wielding

Blaise we met above. Only her aunt Maggie May offers the solace she seeks, but Maggie May is an outcast, a 'rusty tandem' who turned tricks in London until she met her wimpish husband Senchil, and now champions an early brandy. Portia Coughlan is all about speaking the unspoken. Voices are everywhere, from the deadly boy-soprano strains of Gabriel's ghost to Granny-from-hell's passion for the tenor, John McCormack. Language is damaged save when spoken by Portia, at which point it leaps into poetry with a jolt that twists the action and sends the other characters scurrying even further into incomprehension. When the others do use words or images out of the ordinary, the language can get stuck in their craws, making at times for a touch too much of the 'shiny new moon' syndrome, but acceptable in context.

As spoken by Carr's characters, words are weapons designed to inflict hurt and cruelty – nothing is saved for the pillow. Maggie May retaliates against Blaise Coughlan's taunting by telling how she had Blaise's husband up the back lane, paid for by Blaise's own egg money and the jeer that 'he'd rather hump a bag of rats in a bed of nettles' than his own wife. Portia tells Raphael and her mother exactly what she thinks of them and, for the only time, delivers on her threatened violence by wrestling her mother to the floor. Yet the hint of physical violence is everywhere: Raphael lost a foot, Stacia had her eye gouged out and even the blistering Blaise was battered by her dead husband. Whether physically or psychically, every character is damaged; one turn of the screw and the joins begin to show.

There's a passing family resemblance to the work of Tom Murphy. Yet *Portia Coughlan* is written and performed in a woman's voice, from the vision of Marina Carr to the superb production by Garry Hynes and the mega, towering performance of Derbhle Crotty as Portia. Peter Boylan, master of Holles Street Hospital, which commissioned the play, writes that it is 'essentially a woman's story', but this is far more than Maeve Binchy with teat. So few plays by women make it onto the stage of Ireland's hallowed theatres that Carr risks being characterized as flag-carrier for all those voices which – even in post-Robinson society – remain silent. Can you name ten women dramatists who have had work produced in Ireland in the past five years? *Portia Coughlan* is not a woman's story, even though it tells the story of a woman. There's no sentiment, no frills and absolutely nothing ladylike about it. If anything, the play's few flaws derive from its attempt to hit that quasi-heroic note which sounds throughout the Irish theatrical tradition, that mixture of love and death which makes everyday intimacy seem less worthwhile. Presenting Portia as both victim and heroine, the play eventually opts for a mechanistic, causal explanation of her suffering, creating certain dramatic benefits but extracting it from the very cultural throes that signalled audience identification in the first place. That she's not a 'natural mother', that she despises her husband, that she feels the life being sucked from her by the society in which she lives, is truth enough. Pinning her tragedy onto the hook of genetics yields powerful theatre but leaves the rest of us with only our pillows to cling to.

Portia Coughlan comes from a territory where Phaedra and Margo walk hand in hand. It's got all the qualities of Greek drama, save that DNA takes over where the Gods left off. Visualized so clearly you can almost see neo-Doric columns outside Portia's house, or veneered beauty board at the High Chapparel. Kandis Cook's set remains sensitively simple, working with surfaces which reflect and glow as Jim Simmons's lighting strikes them. The impact is so powerful you're tempted to believe only Garry Hynes could produce such work (particularly the second act staging, where Pietà meets *The Quiet Man*), yet you sense that amateur drama groups will be doing *Portia Coughlan* for the foreseeable future precisely because of its upfront human impact and that mischievous writing which makes you laugh just as it shocks your soul.

But it's the sweating, angry torment of Derbhle Crotty's performance that drives the production. Crotty plays Portia like a marathon runner, incarcerated so firmly in the character that she never misses a beat. Marion O'Dwyer's Maggie May is equally well wrought, Bronagh Gallagher underplays Stacia perfectly, Pauline Flanagan is a malicious delight. Tom Hickey and Stella McCusker, a controlled Sean Rocks, the sexy Don Wycherley and the would-be sexy Charlie Bonner along with a ditheringly pathetic Des Keogh make a perfect cast for *Portia Coughlan*'s premiere. You don't often find such passion on an Irish stage.

Writing in Greek: *By the Bog of Cats...*
Programme Note: Abbey Theatre, 1998

Frank McGuinness

I wonder what Marina Carr believes? I think it might be the Greek gods – Zeus and Hera, Pallas Athena. She knows what the Greeks know. Death is a big country. And hers is a big imagination, crossing the border always between the living and the dead. She speaks in a strange language, but has no truck with the gift of tongues. In her plays words are like boiling water. They scald you if they so choose. And she knows playwrights have to be in the business of discovering fire, for without it there is no passion, no comfort, no terror, no light.

I love her plays for the light they cast on darkness. Their passions are terrible, but they are confronted. She has listened to the stern voice of her true literary ancestor, Emily Brontë. No coward's soul is hers. In confrontation with terror, she is without fear. Her theatre is, in the most brutal sense, heroic. Her brave women look into the face of those that have gone before them – Medea, Hedda Gabler, Miss Julie – and they can hold their own in that tough company who took on their world and tore it to ribbons, for that was their destiny. They swallow wedding rings for breakfast. If they have pity, it is not for themselves.

There is no knowing what is going to happen in any play by Marina Carr, except the inevitable. *By the Bog of Cats...* is a play about sorrow. Therefore it must be funny. A play about death, so a wedding shall be at the centre of it. A play about saying things that need to be said, so there will be silence at the end of it. A play about hatred, so love is at its heart. A play whose philosophy is that Carthage must be destroyed, but what happens to the destroyers? That is what *By the Bog of Cats...* tells us.

I wonder what Marina Carr believes? I can't say for certain, but I am certain in this play she writes in Greek.

Review of *Ariel*

Abbey Theatre, *Irish Times*, 4 October, 2002

Fintan O'Toole

After the first few minutes of Marina Carr's new play *Ariel*, we
know that we are in a crumbling world. The very title comes
from the feverish version of the Biblical prophet Isaiah, fore-
seeing the destruction of a city. On stage, at the sixteenth birthday party of the eponymous daughter of a rising Midlands
politician, the three pillars of the old Ireland – Church, State
and Family – are in an advanced state of decay. The politician,
Mark Lambert's Fermoy Fitzgerald, is a strange beast, driven by
dark compulsions and fanatic visions of destiny. His brother
Boniface (Barry McGovern) is a monk whose sole remaining
duty is the care of his decrepit and demented colleagues. And
the wider Fitzgerald family is a cauldron of simmering resent-
ments. In all of this, Carr is laying out the ground that the best
Irish dramatists of the younger generation must now occupy.
The society that gave form and meaning to the work of their
older contemporaries is in disarray. Playwrights such as Carr
and Sebastian Barry, whose recent work, *Hinterland*, bears many
resemblances to *Ariel*, have to start almost from scratch. They
have to find a way to make their own private myths fuse with
the public world they now inhabit. This is a journey into un-
mapped territory, and when you have no map and no clear
sense of a destination, you tend to wander. It may well be that
Ariel is the kind of play we will have to get used to: a meander

into an unknown landscape where we see some breathtaking views and stumble into some treacherous bogs. The grand house that the Fitzgeralds have built with the fortune they have made in the cement and gravel business is, we are told, fronted with Greek columns. So is Carr's play. Given her recurrent concern with family dynasties riven by violence, death and inescapable destiny, it was perhaps inevitable that she should seek her public myth in the Greek tragedies. *Ariel* is clearly a version of the story of Iphigenia, sacrificed by her father Aga-memnon to appease the gods and gain a fair wind for the voyage to Troy. The Fitzgeralds are a twenty-first century Irish House of Atreus, with Fermoy as Agamemnon, Ingrid Craigie's precise, contained Frances as his disaffected wife Clytemnestra and Elske Rahill's Ariel as Iphigenia. There are elements of Electra and Orestes in the Fitzgeralds' other children, Stephen (Dylan Tighe) and Elaine (Eileen Walsh). This in itself is an enormously ambitious undertaking, but Ariel is also trying to be an Irish version of Tony Kushner's *Angels in America*. Carr, too, is trying to fuse an immediate vision of political crisis with a large sweep of religious and Biblical images. She tries this, moreover, over a span of ten years, with the first act set in the present and the other two in ten years time. This is quite simply too much for one play, even for a dramatist of Carr's bold and relentless imagination. Euripides and Aeschylus – no mean playwrights – felt it necessary to unpack the myth in a series of plays. Kushner split *Angels in America* into two very long epics. By squeezing it all into one evening of conventional length, Carr risks the kind of literal overkill that comes when bodies pile up in a rapid succession of catastrophes. Nor does she manage to get to the core of the Greek plays: a sense of neces-sity. In the Greek world, the killing of Iphigenia is as necessary as its terrible consequences are inevitable. Here, Fermoy's sacrifice of his daughter is driven, not by the logic of the story, but by a rhetoric drawn from psychotic visions. We never get a convincing reason why it has to happen.

These are serious problems, all the more so because the play does not pretend to work on the level of social realism. Fermoy is not remotely convincing as a contemporary Irish politician, and his religious ravings in an extended television interview don't sound like the kind of stuff that could make him the next Taoiseach. What is most remarkable, however, is that with all of these gaping flaws, *Ariel* is still curiously compelling. This is partly because of the sheer, gutsy integrity with which director Conall Morrison and his cast engage with Carr's quest. Lambert and Craigie in particular don't just push the boat but steer unflinchingly into the uncharted waters. It is also, though, because of Carr's own courage. It takes vision and generosity to accept the task of trying to find public myths for a society that no longer knows what anything means. If *Ariel* doesn't find them, there is nevertheless an excitement in the search.

6 | Reflections Across Water:
New Stages of Performing Carr.

Melissa Sihra.

> Truth has a short life-span, mysteries survive.[1]

2001 was a significant year in the career of playwright Marina Carr in terms of the production and critical acclaim of her work in the United States. In March of that year Carr was awarded the E.M. Forster Award for Literary Achievement from the American Academy of Arts and Letters. There were three major productions of her plays; Portia Coughlan was produced in March by the Pittsburgh Irish and Classical Theatre company (PICT), *By the Bog of Cats...* had its U.S. premiere in Chicago in May for Irish Repertory (IRC), and was produced again in September by San Jose Repertory Theatre (SJR) with Academy Award winning actor Holly Hunter in the lead role. In the academic field Carr's plays are achieving an increasing presence on literature and drama courses in the major universities across the United States, and November saw the first American publication of her 1998 play *By the Bog of Cats...* by Syracuse University Press in New York. The trajectory continues with Carr's appointment to the Heimbold Chair in Irish Studies at the University of Villanova, Philadelphia, in 2003.

---

[1] Olwen Fouéré in *Chair*, for Operating Theatre, Peacock Theatre, Dublin, October 2001.

As dramaturg on the above mentioned productions I wish to consider the appeal of Carr's plays for American practitioners and audiences. Issues of representation and reception, and the ways in which the performances articulate and explore, perpetuate or contest, received or distinctive notions of 'Irishness', necessarily arise. In highlighting some of the key issues that arose during rehearsal, I will address the ways in which Carr's plays 'translate' in an international context, and outline the diverse modes of staging, design and production choices. I will also consider how these issues relate to questions of identity, cultural specificity and the traditions of Irish drama, and what aspects of the work American audiences may have found problematic or questionable.

Most American directors work with dramaturgs, yet the role is notoriously loosely defined in Ireland. A dramaturg is, traditionally, a 'playwriting specialist' who works closely with a playwright in terms of drafting a new piece for production. If the play is already in its final draft, or indeed, already published, the dramaturg will then work with the director, actors and designers in a consultancy capacity, contextualizing the play socially, politically and historically, advising on set and costume design, musical score and so on. The dramaturg will also offer input on narrative and thematic interpretation, in addition to writing programme notes, subscribers' newsletter essays, mounting exhibitions, and participating in post-show discussions. My role in the three productions involved all of the above.

Before confronting the recent American productions of Marina Carr's plays, it is perhaps useful to consider how her plays operate within the context of theatre in Ireland. As contemporary Ireland rapidly evolves into an ethnically diverse, technologically advanced, economically viable member of the European Union, the modernity remains superficial – old preoccupations prevail. Irish playwrights tenaciously draw on a sense of the past to articulate the present. Pre-Christian systems of belief, the landscapes of ghosts and the dead, of myth and historical reference are repeatedly evoked in the narratives of McGuinness, Murphy, Kilroy, Friel and Carr. Identity, national and individual, is ritually represented on the Irish stage as split, discordant and performative. The Irish theatrical tradition remains a literary one: there is a continual emphasis on storytelling and language, as a means not simply to communicate, but to investigate the intricate, mutually dependent processes of memory and identity.

While Carr's dramas can be considered within this legacy of representation, her narratives reveal the rupture or increasing gap created by the diminished roles of the traditional authorities, displayed by the radical rejection of a nostalgia for the past, monological notions of maternity, domestic security, community and fellowship.[2] Characteristic of her work is the representation of individual, familial and religious authority and stability in crisis. In terms of style, Carr's dramas operate within a kind of 'heightened realism', working on mythic, densely metaphoric levels, where lyrical narratives of memory and flashback, disrupt temporal and 'historical' linearity, effecting a repeated discordance between subjective 'truth' and speculative invention.[3]

How does Carr's representation of contemporary Ireland interact with typically received, pastoral-kitsch commodifications of Irishness abroad? *Mise en scène* is a key factor in Carr's renegotiation of cultural stereotype. The seemingly traditional, rural familial settings of Carr's dramas are fundamentally recalcitrant to any notion of a romantic, de Valerian Irish bucolia. The interaction between place, character and narrative in Carr's plays, where the poetically charged topography becomes the site of infanticide, incest, domestic violence, rape, prostitution, infidelity, violation and suicide, offers depictions of Ireland less concerned with filtering the past through a fractured golden lens, than reflecting contemporary social images of turbulance and anomie.

---

[2] There is a marked absence of religious authority in Carr's plays: where present, as with the figure of Father Willow in *By the Bog of Cats…,* it is depicted as unconventional, operating on the level of carnivalesque inversion.

[3] Interview with Melissa Sihra. *Theatre Talk: Voices of Irish Theatre Practitioners,* (Dublin: Carysfort Press, 2001), p.60.

Carr's characteristic representation of the Midlands of Ireland renegotiates the 'stability' of dominant cultural tropes of a romantic, *green* Irish landscape. This *mid*-lands, or *between*-lands, displays an ambivalent poetics of Irish topography in its negative relation to the popular, romantically constructed landscapes of East and West. The indistinctiveness of the flat, black Midlands bog, 'always shiftin' and changin', and coddin' the eye' (*BBOC*: p.267), radically counteracts depictions of the 'fixed' Irish pastoral scene, incorporating a simultaneous politics of geographical centrality and cultural marginality.[4] Referring to the central triangle of Ireland, the area between Tullamore, Athlone and Clonmacnoise as 'the cross-roads between the worlds',[5] Carr notes the liminality and symbolic potentiality of her theatrical landscape.

In tracing the appeal of Carr's work for American producers, I noted that the lyrical language and strength of characterization was repeatedly commented upon. In the *Chicago Sun-Times* review of IRC's *By the Bog of Cats...* critic Hedy Weiss notes: 'One sure sign you are in the presence of a gifted playwright is that you can laugh wildly one minute [and] cry in horror the next [...] the glue is Carr's blood-rich language and her characters' absolute fierceness and fearlessness.'[6] Producing Director of Irish Repertory of Chicago Matt O'Brien, noted that: 'along with McGuinness, Murphy and Friel, Carr has an innate theatrical skill. While the plays may be 'Irish', they are universal in meaning.'[7] Artistic Director of San Jose Repertory Theatre, Timothy Near, noted the 'theatricality, rich poetic scope, and vast landscape of the piece' after staging a reading of the play at the Magic Theatre's Festival of Irish Women Playwrights in San

---

[4] From early representations of Irish landscape in Boucicault, Shaw, Synge, O'Casey, and John Ford's *The Quiet Man* to Friel and McDonagh.

[5] Carr, Marina, *The Dazzling Dark,* ed. by Frank McGuinness (London: Faber & Faber, 1996), p.310.

[6] Hedy Weiss in *Chicago Sun-Times,* 5 June, 2001.

[7] Conversation with Melissa Sihra, Chicago, 1 June, 2001.

Francisco a couple of years ago.[8] The mythic context was fore-grounded again by Holly Hunter who referred to Carr as 'a gifted poet [...] To find a play like this is rare, no one has this kind of powerful voice. You have to go back to the classics.'[9]

Significantly, Carr's recent plays have received their pre-mieres primarily at the Abbey and Gate theatres in Dublin. [10] New plays are necessarily framed by their association with the theatre spaces in which they are first produced. The cultural and historical ideology of the theatre building instantly contextual-izes the work, informing both meaning and reception. Thus Carr's dramas are placed in such a way as to become contempo-rary classics within Ireland, since most have been produced in the mainstream theatre, rather than in independent or more experimental spaces. Such positioning and association is attrac-tive to international practitioners and audiences. The Abbey and Gate theatres have instant name-recognition in the United States which offer 'authenticity' to the marketing project abroad in offering a product that can be seen as the 'best of contempo-rary Irish theatre'.

Yet the programming of Carr's dramas, while artistically challenging, has not always been commercially unproblematic. Andrew Paul, Artistic Director of the Pittsburgh Irish and Classical Theatre company, who produced *Portia Coughlan* says: 'It took me several years to develop the company to the degree that I could take risks with this type of raw drama. I think the play will challenge Pittsburgh audiences, and that is a good thing.'[11] Paul, who had seen *On Raftery's Hill* at the Festival of Irish Culture in Washington the previous year, noted how 'its disturbing tone clearly unsettled the audience.' He went on to

[8] Conversation with Melissa Sihra and Marina Carr, Dublin, 11 April, 2001.

[9] Holly Hunter, 29 August, 2001.

[10] *Ullaloo,* Peacock Theatre, 1991, *The Mai,* Peacock Theatre, 1994, *Portia Coughlan,* Peacock Theatre, 1996, *By the Bog of Cats...,* Abbey Theatre, 1998, *On Raftery's Hill*, Gate Theatre, 2000, *Ariel,* Abbey Theatre, 2002.

[11] E-mail, 22 January, 2001.

say, 'I think Carr's voice is unique, and will take time to establish itself among American theatre-goers. Her vision of Ireland is certainly not one the Irish Americans want to see and embrace. We seem to prefer Frank McCourt.'[12]

In terms of the reception of these plays in the United States, I perceived a tension between what critics and audiences have praised as Carr's 'theatrical skill', and the content of the plots, which have often alienated, and in some cases, revolted, audience members, who have difficulty reconciling the lyrical elements of the plays with the uncompromising nature of the story-lines. These tensions became apparent with *Portia Coughlan* (and *On Raftery's Hill*), where audience reception proved extremely mixed. This begs the question as to whether on-stage infanticide, suicide and attempted rape (as represented in *By the Bog of Cats…*), are less controversial when filtered through a Euridipean lens, than off-stage, 'un-Classically' mediated suicide, as in the case of *Portia Coughlan*. While *By the Bog of Cats…* is considered 'fearless', 'sweepingly theatrical', 'courageous', *Portia* is viewed as 'grim, unrelenting, 'hopeless' and 'despairing'.[13]

By the Bog of Cats…, which is loosely based on Euripides' *Medea,* and Carr's forthcoming new drama *Ariel,* which is loosely based on Euripides' *Iphigenia,* seem to be less problematic depictions of contemporary Ireland than *On Raftery's Hill* or *Portia Coughlan,* due to the 'mythic-distance' which is afforded them. A contemporary 'version of *Medea*' culturally contextualizes and, in a sense, validates, the narrative content of infanticide, on-stage suicide, attempted rape and incest contained in *By the Bog of Cats…* While many audience members left at the interval, or indeed walked out of *On Raftery's Hill* when it played in Washington in 2000, the same action of attempted rape, which occurred in the staging of both US productions of *By the Bog of Cats…* (with Xavier physically forcing himself on an incapacitated Hester in Act Three, graphically simulating an act of sexual violation), did not cause the same audience reaction.

---

[12] *ibid.*
[13] PICT audience survey (unpublished), April, 2001.

Portia Coughlan was presented by the Pittsburgh Irish and Classical Theatre Company at Chatham's Eddy Theatre, 22 March – 7 April, 2001, and was directed by Timothy Douglas, currently the Associate Director of the Actors' Theatre of Louisville, Kentucky. My role in the production was primarily as an informational and contextual resource for the cast, crew and director. While all three productions used the significantly revised 1999 Faber and Faber published scripts, for *Portia Coughlan* director and actors were also familiar with the earlier dialect versions[14], Douglas noting the texts as being 'so much saltier, and with substantially different endings'.[15]

As an African-American, Douglas spoke about his own connection with the work, and of the resonances of Portia's sense of dislocation and abjection. For him, Portia is 'a strong woman in crisis', in 'a world of secrets, where dominant culture doesn't want to hear the truth'.[16] With the rhythms of the dialect versions being of particular appeal to him, and the Belmont River having resonances of Old Man River, Douglas noted how he would like to direct a black Portia, or to bring an all black cast of the play to Ireland.[17] Andrew Paul also commented on the dialect versions, comparing the speech rhythms of the African-American Pittsburgh playwright August Wilson to Sean O'Casey, and to the earlier dialect editions of *Portia*.

Carr's narratives are interwoven with threads that reveal the bigger picture subtly, and often ambiguously, and my earliest dialogues focused on this characteristic in her writing. That Carr's dramas abound in open-ended references is challenging for the actor. What became apparent in my initial dialogues

---

[14] Earlier editions of *Portia Coughlan* are published by the Royal Court (1996), Gallery Press (1998), and Faber and Faber in Frank McGuinness, ed., *The Dazzling Dark*, (London: Faber & Faber, 1996).

[15] Q&A session with Melissa Sihra, University of Pittsburgh, 23 March, 2001.

[16] ibid.

[17] ibid.

with Douglas was the impulse to tie up the countless stories and tacit suggestions that populate *Portia Coughlan*. Queries over non-expositionalized references such as, for instance, Raphael's limp, came up in rehearsals. Cast and director were curious as to whether Raphael was wealthy before his compensation cheque for the 'accident'. Other queries which arose included: 'Who was the "Boston McGovern?" and why is he mentioned?' 'What is the meaning of "the hoor with the broken bottle"?' 'What "shame" is Sly Scully specifically referring to regarding Gabriel?'; and 'What about that drunken night when Sly got Tom Lahane to sign-over his land?'

Circumspection and speculation are national past-times. Since Gregory's *Spreading the News* and Synge's *The Playboy of the Western World* we see how stories become conflated so as to eventually perpetuate new, often fantastical modes of reality. A recurring characteristic of Irish plays is that resistance to definition and closure. Like Synge's *The Playboy of the Western World*, seemingly extraneous stories often layer *Portia Coughlan* in a highly non-literal way, lending an absurd, often non-sensical quality to the work. That the stories in *Portia Coughlan* are of a particularly violent nature, often graphically detailing bodily mutilation, sexual 'deviancy' and domestic violence, is also significant. As in *The Playboy of the Western World,* itself a study in absurd reference and poetic anecdote, the countless incidents in *Portia* are often referred to without any specific contextualization, imbuing the lives of the characters with both spoken and unspoken histories.

Crucial to *Portia Coughlan* and *By the Bog of Cats…* is the characters' capacity to speak without qualification; to leave things open to conjecture. In performance there needs to be an imaginative space which can allow for *dis*-closure, so that there is a kind of a 'third-space' created and offered to the audience *between* what the characters say and what they potentially *mean* or know. In a recent interview Carr speaks about characters having 'to carry the inner and the outer world. To really work, your character has to carry the spoken *and* the unspoken.'[18] The actor

---

[18] Interview with Melissa Sihra, *Theatre Talk*, p.61.

must have a relationship of trust with the script and the play-wright – that they *will* be carried-through by the *spoken* words, that it *will* make sense, in the final instance. Performers and spectators alike are left to conclude. How did Stacia, 'the Cyclops of Coolinarney', have her eye gouged out? What were the circumstances? How do we construct her past on what we are offered? Did Sly Scully hoodwink Tim Lahane into signing his land over, and is Raphael also a con-artist? We will never know who Tim Lahane is, but we are given enough with which to actively imagine. Everything is left open to conjecture, so that the audience plays a vital role in constructing the story. Mystery, suggestive polysemy, the quest for a character's motivation – this is the journey on which great storytelling must bring us. Historical 'fact' is never accessible; because with absolute closure, comes a negation of mythic possibility and licence, and, above all, the agency of the audience.

Carr's *mises en scène* similarly operate on multiple layers of possibility. Are they located in the 'real', the fantastic or both? The tiny village of Belmont is not far from where Carr grew up in County Offaly in the Midlands of Ireland, yet specificity can constrict the work. Carr's landscape hovers between memory and imagination; between literary allusion and topographic realism. In one of our first discussions, Douglas asked about the links with *The Merchant of Venice* – was this a sub-plot? My response suggested that while the allusion is there, it is not a narrative or structural template. While *Portia Coughlan* was 'inspired' by the suitor's speech, crucial from a directorial standpoint is that this play and *By the Bog of Cats…* , are 'loosely' based on *Merchant* and *Medea* respectively.[19]

Many interesting decisions were made in the staging of *Portia Coughlan*. With no interval, and all of the actors present throughout, seated around designer David M. Maslow's abstract circular, blue, polyurethane highly-raked stage, there was an unrelenting sense of interiority, omnivoyance and claustrophobia. The Brechtian effect of having the actors present through-

---

[19] William Shakespeare, *The Merchant of Venice*, Suitor's Speech, Act One, Scene One.

out, witnessing Portia's every move from their high-backed chairs, effectively underscored the menacing insularity of the tiny and remote village of Belmont. And yet the staging also seemed to imply that Portia (Deirdriu Ring) was the only figure on stage, summoning up these characters as if ghosts in the seance of her purgatorial memory-landscape.

Carr's language of metaphor and image works most effectively when staged conceptually. Douglas noted the circle as having the effect of 'looking through a telescope backwards'.[20] The extremity of the rake seemed a precarious playing space for the actors; one had the feeling that they were teetering unsteadily – a deliberate move on the part of Douglas: 'I never wanted to make this easy for the actors', he commented. In a notes session after the final preview Douglas told his actors: 'I've given you nothing, I've given you a slippery slope to act on [and] uncomfortable chairs to sit on. You need to trust one another now.'[21]

The Belmont River was placed down-stage, facing the audience. Light reflected on the water throughout, illuminating Portia's face. The ghost scenes worked particularly well, with the twins mirroring one another perfectly. The rake offered a natural slope from which Portia rolled to her death in one balletic movement to lie, Ophelia-like, amongst the swale. Andrew Paul noted Ring's 'slightly emotionally detached performance'[22] and sylph-like Ring, with her ceramic-white, ethereal presence portrayed a Portia 'as much *not* of this world', as of it.[23]

How did Pittsburgh audiences and critics receive the show? In a post-production discussion, Artistic Director Andrew Paul, noted that 'Audiences [had] some difficulty with the structure of the play, and with the relentless intensity of the performance. Several patrons commented on their inability to connect or

---

[20] Conversation with Melissa Sihra, Pittsburgh, 23 March, 2001.
[21] Preview, *Portia Coughlan*, Eddy Theatre, Pittsburgh, 22 March, 2001.
[22] E-mail, 10 April, 2001.
[23] Interview with Melissa Sihra, *Theatre Talk*, p.57.

empathize with the characters.'[24] During the performances that
I attended, audience members laughed uncomfortably at swear
words and, in particular, at the image of Portia and Gabriel
making love in the womb. In a PICT audience survey one
patron commented: 'Very positively disgusting. The Irish may
drink and swear and fight but surely not as they were portrayed
in the play (if that's what you call it). My kind of Irish are not
interested in such *trash*.'[25] While positively received by the
critics, the reviews tended to cast the writing in a 'rather
gloomy, grim light.'[26] Chief critic of the *Pittsburgh Post-Gazette*,
Christopher Rawson, who headed his notice 'Portia is
Drenched in Grim Truths', commented: 'Carr reminds me of
Beckett – a great desolation is painfully and poetically probed
without hope of deep change.'[27]

Interestingly, it seems that the word 'grim' is a death-knell to
shows in the United States. Paul feels that the tone of the critical response was a 'deterrent to the relatively conservative
Pittsburgh casual arts consumer'. He went on to say '[c]omedies
and titles with instant name-recognition always perform better
at the box-office.' He saw the humour inherent in the writing
emerge as the run progressed, until later audience members
described the play as 'hilarious':

> Once the actors settled into their roles, the humour emerged
> unscathed. Senchil (E. Bruce Hill), Stacia (Catherine Moore)
> and Blaize (Ginger Lawrence) in particular saw their per-
> formances grow substantially through time.[28]

In considering the reception of *Portia Coughlan* it seems that
the lyrical quality of the writing, the women's roles and the
ebullient moments of humour are what most resonated with the
audience, while the structure, with Portia's death revealed *in
medias res,* and the subsequent, apparent lack of hope for change
or transformation (and in the case of this production, the fact

---

[24] E-mail, 10 April, 2001.
[25] Unpublished PICT audience survey, March-April 2001.
[26] ibid.
[27] Christopher Rawson in the *Pittsburgh Post-Gazette*, 28 March, 2001.
[28] E-mail, 10 April, 2001.

that there was no interval), the subject-matter of incestuous relations, abundance of alcohol and cursing, are what prevented audiences from relating fully to the work. The reception of Carr's representation of death in both this work and in *By the Bog of Cats...* is something that I will consider in the final part of this essay.

On 3I May 2001 Irish Repertory of Chicago presented the U.S. premiere of *By the Bog of Cats...* at the Victory Gardens Theatre. My dialogue with Director Kay Martinovich, (who directed *The Mai* for Irish Repertory in 2000), began in Ireland in January and included research trips to the Midlands and meetings with Irish travellers. We heard stories from locals who lived on the Bog, and visited the villages of Carr's childhood landscape such as Pullagh, Mucklagh, Coolinarney, Pallas Lake and so on. As well as reminiscences about the older ways of life and the relationship between travellers and the settled community, we were told of ghostly presences and sightings. One elderly gentleman recounted a tale about the ghost of a woman he had seen in a house near the bog, repeatedly emphasizing that his friend had also been there, and had seen the apparition, by way of proof as to the veracity of his tale.[29] This is the landscape from which Carr writes, where the ethereal cohabitates with the mundane, where the imagination is as vital and revered as the rational, and where the world of poetry and storytelling is a necessary part of the everyday.

From the outset it was clear that Martinovich had a definite sense of the *mise en scène,* emphasizing a vision of 'vast, purgatorial space'.[30] Through simplicity and spareness set-designer Michelle Habek elicited the abstract and the material nature of a peat-bog, with a single slab of ice-impacted 'turf'; rough, crunchy and sensual. The three-quarter thrust stage of the intimate 200 seater auditorium allowed for a sense of fluidity not as easily attainable with proscenium staging, enabling the 'island' of raked bog to ooze or overspill into the auditorium, 'floating', it seemed, in oblivion, evoking a world that exists

---

[29] Blue Ball Pub, Co. Offaly, 18 April, 2001.
[30] Conversation with Kay Martinovich, Dublin, 12 April, 2001.

both 'within [time] *and* outside of it.'[31] The effect was of a Beckettian 'no-man's land', a site of limitless symbolic potentiality. Props were kept to a minimum, with no house or caravan, just a simple table and bench when needed, and the presence of the actors, evocative lighting and the strength of the language conjuring up the world.

For American audiences, Irish travellers, or more colloquially 'tinkers', and Irish peat bogs were given a context in the program note.[32] Other metaphoric allusions, such as the Ghost-Fancier, the black-swan, and the resonances of Catwoman were referenced. While interest in these images and characters arose in the post-show discussions to both productions of *By the Bog of Cats...,* the fantastical realm from which Carr's dramas operate was never questioned or contested. That Carr frames her plays as occupying several dimensions simultaneously allows an audience to know immediately what imaginative leaps are expected of it. In a recent interview Carr said: 'I [...] don't think we give people enough credit for actually encompassing all the worlds. [...] I think that people have never been more open since, possibly, the Greek world.'[33]

In this production I had a full-time presence in the rehearsal room and saw the performances evolve in depth as the actors excavated the past lives of their characters. What were the key things that actors sought to explore? In a script where again so much is implied and very little explicated definitively, I urged the actors to seek out the multiple possibilities contained within or simmering beneath the script, but to come, finally, to their own conclusions. Martinovich and I both felt it would be useful, particularly for the actors playing Hester (Tracy Michelle Arnold), Xavier (David Darlow) and Caroline (Amanda Archilla) to be familiar with *Portia Coughlan* and *On Raftery's Hill,* in order to get a sense of how Carr has developed certain themes, such as incest.

---

[31] Interview with Melissa Sihra, *Theatre Talk,* p.57.

[32] Melissa Sihra, 'shifting Landscape', Program Note to *By the Bog of Cats...* in *Stagebill,* June 2001, ed. John Istel.

[33] Interview with Melissa Sihra, *Theatre Talk,* p.57.

Incest is ambivalently represented in *Portia Coughlan* as being on the one hand a mythic and romantic allusion to Isis and Osiris, or Hera and Zeus, while on the other hand dramatizing a teratology of 'poor haunted monsters who've no sense of God or man.' The explicit reality of interfamilial sexual violation is stripped to the core in *On Raftery's Hill.* Sly Scully, Xavier Cassidy and Red Raftery are three degrees in Carr's exploration of this taboo, moving from Sly's masturbatory voyeurism, ('gawkin' […] from behind hedges and ditches and sconces', and procreating with his sister [34]), to the inferences of the past actions of Xavier Cassidy ('G'wan home and do whatever it is ya do with your daughter, but keep your sleazy eyes off me and Josie' (*BBOC.* p.293)) to an almost on-stage enactment of rape between father and daughter in *On Raftery's Hill.*

It is never explicitly articulated in *By the Bog of Cats...* that Xavier has raped his daughter Caroline, but it is implied on numerous occasions, particularly in Act Three when Hester says to Caroline 'There's no need to break you, you were broke a long while back.' (*BBOC.* p.337) Whether the abuse was physical or psychological, there is a need for it to resonate in performance. For Darlow, observing the character of Red Raftery enabled him to roughen the edges of Xavier, to give him the darker nature that he possesses, sloughing-off any niceties, and saw his character develop dramatically. For Archilla's Caroline, knowing what *actually* happens to Sorrel Raftery, gives her that possible history with her own father, and the burden of pain that knowledge like that exacts was brought movingly into her performance. Olwen Fouéré, who created the role of Hester for the Abbey Theatre premiere, notes that: 'There is a common experience between Hester and Caroline, and Caroline knows that Hester knows of her unspoken trauma'.[35]

For this production, Carr offered re-writes in order to loosen up some of the expositional content of the narrative. Additionally Carr offered some significant unforeseen changes,

---

[34] Marina Carr, *Portia Coughlan*, (London; Faber & Faber, 1999) Act One, Scene Five, p.214.

[35] Conversation with Melissa Sihra, Dublin, 25 January, 2002.

most notably regarding Hester's response to meeting the ghost of her murdered brother Joseph. In the previously published versions of the script, Hester displays no remorse at killing her brother, whereas now, she is filled with guilt and regret:

Act Three:

> **HESTER**: Well be off wud ya now sir, I've natin to say to ya.
> **JOSEPH**: Haven't ya?
> **HESTER**: Alrigh I'm sorry, now go away please.
> **JOSEPH**: Ya don't look wan bih sorry.
> **HESTER**: Well I am. Belave me Joseph Swane I'm noh the sorryin kind, buh you, if there was wan thing I could undo, ud's whah I done to you. I've barely slept a nigh this ten yare.
> **JOSEPH**: Haven't ya. Whah I can't make sense of if why ya killed me.
> **HESTER**: Ya think I can?
> **JOSEPH**: Wan minuh I'm rowin' across Bergit's lake and the next I'm a ghost.
> **HESTER**: There's a devil in me Joseph, comes ah me ouha nowhere, takes me over, I'm only hees soldier.

Carr's re-writes offered moments of unanticipated poetry, particularly in her elaboration of the unimaginable purgatorial landscape to which the dead soul of Joseph is consigned to traverse for infinity. In this added dialogue, Joseph describes the non-human, the non-knowable, a Boschian hell-mouth, somewhere out of the bounds of decency, 'before rules was made':

> **JOSEPH**: Ya'd want to geh an eyeful a the devils here. They sih along the avenues, perched on glass, fall on ya, try to suck ya, the faces of them where faces should be, jealous of anywan thah was ever born. Ya see they'll never make ud to the earth, noh if they were to live a millin, millin yare. And their howls ah nigh, 'make me human', they cry in their terrible voices that aren't voices ah all buh somethin before a voice, 'make me human just for an hour.'

> **HESTER**: I've often whispered the same. Mebbe I'm wan a them thah somehow goh pupped on the world. [36]

Critics of both productions of *By the Bog of Cats…* noted the allusion to Medea, and the position of Irish travellers as a means of contextualizing Hester's social position as outsider and exile. Chicago Tribune chief-critic Richard Christiansen commented on 'the stinging force [of the] drama's many furious confrontations.'[37], while Hedy Weiss, for the Chicago Sun-Times wrote: 'Shakespeare was the master at orchestrating […] volatile moods. The young Irish dramatist Marina Carr clearly shares his gift.'[38]

For the *Irish Theatre Magazine* Enrica Cerquoni noted the production's 'daring and innovative' representation of 'racism, physical abuse, murder and fratricide' with particular reference to the 'Act Three rape scene – and the play's closure.' Of the re-writes Cerquoni noted that 'while cuts in the exposition of Joseph Swane's character drive the action faster towards its tragic denouement, the decision to indicate that Hester is re-morseful for having killed her brother, where she was unbending before, becomes problematic. Is Carr trying to make this a more likeable character to a non-Irish audience or does the playwright now see it differently?'[39] The turn-around in Hester's response certainly radically alters her characterization, lending a new ambivalence to the action.

Just three days after the terrorist attacks on the World Trade Center in New York City, San Jose Repertory Theatre's production of *By the Bog of Cats…* opened as scheduled in California. The show ran for a month resulting in an overall attendance of eighteen thousand people. As a playwright, Carr was not familiar to West Coast audiences, but unsurprisingly the casting of Holly Hunter in the lead role of Hester Swane allowed for the

---

[36] Marina Carr, *By the Bog of Cats…* Unpublished re-writes; reproduced by permission of the author.

[37] Richard Christiansen in the *Chicago Tribune,* 5 June, 2001.

[38] Weiss in the *Chicago Sun-Times*, 5 June, 2001.

[39] Enrica Cerquoni in *Irish Theatre Magazine*, Volume 2 (9), Summer 2001, pp.70-72.

show to sell out before opening. Director, cast and crew were highly concerned about the potential emotional impact of the tragic proportions of Carr's play at this time. In retrospect *By the Bog of Cats...* offered a sense of comfort and catharsis to audiences, where a lighter drama or comedy would certainly have been inappropriate at this time.

My dialogues with Near and Hunter began in Ireland in March 2001, when they visited for research purposes. Among their primary concerns at that point was to research the origins and traditions of Irish travellers, and for Hunter, to get a feel for the landscape of the bogs and dialect of the Midlands. Director and performer wished to learn about the origins, lifestyle and customs of the travelling people, and in particular, the position of women within this culture and to learn about Shelta, or Cant, the language of travellers which descends from Old Irish.

Near was curious about Irish identity in general – how might it be defined? Acutely noting a tension between public and private sensibilities within the Irish people, Near wondered if exterior traits of friendliness and generosity 'covered up a more private nature.'[40] In our discussions I pointed to the transitional position of contemporary Irish culture. My responses suggested that an overview of the Irish 'national character' is problematic due to the fact that it has always been a cultural and political construction, which can be viewed, like the bog itself – 'always shiftin' and changin' and coddin' the eye'.

While Near used the published version of the script, she was concerned with the expositional details of the blood-money, the mystery of Jack Swane of Bergit's Island, and Carthage's role in the murder of Joseph. While much information is offered in the narrative, the impulse was to define character motivation and narratival suggestion. Queries such as 'Was Carthage implicated from the outset?', 'Did he premeditate the murder with Hester?' arose in discussion. I suggested that Carthage was completely unaware that Hester was going to kill her brother, just as she herself was; but that this then bound them together forthwith.

---

[40] E-mail, 5 June, 2001.

Near also wondered as to Hester's motivation in killing her daughter – was this a revenge act? Again, the actions and words must speak for themselves, so that each audience member may come to their own conclusion. In my own opinion, this is unequivocally not a revenge killing. Hester cannot stay in the world under present circumstances, and her action is one of love, motivated by the primal desire to liberate Josie from the heartbreak of abandonment, and feelings of self-fracture, which inevitably accompany such primary loss as that of a mother.

In *By the Bog of Cats...* and *Portia Coughlan,* memories, stories and open-ended references compete for authority, challenging the very notion of 'authenticity'. The inherent lack of closure and discordance at play in the narrative was remarked upon in a post-show discussion. An audience member remarked on the mythical nature of Big Josie Swane: 'Why are Catwoman's memories of Big Josie so at odds with others?' 'Why are Hester and Joseph discordant in their memories also?' With no access to singular 'truth' in the play, *By the Bog of Cats...* is a poetic study in the subjectivity of memory and historical narrative. In a play that is primarily a series of duologues, whose version can we trust? The answer is, quite simply, no-one's; we are cautioned, once again, as to the fallible and precarious nature of narrative and, consequently, identity. Culturally specific references, such as the Industrial School, in which Hester spent her childhood from the age of seven to eighteen, and the implications of this for her childhood, were also discussed.

The opening moments of Joe Vanek's award-winning set allowed for the immensity of Carr's mythic world: huge black plastic sheets billowed under falling snow, ambivalently protecting the bog, yet evoking a claustrophobic sense of entrapment and suffocation. The show was highly technical in terms of props and engineering, lending a cinematic scope to the proscenium staging. Early discussions with Near arose regarding the *mise en scène:* 'Where is the house in relation to the caravan? How would this be staged? What specific year is it set?' and, 'What objects would be in Cassidy's house to indicate the year in which it was set?' What is striking about *By the Bog of Cats...* is how 'open' the play is temporally, that it is set in a kind of past, present *and* future, both within and *beyond* time, in which details of realism need not be strictly adhered to. Carr notes that: 'I have never believed that time is linear'[41] and elaborates: 'we are of time, but also beyond it. And to forget that is the problem. Everyone forgets that they are also outside of time – that they are both within it *and* outside of it.[...] We are as much *not* of this world, as we are of it. And how to capture that in the theatre is the huge challenge.'[42] There was a need during final rehearsals to maintain the vastness of the scope: the house and caravan did not appear as often as it is mentioned in the script, for instance, and the green make-up of the ghost of Joseph Swane was reduced, so that he looked more ordinary. In final previews, I urged for an acceleration of the pacing to increase the dramatic drive of the narrative, effectively reducing the running time from nearly three hours to two.

In exploring the characters, there was a need to highlight the sinister, threatening potential of Xavier Cassidy (J.G. Hertzler) which is revealed in the third act, but needs to be indicated in earlier scenes, particularly the latent underpinnings contained in his wedding speech. A striking image of loneliness and isolation, Hester (Holly Hunter) entered, a strong yet vulnerable figure dragging the corpse, her soul, the dead swan, across the bog. Hester's sexuality was foregrounded in this production. Salomé-like, her veiled entrance in Act Two to the wedding party was a dance of revelation, as she climbed feral-like onto the table, in a display of seductive and sexual dominance. In Act One Hester and Carthage (Gordon McDonald) punctuated the dialogue with a choreographed sexual simulation, performing the characters' shared history as lovers, and iterating by comparison, the contractual, economic nature of the union between Carthage and Caroline. Yet the drive to physicalize the relationship seemed at times over-literal.

Imperative to the character of Caroline Cassidy, again, is an indication of the possible traumatic past events which may have shaped her early life. While the character *may* read as a pawn,

---

[41] *Theatre Talk*, p.59.
[42] *Theatre Talk*, p.57.

plot device and objectified patriarchal commodity, the levels of instinctual knowledge, experience and integrity that the character possesses must be excavated in performance, so that her situation can be realized as one of the most tragic elements of the narrative.[43] If played without any signification of an unspoken past, Caroline is reduced to the one-dimensional, robbing the drama of its subtler, and complex nuances of emotional conflict. Gretchen Cleevely developed the role sufficiently from the doll-like, so that Caroline did not appear singularly innocent, naive, or purely as comic foil to Hester's crises.

West-coast critics commented repeatedly on the desirability of the role of Hester: 'It is a role that every great actress would love to obtain', noted Richard Connema.[44] Similarly with the other productions, the uncompromising scale of the narrative was praised: 'Carr [has] emerged quietly as one of Ireland's finest on the strength of her ability to draw characters and situations on an operatic scale', in, what another critic commented was: 'a tough week [that] introduced us all over again to feelings of terror and pity.'[45] Lack of closure was again an issue in the reception of the play. One critic commented:

> At times, Carr supplies too many vaguely sinister references; although a sense that all may never be revealed is fitting for this morass of high emotion and dark secrets, it can also be alienating. [The] many hints at incest, perhaps rampant in this very small town, almost seem at odds with such an 'Earth Mother' sensibility.'[46]

At the second post-show discussion an audience member commented on how they had hoped the 'pattern would be broken', that the play could end on a note of hopeful possibil-

[43] Michael Scott Moore in the *San Francisco Weekly* comments that the characters of Caroline and Carthage are 'mostly one-note foils for Hester's nuanced, self-contradictory Fugue.' 26 September, 2001.

[44] Richard Connema in *Regional News & Reviews: San Francisco,* 27 September, 2001.

[45] Michael Scott Moore in the *San Francisco Weekly,* 26 September, 2001.

[46] Heather Zimmerman in *The Metro,* 26, September, 2001.

ity.[47] This brings us to the prevalence of death in Irish drama. A response that I note continually from American students of Irish drama is that desire for a 'positive' resolution. The most frequently asked question is 'Why is there so much tragedy in Irish theatre, why are there not more comedies? Why so much death?'

In order to shift the emphasis from death as purely negative closure, it needs to be considered in terms of performance. Death on stage does not indicate finality, but *movement*; it is a poetic drive to excavate what it means to live. With *Portia Cough-lan* too, the difficulty for American audiences was, in a large part, due to the 'unrelenting' nature of the tragedy. By having the protagonist's death in the middle it seemed to reach depths of despair that were too 'grim' to enter into and survive. What is the pay-off for the audience if death is revealed *in medias res*? Quite simply, there is none, if Portia's death is regarded in terms of plot rather than poetics. 'Death' *per se*, can offer no resolution unless it is viewed as a symbiotic dynamic of living.

In a 2001 interview Carr expands on this notion: 'Death is just a moment, like two seconds. It is almost like the starting block of the race [...] The fact that we are dying is probably the only significant thing about us. And *how* we live and *how* we die[...]I love biography because I love reading about how people die. I think it says everything about how they have lived.' Seen as such, Carr's treatment of death in her work from 1994 to 1998, can be regarded other than literally. Beckett's aesthetic similarly contemplates the journey towards death (as the domi-nating impulse from the moment of birth), yet it centres around the act of *being*, and of how each of us negotiates the journey that is life. It is neither negative nor celebratory, simply prag-matic.

In looking at the most recent approaches to Marina Carr's plays in the United States, I hope to have indicated some of the key issues in the diverse stagings and receptions of her work. Of Carr, Olwen Fouéré says: 'she is probably the only [Irish] writer who sees rehearsals as a voyage of discovery for herself,

---

[47] San Jose, 15 September, 2001.

as much as anything [...] She sees what she has given as being something to come to life through performance.'[48] International productions of Irish drama offer different perspectives, confirming or disputing, and always complicating received notions of 'Irishness', holding a lens to Irish culture, reflecting images which are, like the Belmont River, ceaselessly in motion and ever-renewing.

---

[48] Interview with Melissa Sihra, *Theatre Talk*, p.163.

7 | The Mythical and the Macabre:
The Study of Greeks and Ghosts in the Shaping of the American premiere of *By the Bog of Cats...*

M. K. Martinovich

> She knows what the Greeks know. Death is a big country. And hers is a big imagination, crossing the border always between the living and the dead...I wonder what Marina Carr believes? I can't say for certain, but I am certain in this play she writes in Greek.[1]

> ...they (*Barry's descendants*) exist here in an afterlife, in another life, in a gallery of pictures painted freely, darkly. They are ghost plays, if ghosts are the images lingering of the vanished and the dead...[2]

Several images of 'the vanished and the dead' linger in Marina Carr's haunting play *By the Bog of Cats....* Tormented memories and sorrowful spirits drift over the landscape of the mythological bog. Yet, more than simply hovering, the undead co-exist with the living in Carr's poetic yet realistic world. Carr's *By the Bog of Cats...* re-sets Euripides' *Medea* in the midlands of contemporary Ireland. Familiar traits of ancient Greek tragedy and modern Irish drama are uniquely combined through the play-

---

[1] Frank McGuinness, 'Writing in Greek', programme note for *By the Bog of Cats...,* Abbey Theatre, October 1998.

[2] Sebastian Barry, 'Preface' in *Sebastian Barry Plays: 1*, London: Methuen, 1997, p.xv.

wright's ability to interweave elements of the supernatural and the mystical with the classic themes of prophecy and fate. By virtue of her source material and its universal concerns, Carr's canvas extends beyond the bare setting of a bog and the age-old story of a woman wronged.

Marina Carr is one of several Irish playwrights who have written over thirty adaptations of Greek tragedy since 1984.[3] Marianne McDonald ventures an explanation for this trend in her article on the subject, suggesting that the literary classic allows for a 'heightened mode of communication' and can be used as a means of expression of the Irish people and their social concerns.[4] In *By the Bog of Cats...*, Carr uses the structure of Greek tragedy to stitch together her tale of abandonment, betrayal and finally revenge in her contemporary reinterpretation.

After deciding to direct *By the Bog of Cats...* for Irish Repertory of Chicago in the spring of 2001, I questioned how to make this very Irish text 'readable' for an American audience. Despite cultural specificities, a human universality resonates throughout *By the Bog of Cats...*, just as in the Greek original. However, the midlands dialect, the struggle for land, the traveller community,[5] and life on the bog were all issues that would have to be made intelligible to Irish Rep theatre-goers not well-versed in such subjects. These topics dominated my research. As a director, I consider a thorough and intensive investigation of the subject matter to be of the utmost priority. For the production of *By the Bog of Cats...*, I determined that the design team, the actors and myself should have an extensive grasp of those issues listed above. We further acknowledged a need for both the re-discovery of Euripides' *Medea* and the exploration of spectral and mystical figures that are indebted to Irish folk

---

[3] Marianne McDonald, 'Classics as Celtic Firebrand: Greek Tragedy, Irish Playwrights, and Colonialism' in *Theatre Stuff: Critical Essays on Contemporary Irish Theatre*, ed. by Eamonn Jordan, Dublin: Carysfort Press, 2000, p.16.

[4] McDonald, p.16-17.

[5] Irish travellers are a minority group who lead an itinerant lifestyle.

tales and legends. As a result, intensive scrutiny of these two essential issues helped to inform the work for me as a director.

The classical associations to be considered in this essay include the prominent similarities between the two plays, with an emphasis on both landscapes. The landscape of *By the Bog of Cats...* plays a significant role in understanding the importance of the Greek model on the Irish re-telling, for the bog can be read as a mythical space. The challenge for the designers and myself was how to activate Grecian aspects into the Irish setting. The ghostly influences to be investigated include the characters of the Ghost Fancier and Joseph Swane, as well as the approach to the bog as a purgatorial space and the tormented longing of Hester for Big Josie, her absent mother. The purgatorial space of the bog suggests the transitional stage in which Hester finds herself – lingering between this world and the next. Questions posed and answered in production included how this liminal space was realized, how the various ghost-like figures were represented, and how the plagued protagonist was haunted by maternal figures, mystical creatures and ghosts. The focus of this essay is my directorial approach to addressing these Greek elements and ghostly environs within Carr's text and through theatrical performance.

The Greeks

Why does Carr need to tell her tale through the story of the Medea? One hint may be in what Carr says herself about the pillaging of dead authors' works:

> [Shakespeare] took from everywhere, but what he did with his plunder! [...] This points up something [...] about all these great dead writers. It seems that you are allowed to steal what you need while learning the craft and that there is no crime in that. The crime would be to diminish or desecrate what you have stolen.[6]

---

6 Marina Carr, 'Dealing with the Dead', *Irish University Review*, Vol. 28, (1), Spring/Summer 1998, p.196.

Multiple affinities exist between the Medea and *By the Bog of Cats*.... The ideas of fate, prophecy, rejection, revenge and infanticide are all played out in Carr's script. In taking her basic plot from Euripides, she looks back on a classic work that presents a strong, aggressive woman. In 'The Impact of Feminism on the Theatre', Michelene Wandor states 'in theatre there are no female 'classics' to which to point.'[7] For Carr, there are no female-authored 'classic' texts from which to extract her story. Many modern critics, such as Sarah B. Pomeroy, however, consider the work of Euripides to be sympathetic to the woman's position. He created female characters that were strong, assertive and successful even if at the same time they might be selfish or villainous.[8] As the female protagonist in *By the Bog of Cats...*, Hester Swane is raised to the status of a tragic heroine by her defiant and determined – yet ultimately destructive – nature.

A brief overview of the two plays shall serve to highlight the similarities. Euripides' Medea is an outsider from the distant land of Colchis. After ten years together, Jason abandons Medea and their two sons. She considers herself a legitimate wife, though technically as a foreigner, this is not so.[9] At the opening of the play, Jason has secretly married the princess who is the daughter of Creon. Medea has been asked to leave her home and go into exile with her children. In an act of revenge, Medea first poisons the princess and her father, Creon, and then murders her own sons. She then escapes to Athens on the chariot of her grandfather, the Sun God. In *By the Bog of Cats...*, Hester Swane is a traveller; one of a group of people often

---

[7] Michelene Wandor, 'The Impact of Feminism on the Theatre' in *Feminist Literary Theory: A Reader*, ed. by Mary Eagleton, Oxford: Blackwell Publishers, 1996, p.171.

[8] Sarah B. Pomeroy, *Goddesses, Whores, Wives and Slaves: Women in Classical Antiquity*, New York: Schocken Books, 1976, pp.107-108.

[9] Pietro Pucci, *The Violence of Pity in Euripides' Medea*, Cornell: Cornell University Press, 1980, p.198 as quoted in Gilbert Murray, *The Medea of Euripides*. Foreigners in Greek society were denied the rights of citizens.

referred to as Ireland's 'national outsider[s]'.[10] After spending fourteen years together and giving him a daughter, she has been abandoned by her lover Carthage Kilbride. *By the Bog of Cats...* opens on the morning of the wedding between Carthage and Caroline, a rich daughter of the landowner Xavier Cassidy. Due to a contractual commitment, Hester must leave her home on the Bog of Cats and move into town. Outraged, Hester sets fire to Carthage's house and livestock. As a final act of defiance she commits suicide, but only after killing her seven-year-old daughter, Josie.

Another resemblance between the two plays is their respective settings. The relationship of the inside domain (feminine) to the outside world (masculine) of Heroic age Greece is vital to the action of the *Medea*. When Medea steps out of the female household into the male dominated society, we notice a fundamental change in her character. In the beginning segment of the play Medea is never seen, but is only heard wailing from inside her home. When she steps outside however, she becomes a dominant force intent on revenge. Likewise, in *By the Bog of Cats...*, exposure to the outside environment has a particular effect on the protagonist. Hester has a strong attachment to the Bog of Cats: it becomes a source of spiritual fulfilment for her. Hester says herself that she can never leave her place on the land: '... everythin' I'm connected to is here. I'd rather die.'[11] The outside world plays a crucial role in determining the fate of both women. Medea gains strength from confrontation in this outer, masculine space, while Hester is empowered by roaming on the natural expanse of the bog. Both Hester and Medea, however, are in a sense ultimately destroyed by their need to belong to these outer realms.

In pre-production discussions, set designer Michelle Habeck, lighting designer Jaymi Smith, costume designer Lisa Lewandowski and I spoke extensively about the Greek influ-

---

[10] Eileen Battersby, 'Marina of the Midlands' in *Irish Times*, Thursday, 4 May, 2000.

[11] Marina Carr, *By the Bog of Cats...* in *Marina Carr: Plays 1*, London: Faber and Faber, 1999, p.273.

ences on the physical reality of the world of the play. The heightened poetic language, the Grecian antecedent, and the black and white costumes[12] propelled us to respect the classical linkage. First, we used the term 'mythical realism' as a conceptual starting point to highlight the connection. For the set and lighting designs, this was defined as embodying both the reality of the Bog of Cats locale (a squishy, yet textured and rough surface) and the otherworldly nature of that place (top and atmospheric lighting utilized, as well as fog and smoke).[13] To make the set and lighting designs too realistic or literal would be to lose the heightened sense of theatricality and magic that both the bog and the stage hold. Second, the idea that a raw or bare playing area would best evoke not only the neutral playing space of the ancient Greek stage but also the desolate nature of this particular Irish setting was a central design concept throughout the production process.

During the early phases of rehearsal, the actors and I discussed at length the issues and ideas that Carr's play generated. We began our discussion however, with the topic of *Medea*. In preparation for directing *By the Bog of Cats...*, I had flown to London in early 2001 to watch the Deborah Warner/Fiona Shaw production of *Medea*. Bringing that experience to the table instigated an exploration of the above noted similarities in character and plot. The actors were inspired by these and other discoveries. When we arrived at the point of staging, *Medea* was rarely mentioned. Yet the Greek text continued to be an underlying influence and worked through all of us on a subconscious level. Familiarity with the *Medea* myth played a crucial part in the production's development.

---

[12] Since Carr has outlined specifics in terms of costume, a classical palette of black, white and gray was easy to embrace for the design. Josie was the only character who wore the additional color of red in her opening costume, symbolizing her as sacrificial lamb.

[13] Other words and impressions the designers and I used to describe the play and the place included vastness, simplicity, barrenness, cold, darkness and shadow, heightened emotionality and the idea of the landscape as a character unto itself.

Mother-Love – Grecian and Ghostly Matters

Over the passage of one day, the troubled Hester Swane is disturbed by the phantom-like Ghost Fancier, forewarned by the mysterious creature Catwoman and visited by the spectre of Joseph, the dead brother she murdered out of jealousy and spite. These characters wreak havoc on Hester's present state of mind. However, the wraith that most plagues Hester is never seen, but lies deep in her soul. Hester's mother, Big Josie, abandoned her when she was a child. Unable to face the fact that her wayward mother deserted her, forty-year-old Hester awaits her mother's return to the Bog of Cats. The haunting memory of Big Josie, reconstructed by the recollected stories of her by the Catwoman and Monica Murray, plagues Hester until her own death in the final moments of the play. While the drama of *By the Bog of Cats...* features ghosts, the narrative of the motherless child can also be read as a ghost story, for the absent mother becomes a shadow figure, illusory and unreal.

The absent Big Josie and the animal-like Catwoman, both liminal subjects between the legendary and the real, offer Hester a prophetic directive to alter her destiny.[14] Yet, Hester remains reluctant to leave the bog. Her continuous search for and anticipation of a suitable mother figure contributes to her despair. One primary trope of *By the Bog of Cats...* is the representation of 'mother' and how this image is utilized. In *By the Bog of Cats...*, several of the women perform the role of mother. Hester is haunted not only by her absent mother, but also by other maternal figures and associations in the play. These matriarchal associations include: the loving and affectionate attachment between Hester and her own seven-year-old daughter, Josie; the over-enthusiastic Mrs. Kilbride as a clinging mother towards her son Carthage; the ineffectual yet well-meaning neighbor Monica Murray as surrogate mother to Hester; and the mystical Catwoman as an alternative confidante who appeals to Hester's dark side. Mother-love, as the Greek construc-

---

[14] Big Josie's prediction is told via Catwoman. Also, Catwoman is blind, but can 'see' the future, contributing to her liminal status.

tion of gender proposes, is the 'most powerful 'natural' emotional bond.'[15] None of these bonds, however, are satisfactory for Hester. The enigmatic Catwoman is not the type of creature to give Hester the mother-love that she so desires and Monica Murray is preoccupied with her own trauma of loss due to her son's tragic death years earlier. Also, the impulse towards mother-love is continually thwarted in these corporeal relationships because of the powerful intangible hold of Hester's spectral mother, Big Josie.

The Ghosts

By the Bog of Cats… opens at dawn on the day of Carthage and Caroline's wedding and proceeds through the tragic events of that day. While the play adheres to the structure of *Medea*, several factors brand it as unmistakably Irish. These include the 'surreal comedy of Irish rural life'[16], the Irish midland dialect (written into the text) and the supernatural figures of Irish fiction and folk tales. The arrival of the Ghost Fancier, an Irish Grim Reaper, suggests the dead living among us, a mainstay of Irish folk tradition. The Ghost Fancier may be read as a materialization of Hester's unconscious, but the ghosts in this play are also a part of the purgatorial world of the bog. Hester belongs to and feels at home in this world.

The ancient landscape of the bog makes up this realm, which is the threshold between the living and the dead, the natural and the unnatural. The bog is not only a haunted liminal space, but also a psychological space, where layers of Hester's psyche can unfold. For example, in the Chicago production the specific area where Black Wing was buried, located upstage left, served as one of many purgatorial places. The actress Tracy

---

[15] Ruby Blondell, 'Introduction' in *Women on the Edge: Four Plays by Euripides*, ed. and transl. by Ruby Blondell, Mary-Kay Gamel, Nancy Sorkin Rabinowitz, Bella Zweig, New York: Routledge, 1999, p.155.

[16] Joyce McMillan, 'Beyond Blarney' in *The Scotsman*, Abbey National Theatre of Ireland Archives, 21 October, 1998.

Arnold as Hester stepped into the grave during her scene with the Catwoman (played by Mary Ann Thebus), foreshadowing both her impending death and her need to escape to this ghostly world. The Bog of Cats is the closest space where Hester can get to her mother's memory, for it was on the Bog of Cats that her mother left her. Both liminal and psychological, Carr's bog is the perfect traipsing ground for ghosts. In *Ghosts: Deconstruction, Psychoanalysis, History*, Peter Buse and Andrew Stott suggest ghosts are absent presences and represent both the past and the present:

> Ghosts arrive from the past and appear in the present. How-ever, the ghost cannot be properly said to belong to the past, even if the apparition represents someone who has been dead for many centuries, for the simple reason that a ghost is clearly not the same thing as the person who shares its proper name.[17]

Through ghostly images Carr suggests the complicated inter-weavings of the living and the dead, the past and the present.

Hester finds the swan Black Wing, her animal friend and al-ter ego, dead in a bog hole before the play begins. Hester is aware of her psychic connection to the black swan, just as she is metaphysically linked to the animal-like Catwoman. When she finds Black Wing dead, she knows it is an omen of her fate. At the beginning of the play, while dragging the black swan to a burial space, the Ghost Fancier 'appears' in order to bring the ghost of 'a woman be the name of Hester Swane' (*BBOC*: p.266) to the other side. In the Chicago production, the lights came up slowly at the top of the show to a very dim level, revealing Hester dragging the black swan across the bog. Posi-tioned far upstage, Ed Zeltner as the Ghost Fancier could barely be seen, as there was a thick layer of fog and only a top light, highlighting his otherworldliness. The Ghost Fancier's eyes and body were directed towards Hester as she moved across the stage. Hester stopped centre stage, in line with the

---

[17] Peter Buse and Andrew Stott, 'Introduction: A Future for Haunt-ing' in *Ghosts: Deconstruction, Psychoanalysis, History*,. Peter Buse and Andrew Stott, (London: Macmillan Press Ltd, 1999), p.11.

Ghost Fancier, who was directly upstage of her. /
taken as Hester looked out over the bog, nev
wards the Ghost Fancier. This frozen moment ᵤᵤ
gested Ghost Fancier as Hester's unconscious, but also repᵣᵤ
sented death itself lurking in the background. Once the Ghost
Fancier did approach Hester, their bodies were relatively close
to each other during the scene, indicating the Ghost Fancier's
invasion of her personal and psychological space. Finally, they
both lingered over the place that would become the dead
swan's grave suggesting an intimate purgatorial space of the
psyche within the larger liminal space of the bog.

While the Ghost Fancier does not mistake Hester for a
ghost, his declaration that 'where there's ghosts there's ghost
fanciers' (BBOC: p.265) implies that even though alive, Hester is
liminal: her status also complies with her later admission to her
dead brother Joseph, that for a long time she has been thinking
she is 'already a ghost'. (BBOC: p.321) Deep within her lies the
foresight of her fate, a physical death to mirror the emotional
death she experienced when she was seven. By the time of her
encounter with the Ghost Fancier, Hester is clearly hovering
between two worlds. This liminality corresponds with Fiona
Macintosh's definition of the tragic character, "'absent and
present" in the world at one and same time.'[18] Macintosh maintains that in Ireland,

> it is the conception of death as a process that makes death
> and dying a part of the processes of living [...] it is also this
> conception that brings the dead themselves into the world of
> the living.[19]

The Ghost Fancier therefore occupies many roles – as the
undead, as unconscious, as prophecy.

In the revised text for the American premiere, the scene fea-
turing the ghost of Joseph Swane and Hester was the most
substantially rewritten. In the new scene, the reasons for Hes-

---

[18] Fiona Macintosh, *Dying Acts: Death in Ancient Greek and Modern Irish
Drama*, Cork: Cork University Press, 1994, p.78.
[19] Macintosh, p.37.

ter's murderous actions towards Joseph are more vague. The scene seems to suggest that Joseph's ghost could act as a warning from hell. While she is sorry she killed him, Hester wants nothing to do with her undead brother. Yet when pressed by Joseph as to why she killed him, Hester responds: 'There's a devil in me Joseph, comes ah me ouha nowhere, takes me over, I'm only hees soldier.' (*BBOC*: p.319, revised text 2001) Joseph's devil-filled response to Hester is strangely beautiful in its horror:

> Ya'd want to geh an eyeful a the devils here. They sih along the avenues, perched on glass, fall on ya, try to suck ya, the faces of them where faces should be, jealous of anywan thah was ever born. Ya see they'll never make ud to the earth, noh if they were to live a millin, millin yare. And their howls ah nigh, 'make me human', they cry in their terrible voices thah aren't voices ah all buh somethin before a voice, 'make me human just for an hour'. (*BBOC*: p.319, revised text, 2001)

In performance, the revised scene is relatively short. Joseph Swane, played by Christopher Grobe, and Hester can see each other, so much was made of their physical proximity. Although Joseph could be heard, the smoke from the burning house and livestock as well as the dusk-like lighting made it difficult for him to be seen by Hester. When she did finally recognize her brother, she was frightened and wanted to get far away from him. She backed away but still faced towards him. Hester, while frightened at this confrontation with her past and with the memory of her mother, could not turn her back on him. Joseph walked straight towards her and got in her physical and psychological space forcing her to confront him. During Joseph's devil speech (above), he stood centre stage, facing front, and looked straight at Hester. She, downstage of him, was turned directly stage left, in profile towards him. Her body, neither facing towards him or away from him, reflected her conflicting attitude: Hester was unable to face her destiny but simultaneously compelled not to turn away.

This revised scene consolidates the structure of the play and also sheds terrifying light into the workings of Hester's psyche.

Carr's alteration for the Chicago production distorts the trope of mother-love. Hester admits that a 'devil', which can suggest an 'evil spirit', possesses her: 'Mebbe I'm wan a them [devils] that somehow goh pupped on the world.' (*BBOC*: p.319, revised text 2001) The evil spirit suggests that Hester is her mother's daughter. While the word 'evil' is not mentioned, Big Josie did put a curse on Hester when she was a baby. Monica Murray says that there was 'something cold and dead' about Big Josie, and that she was never comfortable around her. Xavier says that he heard Big Josie once 'croonin' towards Orion in a language I never heard before or since.' (*BBOC*: p.94) Cat-woman turned against Big Josie when she put the curse on Hester and says that Hester is 'her match in witchery...same as your mother.' (*BBOC*: p.273) These comments give some insight into the dark presence lurking within Big Josie. Yet, this evil spirit within Hester also solidifies the notion of her being on the threshold between life and death and ultimately, not long for this world. In telling her that she should have never done what she did, Joseph is warning her about the other side before she gets there.

As the play draws to its conclusion, Hester continues to be haunted by the past and her spectral mother. Hester must acknowledge the fact that her mother is not returning to the Bog of Cats. Hester cannot admit that truth. Through Joseph, the past catches up with Hester because she does not take action against the memory of her mother. Thus Hester's interaction with the ghost of her brother Joseph takes its form as a battling with herself against her mother's memory. She tries to find the will to seek a resting-place within the world in which she already exists. Hester's psyche clashes with itself in both attempting to 'remember' and striving to 'forget'. As Nicola King attests in *Memory, Narrative, Identity*, the work of memory 'involves a complex negotiation between remembering and forgetting, between the destruction and creation of the self.'[20] For the tragic Hester, this negotiation results in only the de-

---

[20] Nicola King, *Memory, Narrative, Identity: Remembering the Self*, (Edinburgh: Edinburgh University Press), 2000, p.180.

struction of her self. Without a mother bond, Hester is empty inside. In the final moment of the play, Hester stabs herself, and as she is dying she whispers, 'Mam, Mam'. Forced to leave the Bog of Cats without her mother, she chooses death. In 'dying into death,' the tragedy for Hester is evident. Hester the little girl is still waiting for her mother. Hester the woman is still waiting for her mother's love.

Dramatist Marina Carr creates 'a kind of uncertainty' as she takes us on her ghostly journey into the liminal realms of the real and the fantastic, the worldly and the spiritual, the corporeal and the intangible. As the lights come up on this unsettling world, the purgatorial space of a bog enables the playwright's supernatural creations to interact with their mortal counterparts. *By the Bog of Cats…* opens with a woman dragging the corpse of a black swan behind her, blood trailing in the snow and the character of the 'Ghost Fancier' watching her every move. In this playwright's hands, we 'bow' to her ghoulish inclinations and embrace her settings for the real/unreal environs as they have been authored. Ghosts and ghost stories have a long history in Irish folk culture, but they also have a presence in the Irish dramatic tradition, from W.B. Yeats' *Purgatory* to Conor McPherson's *The Weir*. Carr uses the theatrical convention of a ghost and a 'ghost fancier' to tell her tragic story of a despairing, heartbroken and sorrowful individual.

Euripides' *Medea* is one of the greatest of Greek tragedies. Carr authors *By the Bog of Cats…* in the tradition of Shakespeare by 'robbing' the plot of *Medea* for her 'well-disguised' interpretation. During the original run of *By the Bog of Cats…* at the Abbey Theatre in Dublin, many members of the audience did not recognize the *Medea* in Carr's play. As Carr herself says, 'The plot is completely *Medea*. It was surprising how few people picked up on that initially.'[21] In Hester we find a woman who, as Aristotle maintains, through her suffering is 'someone like ourselves'. It is through Hester's status as a tragic heroine that

---

[21] 'Marina Carr' in *Reading the Future: Irish Writers in conversation with Mike Murphy*, ed. Clíodhna Ní Anluain, (Dublin: The Lilliput Press, 2000), p.51.

she ultimately attains our sympathy. Hester's tragic fall is brought about by her eternal belief that her mother will return one day and by her hope of a reciprocal manifestation of her daughterly affection and love.

Studying the Greek and ghostly elements was imperative towards a broad understanding of the world of *By the Bog of Cats*.... My overall vision was shaped by this crucial scholarship and as a result, it both consciously and unconsciously influenced many of my directorial decisions. As the lights came down on this American premiere, the world of Greek drama and the realm of Irish ghosts had joined forces to link three distinct cultures. Directing *By the Bog of Cats...* was not only a brilliant 'cross-cultural' experience; it was also an extraordinary venture into the ghostly worlds and haunted imaginings of Marina Carr.

8 | Carr's 'cut-throats and gargiyles'[1]:
Grotesque and Carnivalesque Elements in
By the Bog of Cats...

Bernadette Bourke

Marina Carr, remembering her early theatrical endeavours in the family shed, describes how she and her siblings created another world outside the official realm of their everyday lives, a world which adhered to none of the rules and abandoned itself to a freedom akin to that of carnival. In a sense all child's play has this 'topsy-turvy' carnivalesque quality to it. It is a world to wallow in until order is restored and the child sleepily returns to the realm of rules, unscathed, despite having transgressed beyond its permitted boundaries.

> We loved the havoc, the badness, the blood spillage, but we loved equally restoring some sort of botched order and harmony.[2]

Carr, the dramatist, continues to explore this 'scut's view of things'.[3] Disorder and turbulence permeate her plays, and lend to them a grotesque and carnivalesque dimension, which can be monstrous or poignant, but is absolutely compelling.

---

[1] Marina Carr, *Plays 1*, (London: Faber & Faber, 1999), p.325. All quotes from Carr's plays are from this edition and are indicated in the text by page number.

[2] Introduction to *Plays 1*, pp.ix – x, p.x

[3] *ibid*, p.x

Reversal is the essence of carnival. It is at the heart of grotesque imagery, and the spirit of carnival is alive in the work of Marina Carr, where grotesque and carnivalesque elements produce a drama of subversion, that celebrates the incongruous and the alternative. While Carr's play *Portia Coughlan* (1996) enacts the grotesque note through character and situation, *By the Bog of Cats...* (1998), which is the subject of this study, goes beyond the boundaries of grotesque imagery and launches us into the bizarre world of carnival itself. The traditional carnival is a form of transitory madness, a tumultuous other world which is real while it lasts, but when it ends, is succeeded by order. The freedom of carnival presupposes such eventual restoration, which is why successive regimes permitted it as a way of re-establishing the status quo under the guise of autocratic benevolence. However, Carr's version does not allow for such neat closure, but gyrates out of control leading to devastating consequences, and precluding the restoration of any but a 'botched' sort of order.

Marina Carr possesses a vision that thrives on the grotesque incongruities and reversals peculiar to carnival, and her historical placing allows her to expand these theatrically. She is perfectly poised to exploit the incongruities of modern rural life, which retains strong links with the past while engaged simultaneously on a collision course with the future. Hers is a drama that takes traditions and conventions and subverts them. The 'topsy-turvydom' of carnival is in evidence throughout her work as she mixes genres, attaching equal value to each, while rewriting myths to suit her contemporary disjointed vision. It is a strategy that allows for the blurring of boundaries between the real and the surreal, the natural and the supernatural, the past and the present, and between high and popular cultural influences.

In *By the Bog of Cats...* the Greek messenger of death is subverted in Carr's Ghost Fancier who mistakes dawn for dusk, thus undermining the classical tradition. The blind seer Teiresias is degraded in the grotesque figure of Catwoman who eats mice and has mouse fur growing out of her teeth. Even the Medea myth, on which the play is loosely based, is reversed so that a girl child is sacrificed instead of the traditional boys, and the legend is further subverted, when the motive for the killing is love, and not hatred or revenge. Character types are flagrantly reversed in the hellish grannies, negligent mothers, incestuous fathers and murderous siblings who crowd the shadows of Marina Carr's plays.

At the turn of the last century J. M. Synge's work had displayed a similarly 'mixed mood', and when attacked for *The Playboy of the Western World*[4] in 1907, and called upon to defend this ambivalent quality Synge referred to,

> the romantic and the Rabelaisian note [...] working to a climax through a greater part of the play, and [...] the Rabelaisian note, the 'gross' note if you will, *must* have its climax no matter who may be shocked.[5]

By invoking the name of François Rabelais in this now famous defence, Synge was justifying his seemingly incongruous choice of matter and mood. Rabelais, the sixteenth century French humanist, whose novel *Gargantua and Pantagruel* is a celebration of the pre-modern carnivalesque folk traditions of the European peasantry, has given to the English language the two words – gargantuan and Rabelaisian – which sum up his alternative world view. Rabelais had tapped into a rich culture of unofficial folk humour, which celebrated the body in its material physical existence, contrary to the official medieval and emerging modern aesthetic, which was to drive the essential animal nature of man underground. Rabelais's work brought to the surface a way of life that had hitherto been invisible in official literature. This was the culture of the medieval peasantry, a thousand-year-old subversive folk tradition of rituals and carnival excesses, which existed in an unofficial capacity alongside the official culture of church and state. The medieval

---

[4] J. M. Synge, *The Playboy of the Western World*, in *Plays, Book 2,* ed. Ann Saddlemyer, (London: Oxford University Press, 1969). All quotes from Synge's plays are from this edition and are indicated in the text by page number.

[5] Quoted in Katharine Worth, *The Irish Drama of Europe from Yeats to Beckett,* (London: Athlone Press, 1978), p.121.

carnival celebrated temporary liberation from the prevailing truth and the established hierarchical order, and it was the Russian linguist and critic Mikhail Bakhtin who was to undertake a detailed exploration of the carnivalesque tradition in his book *Rabelais and his World* (1965). In this work Bakhtin insists that in order to understand grotesque literature we must comprehend the carnival idiom of the marketplace, which laughs at fear and death. This carnival laughter is always ambivalent, 'gay, triumphant, and at the same time mocking, deriding',[6] and the work of Marina Carr at the turn of the twenty-first century is distinctly Rabelaisian in its celebration of the resilience of the human spirit, through grotesque imagery and carnival rituals.

One of the most important features of Bakhtin's study, which has particular relevance to Marina Carr, is his concept of 'grotesque realism' (Bakhtin, p.195). The body in grotesque realism is presented, not in the private, ego-centred form of modern interpretation, but as something universal, representing all the people, a people who are continually growing, decaying and being renewed. Such a view reflected the folk need for the assurance of continuity in a world which offered them little power, and no opportunity to rise to the status of the dominant culture. This explains why all that is bodily becomes exaggerated and grotesque, representing fertility, growth and abundance. Bakhtin explains how the essential principle of grotesque realism is 'degradation', 'the lowering of all that is high, spiritual, ideal, abstract', and linking it with 'the bodily lower stratum' (Bakhtin, pp.205-206). In Rabelais' novel, grotesque and exaggerated images of food, excrement and the lower regions of the body are all profoundly inter-related, signifying a world that dies to be born; the body that is also the earth, grave and womb. Hard, wild, passionate and ecstatic, grotesque realism proclaims the body's instinctive right to primal satisfaction.

---

[6] Mikhail Bakhtin, in *The Bakhtin Reader: Selected Writings of Bakhtin, Medvedev, Voloshinov*, 'section Four: Carnival Ambivalence', ed. Pam Morris, (London: Edward Arnold, 1994), pp.194-244, p.200. Further quotes from this book are indicated in the text by page number.

Bakhtin reiterates the notion of victory over fear, and pro-
nounces it as an essential element of medieval laughter. In
carnival this defeat is represented in images of comic or monstrous reversal, as all that is terrifying becomes grotesque.
Death and hell are triumphantly defeated during carnival, the
latter when the hell set, an essential prop, is solemnly burned at
the peak of the festivities. Such reversals subvert official authority – religious and secular, and represent victory over fear. In
carnival imagery, death, uncrownings, mock-thrashings, hell
burning, beatings – all simultaneously enact their opposites
leading to renewal, rebirth, and abundance.

When Bakhtin discusses the grotesque body he endows it
with traits common to all carnival images. It is 'a body in the act
of becoming' (Bakhtin, p.233). He compares the grotesque
body, which had prevailed in folklore over thousands of years,
to the post-renaissance bodily creed which presents an entirely
finished, strictly limited body, shown from the outside as something individual. All orifices that were gaping wide in grotesque
realism, offering access to hidden possibilities, are closed. All
protrusions have been levelled. The body now represents an
individual ego, guided by the faculty of reason, and its medieval
cosmic significance is thus diminished. With the loss of the
grotesque imagery that unites all bodies as one, death emerges
once more as victor over the individual, who is subject to its
power, and no longer part of the sustaining, grotesque body of
the people.

The psychological realist drama of the latter part of the nineteenth century expresses this predicament of the individual
facing the void. The communal supports that sustained the
medieval peasant community have been demolished and the
human being must now go it alone. While Synge's post-realist
aesthetic had reintroduced the folk imagination with its strong
emphasis on the natural world as a sustaining and destructive
force, Marina Carr goes full circle. She reworks the folk belief in
the earth as grave and womb, that 'swallows up and gives birth
at the same time.' (Bakhtin, p.206), embracing and defeating
death simultaneously. Carr's doomed heroines return through
suicide to their natural element, to the womb from whence they

Illustration 6
Seán Rocks (Raphael), *left,* and Derbhle Crotty (Portia) in *Portia Coughlan*
at the Peacock Theatre, Dublin (1996)

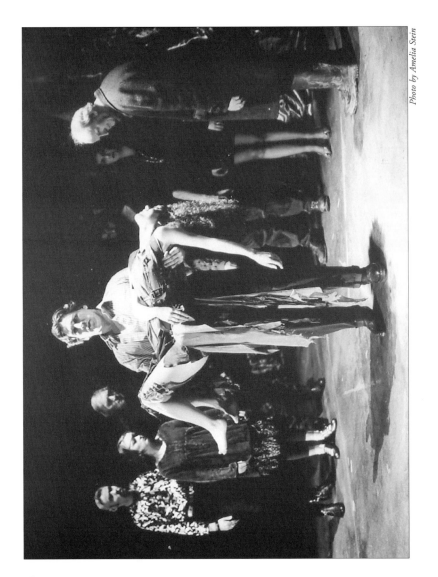

Illustration 7
Act Two, Scene One of *Portia Coughlan* at the Peacock Theatre,
Dublin (1996)

Illustration 8
Bronagh Gallagher (Stacia), *left,* and Marion O'Dwyer (Maggie May)
in *Portia Coughlan* at the Peacock Theatre, Dublin (1996)

Illustration 9
From left to right: Conor McDermottroe (Carthage), Olwen Fouéré
(Hester), and Kerrie O'Sullivan (Josie) in *By the Bog of Cats...* at the Abbey
Theatre, Dublin (1998)

Illustration 10
Fionnuala Murphy (Caroline), *left,* and Olwen Fouéré (Hester) in
By the Bog of Cats... at the Abbey Theatre, Dublin (1998)

Illustration 11
Joan O'Hara (Catwoman), *left,* and Olwen Fouéré (Hester) in
By the Bog of Cats... at the Abbey Theatre, Dublin (1998)

Illustration 12
Olwen Fouéré (Hester) and Siobhán Cullen (Josie) in *By the Bog of Cats...*
at the Abbey Theatre, Dublin (1998)

Illustration 13
Tom Hickey (Red Raftery) in *On Raftery's Hill* at the Town Hall Theatre,
Galway (2000)

came, which is the bog for Hester Swane in *By the Bog of Cats*....
They tread the thin path that separates the worlds of the living
and the dead, and continuity between these worlds is expressed
through the ghosts 'stravagin' the shadows' (*BBOC*, p.321), who
hover on the edges of both, blurring the distinctions between
past, present and future.

Carr's protagonists live in the democratic Ireland of equal
opportunities, yet find themselves trapped and marginalized.
The presence of ghosts, the strong connection with nature
which sustains and ultimately reclaims her tormented heroines –
these ideas are linked to the concept of the earth as both grave
and womb. Carr is re-working folk traditions by suggesting that
her characters die, but are re-assimilated into nature, the Belmont River for the eponymous Portia Coughlan, and the bog
for Hester Swane. Synge, though writing in a realist vein, was
reaching out to a modern post-realist audience by presenting his
vision through a distorting mirror, which gives back a grotesque
reflection. Marina Carr gets rid of the mirror altogether and
gives us the thing itself, unmitigated by the stabilizing demands
of realism.

Her vision does accommodate a critique of the individual
psyche, but her portrayals insist that 'there are a thousand lives
in each of us'.[7] Carr shows, through the shifting nature of
memory in her plays, how there are no absolute certainties. In a
postmodern era, her grotesque carnivalesque aesthetic can
operate in complete freedom, uninhibited by the organizing
rationale of one supreme truth; and perhaps the Rabelaisian
note, central to Synge's aesthetic, reaches an inevitable climax in
the work of Marina Carr.

Joyce McMillan, reviewing Marina Carr's *By the Bog of Cats...*
for the *Scotsman* in October 1998, acknowledges 'a Synge-like
feeling for the surreal comedy of Irish rural life, deftly updated

---

[7] Marina Carr, in interview with Heidi Stephenson & Natasha Langridge, in *Rage and Reason: Women Playwrights on Playwriting*, ed. Heidi
Stephenson and Natasha Langridge (London: Methuen, 1997),
pp.146-155, p.148.

to the nineties'.[8] Two years earlier Jocelyn Clarke had hailed
Portia Coughlan as 'savage in its fierce and violent beauty'.[9] What
connects these responses is an astute perception of Carr's work
as accommodating opposing forces, which clash in the intensity
of their discord, to produce a grotesque vision, reminiscent of
John Millington Synge's. While the grotesque in the work of
Synge has already been explored by Toni O'Brien Johnson in
her book *Synge: The Medieval and the Grotesque* (1982), similar
influences in the work of Marina Carr still invite investigation.
Hopefully this study, by using the work of Synge, and Bakhtin's
theories on carnival as springboards against which to bounce
parallel elements in *By the Bog of Cats…*, will shed some light on
her grotesque impulse. The departure motif and the
fool/outsider motif will be analysed, and their employment by
Carr will show how she is part of a long tradition in Irish
drama, but also how she subverts the very tradition that she
belongs to. The way these motifs are used in her work illustrates how Carr refuses to be confined by rules, and demands
the freedom to operate unencumbered and in defiance of accepted norms, which are invariably subverted in her plays.

Hester Swane, Carr's female protagonist in *By the Bog of
Cats…,* is the forty-year-old 'tinker'[10] woman whose mother
abandoned her on the Bog of Cats at the tender age of seven.
As the action of the play begins she has once more been abandoned, this time by her lover of fourteen years, Carthage Kilbride. The father of her seven-year-old daughter Josie, Carthage
is about to marry into a local landowning family for, as Hester
accuses, 'a few lumpy auld acres and notions of respectability'
(*BBOC*, p.289). Hester is determined not to leave her home,

---

[8] Joyce McMillan, 'Why Can't Scottish Theatre have the Look and
Flair of the Irish?' in *The Scotsman*, 21 October 1998.

[9] Jocelyn Clarke, 'Plunging Bravely Into the Murky Depths', in *Tribune
Magazine*, 31 March 1996.

[10] Before the word acquired the connotations associated with it today,
a tinker was a travelling mender of pots and pans. Hester Swane is
proud of her heritage and claims on p.289 that her tinker blood
gives her 'the edge over all of yees around here'.

despite Catwoman's prophetic dreams. In medieval folklore, death's headless harbinger travels in a black horse-drawn coach which stops at the abode of the victim. Carr presents the post-modern appropriation,[11] with a 'black train motorin'' through the Bog of Cats', scorching and blasting everything in its wake (p.273). Catwoman interprets the dream and urges Hester to leave or she will 'bring this place down by evening' (p.273). Hester Swane contradicts the departure motif central to Synge. His plays usually end with the departure of the hero/heroine whose alternative viewpoint is rejected by a closed society. Nora in *The Shadow of the Glen* chooses to escape from the re-pression of her fruitless life and marriage, and to embrace the wild outdoors with the tramp.The Douls face a similar fate when they choose a dubious freedom at the end of *The Well of the Saints*, and the most famous departure of all is probably that of Christy Mahon. He vacates the space at the end of *The Play-boy*, leaving behind him a static society, which had been tempo-rarily invigorated by the vital energy he brought with him. In Carr's play, Synge's departure motif is subverted, and ultimately expanded, as Hester refuses from the beginning to leave the bog, and avoids the necessity by taking her own life.

At times, one detects in Carr's work grotesque allusions which seem like deliberate appropriations from Synge. Sarah Tansey, who 'yoked the ass cart and drove ten miles' to see 'the man bit the yellow lady's nostril on the northern shore,'(*Playboy*, p.127), strikingly illustrates Synge's fascination with the gro-tesque. This story finds echoes in *By the Bog of Cats...* where Big Josie Swane is recalled as a pugnacious individual, who once 'bit the nose off a woman who dared to look at her man. Bit the nose clean off her face' (p.295). In Carr's play, Synge's gro-tesque image is taken to its most extreme conclusion.

---

[11] Hutcheon says postmodern parody, whether ironic quotation or appropriation, notes the continuum, but also the difference in-duced by the history which separates the two representations. See Linda Hutcheon, *The Politics of Postmodernism*, (London: Routledge, 1989), p.93-94

She does the same with the image of Jimmy Farrell's dog which we are told was left 'hanging from the licence and [...] it screeching and wriggling three hours at the butt of a string', (*Playboy*, p.115), by presenting an horrendously grotesque version in *By the Bog of Cats...* Here Hester recalls finding young James Cassidy 'strychnined to the eyeballs [...] and his dog in his arms' (p.329). She accuses Xavier Cassidy, the victim's father, of lacing his son's dog with the lethal poison, in the sure knowledge that the boy would enfold the afflicted creature thus making contact with the strychnine, which was intended for him. Hester suspects that Cassidy used the dog in order to eliminate a weak and ineffectual male offspring. Just as the vengeful Medea 'anointed' the dress and the coronet, gifts for Jason's new bride, with such a deadly poison that 'all who touch her will expire in agony',[12] so too does Cassidy deliberately smear strychnine on his son's dog, fully cognizant of what that poison does. '[...]a tayspoonful is all it takes, and ya'd the dog showered in it. Burnt his hands clean away' (p.329). The playfulness of Synge's grotesque is absent in these examples, and the perversion of 'normal' female, and fatherly behaviour, no longer provokes congenial laughter in the shock of these mutated accounts.

In her study of Synge's plays Toni O'Brien Johnson shows how the playwright explores the grotesque through a mixture of comedy, incongruity, and ugliness, and by utilizing the fool motif. If Synge's 'fools' are those perceived as such by the 'official community' for choosing to place themselves outside the established social structures, Hester Swane, like her mother before her, is Carr's version. She goes beyond Synge's models however, and possesses even wider mythic associations and possibilities. Hester is not only rejected as an outsider – an itinerant – but feared also, as a woman in possession of 'a black art thing' (p.324). When outlining Synge's use of the literary fool Johnson highlights three important aspects. The fool is closer to nature than the 'insiders', and is instinctive, vital and

---

12 Euripides, *Medea and other Plays*, trans. by Philip Vellacott, (London: Penguin Books, 1963), p.41.

impulsive. The fool is irrational, which leads others, on the one hand to admire his/her visionary ability to see into the heart of things, but on the other, to fear this as madness, and thus reject him/her. Finally, Johnson notes that the fool 'remains an outsider'.[13] Although coined as a description of Synge's early twentieth century outsiders, this account fits perfectly the character of Hester Swane conjured into existence almost a hundred years later.

Hester's bond with nature is symbolized in the opening moments by the lone figure dragging the dead swan, across the raw and corrugated landscape. It is emphasized throughout the play by her inability to settle in either house or caravan, and by her choice to occupy the liminal space between the two. Big Josie Swane, who 'hung around for no wan' (p.320), had prepared her infant daughter Hester for a life in tune with nature, by choosing the black swan as a surrogate mother for the child she knew she would one day abandon. The ritual of placing the newborn baby in the swan's lair, and repeating the exercise for three consecutive nights, creates a bond which can only be broken by death. As the play draws to a close, Hester, anticipating her own impending fate, gives in to her vital instinctive side and burns down the house and stables, letting the bog 'have it back' which is 'what the tinkers do' (p.322). Her final impulsive act of union with nature is to slit her young daughter's throat, and then kill herself with the same knife, still warm and wet with her child's blood. Carr has taken the grotesque possibilities in the fool/outsider figure to a new and powerfully subversive level.

That Hester Swane possesses the second feature of O'Brien Johnson's 'fool' model, and is a visionary, a 'truth-teller',[14] is evident early in the play when Catwoman recognizes this quality as 'the best thing about ya' (p.274). Although Catwoman can find little to praise in the stubborn and turbulent Hester, she is aware that unlike others 'who manage to stay a step or two

---

[13] Toni O'Brien Johnson, *Synge: The Medieval and the Grotesque*, (Gerrards Cross: Colin Smythe, 1982), p.118.

[14] Johnson, p.118.

ahead of the pigsty truth of themselves' (p274), Hester faces her demons, and ultimately overcomes them. Frank McGuinness has pinpointed the paradox inherent in this, noting that while 'tragedy is so often caused by a fatal lack of self-knowledge, Carr's characters die from a fatal excess of self-knowledge'.[15] This irrational side to Hester Swane is probably what attracted young Kilbride to her in the first place. However, the urge towards land and respectability, coupled with the horrible guilt for his part in, and revulsion at her part in her brother's murder, turn him from her to a world that she can never inhabit. When the lure of her unconventional irrationality ceases to attract him he begins, like the others, to suspect her, and to question himself for having stayed with her for so long. He joins ranks with the 'settled' community when he expresses their belief that it is time Hester, the outsider, 'moved onto another haltin' site' (p.289).

This brings us to the third point in relation to the literary fool. She/he remains an outsider. Social assimilation, anathema to Synge's outsiders, is savagely rejected by Hester Swane. Synge's plays, as already observed, generally end with the departure of the outsider. Timmy's final prophetic words, presaging the drowning of the blind couple, in *The Well of the Saints,* offer a diegetic, off-stage possibility only. Nora's choice in *The Shadow of the Glen* does not ignore the attendant dangers, and Patch Darcy's fate hangs over that play as a constant reminder of the elemental forces, which are destructive as well as alluring. While death is always around the corner for Synge's departing outsiders, it is never mimetically enacted. Carr's historical placing allows for the gross note to be acted out on stage. Hester Swane, refusing to vacate the space, makes the choice that Synge had hinted at for his blind protagonists in *The Well*, and for Nora in *The Shadow*, as Carr expands the dramatic possibilities of the fool figure, by presenting onstage, Synge's off-stage suggestion.

---

15 Frank McGuinness, Introduction to *The Dazzling Dark: New Irish Plays*, (London: Faber & Faber, 1996), pp.ix-xii, (p.ix-x).

By the Bog of Cats... is set in a Beckettian no-man's-land and Patrick Mason's 1998 Abbey production chose to incorporate the house, which represents the settled community, and the caravan, which symbolizes Hester's tinker heritage, as offstage extensions of designer Monica Frawley's bleak stepped land-scape of partially-cut, snow-covered bog. This decision effec-tively highlighted Hester's anomalous status, as the space she chooses to occupy is the liminal region between the two, the bog itself, which is a magnet for her, as the Belmont River is for the doomed heroine in *Portia Coughlan*. The cottage kitchen as the domesticated space of 'woman' has been entirely rejected by Hester who first shuns the house, and later obliterates it in her act of vengeance. Carr's troubled characters choose to roam the vast expanses rather than succumb to the asphyxiation of con-fined spaces. The surreal landscape of *By the Bog of Cats...,* provides a realm where the grotesque can flourish.

The opening image of Hester trailing the corpse of a black swan, and leaving a track of blood in the snow immediately strikes the 'gross note' that Synge insisted on, only here it is more stark as the image is presented visually rather than in language. *By the Bog of Cats...* opens with a vivid image of bloody death, and the prediction that more will follow before the cycle is complete. The Ghost Fancier's 'mistake', coupled with Catwoman's injunction to Hester to 'lave this place now or ya never will' (p.276), prepare us for the bloody *dénouement*. The ritualistic death dance is the Rabelaisian climax, which is at once terrifying and jubilant. Hester's death at the end of the play is the carnivalesque enactment of its opposite, representing re-newal in a return to the great nurturing womb of nature, giver of life, death and continuity.

The violent thrust in Carr's work is undisguised, and lends itself readily to grotesque treatment. A brother's corpse is weighted down and lowered into the murky depths of a lake. A man uses a cocked shotgun to grope a woman's body. A boy embraces a dog laced with strychnine and is burnt alive by the contact. Such grotesque descriptions of violence abound, and even Hester's early humane impulse to bury the dead swan is subverted in the violent ripping of the bird from the ice, which leaves half her underbelly intact, while creating the bloody trail of a split-open corpse in the white snow. This opening image anticipates the flesh-ripping violence with which the play will close. Hester's savage nature is never hidden, and she warns Caroline of her capabilities early on as she describes the two opposite poles to her own nature: One, decent and tolerant, and the other who 'could slice a knife down your face, carve ya up and not bat an eyelid' (p.285).

Such savagery emerges against those who take away what she holds most precious. Her brother Joseph, she believes, took her mother's love, and Carthage is about to take her home and her child. Swallowing her pride, Hester begs to be allowed to stay on the bog, and when Carthage refuses her, she feels she has no choice but to wage 'a vicious war' (p.316) against him. Hester goes on the rampage, pouring diesel over everything they once shared and setting it alight.

The evocation of burning stables replete with howling animals at the beginning of Act Three, may be viewed as a reworking of the traditional festive hell-burning. The farm represents the wages of sin, built up from the money taken from the murdered Joseph. This bloody deed has turned Hester's life into a living hell as she grapples with the guilt. Carthage too is haunted, having 'rose in the world on his [Joseph's] ashes' (p.334). Hester's reckless actions at this point symbolize an impulse to eradicate a personal hell, an impulse that reaches its climax in the death dance. The discordant sound of howling animals, tied in, and burning to death, is a perverse reversal of the earlier scene where father and daughter, Carthage and Josie, exit hand in hand, to 'check the calves' (p.282), and 'count the cattle' (p.285), which represent the life-blood of the farm. The incongruity between the homely, and its perverse violent opposite, enacts that clash of opposites which is at the heart of grotesque and carnivalesque imagery.

Hester's final act of violence is prompted by Carthage's decision to take Josie from her. Her efforts to say goodbye to her daughter prove futile, as the child refuses to be separated from her mother, and Hester refuses to sentence her daughter to the limbo she has lived in since her own mother's departure. The killing of her child, by far the most controversial aspect of the play, is ironically perpetrated without overt violence, but with love. Carr has subverted the very notion of violence itself, by couching it in gentle, protective, motherly terms.

The final death, her own, is presented ritualistically in the death dance. The aesthetic beauty of the description of Hester's heart, cut out of her body, and 'lying there on top of her chest like some dark feathered bird' (p.341), introduces a romantic sensibility which clashes with the gross. The hybrid nature of Carr's aesthetic allows for towering grotesque moments, along-side stylized ritual, and the ultimate disruption of carnival itself, which is employed in the superb second act of *By the Bog of Cats*....

Of all of Carr's plays this is the one that most obviously employs the strategy of carnival to generate a deliberate travesty of the social order. The disruptive power of this act represents a sustained attack on the ritual of marriage, which is subverted on every level, as the misrule of carnival is given free reign. Michael D. Bristol identifies the traditional carnival personae including fools, clowns, giants, oversized puppets and effigies, and explains how 'each of these figures represents a variant on the central pattern of travesty and identity switching'.[16] All these ingredients are present in Act Two of Carr's play. The grotesque, rooted as it is in the medieval carnivalesque tradition, sits comfortably in this environment where the spectacle of Catwoman slurping wine from a saucer is perfectly acceptable. This vision can also contain the physical representation of the blood-soaked ghost of Joseph Swane who enters the space in search of company, and reveals the awful loneliness of his purgatorial existence.

The subversive intention is further exposed with the entrance of the bride and groom, and Caroline's uneasy admission that they have 'done the wrong thing' (p.303). Carr does not simply present a carnival festival, which the folk unthinkingly

---

[16] Michael D. Bristol, *Carnival and Theatre: Plebeian Culture and the Structure of Authority in Renaissance England*, (London: Routledge, 1985), p.66.

embrace and partake in. What she offers is a travesty of the tradition itself, where the 'true' bride Caroline is trapped in a parody of a marriage, which bears no relation to the fantasy of 'a big ballroom with a fountain of mermaids in the middle' (p.336). Defeated, she admits to the pretence, resolving to endure the day, which should have been the happiest in her life.

The carnival laughter, temporarily dampened by the veracity of the 'unhappy couple', resumes with gusto as Mrs Kilbride enters, enacting her very surname by usurping the role of 'bride' for herself. 'Disguised' as the bride, she reverses expectations by refusing to part with her son, by assuming the central position beside the groom in the wedding photograph, and by suggesting an Oedipal bond – referring to her 'son' as her 'husband' (p.311). Outrageous and grotesque, such reversals sit comfortably within the carnival tradition.

Catwoman's return, linking arms with the doting Father Willow, introduces a wonderful 'clash of incompatibles'[17] reminiscent of Synge. Here we have the two traditions, Catholic and pagan, arm in arm, and planning a holiday in the sun together. The ambivalent laughter of carnival which is gay and triumphant, and at the same time mocking and deriding can accommodate the spectacle of a Catholic priest, whose adoration is directed not at the God of his church, but at the blind pagan prophetess, with mouse fur stuck between her teeth. That he is unsuited to his pastoral role is indicated in the clothing imagery. The ecclesiastical uniform – black suit and clerical collar – is, for Father Willow, but a festive costume, and the pyjamas that can be seen peeping 'from under his shirt and trousers', (p.306) remind us that what he wears is a disguise, a carnival mask.

Toni O'Brien Johnson describes how, during the Festival of Fools in the Middle Ages, all things sacred were profaned.[18] Marina Carr's priest, a monument to carnivalesque reversal, epitomizes the sacrilegious. By keeping 'a gun in the tabernacle' (p.305), and by wearing ear-plugs in the confession box, he embodies a burlesque subversion of both sacraments, mocking

---

[17] Johnson, p.2.
[18] Johnson, pp.15-30.

the doctrine of transubstantiation, and denying the possibility of absolution for the contrite. The ambivalent laughter reaches a climax when the priest cannot remember the grace before meals, and instead launches into an anecdote, expressing regret at his own unmarried predicament.

Hester's arrival could be said to represent that moment when the carnival goes out of control. Though officially carnival was meant to reinforce the status-quo by offering temporary anarchic licence, Anthony Gash draws attention to several incidents where 'the tensions between the festive and everyday official realms was broken and uprising ensued'.[19] Bristol's study supports this view, acknowledging that 'the transgressions connected with festive misrule are real and that, in the violence of festive misconduct, real and sometimes irreparable damage will be done'.[20] When carnival festivity ends, social order should be restored, but Carr's festival spirals out of control with the dissonant entrance of Hester. This 'bride-effigy' will be destroyed, as all festive effigies are, before deviant impulses are pacified and brought under control.

Roger Caillois believes that the 'underlying purpose of social inversion [in carnival] is to eliminate all dissonant impulses'.[21] Bristol cites the Roman Saturnalia as an example of this type of festive manifestation. He relates how the reversal of social order in this instance concluded with the actual murder of a mock-king. The victim would be an outsider, a slave maybe, who represented the discordant voice in the community which must be eliminated for social equilibrium to be re-established. I would argue that Carr's ending is a variant on the saturnalian model. Although the community does not physically take Hester's life, it forces this outcome by banishing her from the source of her very being, the bog, on which she was born, and where she is predestined to die. Hester Swane is the 'outsider',

---

[19] N.Z. Davis, quoted in Anthony Gash, 'Carnival and the Poetics of Reversal', in *New Directions in Theatre*, ed. Julian Hilton, (London: Macmillan, 1993), p.89.

[20] Bristol, p.33.

[21] Quoted in Bristol, p.34.

the 'piebald knacker' (p.311), the mock-bride, who should, according to local consensus, be moved on to another halting site, and who will be degraded before their festivities are complete. The carnival ends with her suicide, but Carr, unwilling to embrace a neat closure, suggests that the restored order will not bring happiness to the surviving community which has been irreparably damaged by the events leading to this extremity.

All texts must end, and even those that resist closure must physically stop. It is the metaphysical closure of events that Carr prevents in *By the Bog of Cats...* Catwoman has prophesied 'separate tombstones' (p.308) for the bride and groom, and Hester has sworn to haunt the place, and to afford Carthage no peace as long as he lives:

> Ya won't forget me now, Carthage, and when all of this is over or half remembered and you think you've almost forgotten me again, take a walk along the Bog of Cats and wait for a purlin' wind through your hair or a soft breath be your ear or a rustle behind ya. That'll be me and Josie ghostin' ya (p.340).

Although Hester is dead, the ending suggests that her ghost will roam the bog as her brother's does, and her presence will hang over the place like her mother's, as the past continues to exist in the present and into the future. The folk belief in the regenerative power of nature, in the earth as both grave and womb, is reworked here as Hester is re-assimilated into the timeless bog (an apt symbol of continuance), thus embracing and defeating death simultaneously. Carr's ending represents a victory over fear, and concurs with Bakhtin's theories of carnival by subverting official authority – religious and secular – and by proposing the possibility of renewal and continuity through nature.

9 | 'Poetry shite':

A Postcolonial Reading of Portia Coughlan and Hester Swayne

Victor Merriman

The twentieth century saw remarkable historical transformations on the island of Ireland. Fully absorbed in the British Empire in 1900, by 2000 the Republic of Ireland was a sovereign state, a member of the European Union, and an 'economic success story'.

A longed-for independent Ireland was the focus of eighteenth and nineteenth century anti-colonial dreaming. By 2000, the benefits envisaged as the inevitable bounty of national self-determination appeared to have been achieved. It seemed as if the historical moment of the late nineteenth century, in which a longing for decolonization crystallized around a construct of the Irish nation, had been vindicated. At that time, anti-colonial nationalist consciousness elaborated itself across all areas of Irish experience, and the nation was announced as an achievable utopia, should the British depart.

Cultural production was central to the development of nationalist consciousness, and the National Theatre Society occupied a central position in staging – and critiquing – available social models. Gregory, Yeats, Synge and Shaw recognized that the social reality most likely to emerge post independence carried within its genes the inevitable frustration of republican ideals around liberty, equality and social solidarity. The cultural *cul de sac* engendered by this reality was keenly experienced across Irish society. Two significant playwrights, Sean O'Casey and Samuel Beckett, emigrated to Devon and to Paris respectively, and continued to critique the choices made in the Irish Free State with the relative freedom of the exile. Even as the new state's failures produced an unbearable level of economic migration, peaking during the 1950s, playwrights such as M.J. Molloy and John B. Keane depicted the brutalization of rural Ireland by poverty, emigration and late marriage in plays such as *The Wood of the Whispering* and *Sive*. Brendan Behan's *The Quare Fellow* argued bluntly that 'the Free State didn't change anything more than the badges on the (prison) warders' caps'.

The economic caesura of 1958-1959 was accompanied by the retirement from active politics of Eamon de Valera, enabling a cultural caesura to come into being also.

Since that time, the state has pursued an outward looking economic policy, driven by the conviction that 'a small open economy' must be open above all else, to compensate for the disadvantages of being small. Officially, economic openness has meant 'attracting inward investment' from Europe and the USA. The state has accepted the technocratic copying of political and economic forms and conventions from the Anglo-American world as a necessary motor of change. This habit of what J.J. Lee refers to as 'the official mind' installs and legitimizes implication in the global capitalist order as the national destination: the escape route from nineteenth century imperialism turns out to lead directly to collusion with the imperialist project of the twenty-first century. Embracing the New World Order, in gestation since the early 1970s, means living within its neo-liberal ground rules. Those premises are rooted in individualism and the primacy of economic narratives of reality and possibility. They are fundamentally incompatible with the ideals underpinning late nineteenth, and early twentieth century Irish nationalist consciousness. They are openly at odds with the Enlightenment principles underpinning a republic of equal citizens. Contemporary Ireland faces every day a profound historical irony: the diverted teleology of the nation-state demands the abandonment of the egalitarian and communitarian aspirations of anti-colonial nationalism. Such a contradiction ensures an unsettled country.

Inevitably, accounts of Irish experience other than those authorized by the official mind emerge and attract public support. Such accounts appear in both unofficial and non-official forms throughout the twentieth century. Unofficial versions of Irish openness question the received wisdoms of the extremely conservative social order dominant in Independent Ireland. Challenges are mounted to the extraordinary control of the Catholic Church, not only during the 1960s and after, but even in the 1930s, when its compact with de Valera was such that drafts of the 1937 Constitution were proofed and commented upon by the Archbishop of Dublin, Dr. McQuaid. Alongside unofficial narratives and practices, non-official forms of Irish openness proliferate: all the branded products of the global marketplace are enthusiastically embraced, as are sporting, cultural and capitalist heroes. A generally uncritical openness to the world manifests not in liberation from imperial domination, but in the limit situations[1] of neo-colonial social relations. Measured against the yardstick of republicanism, which guarantees liberty and equality for, and solidarity among its citizens, Independent Ireland has not decolonized in any significant sense.

Independent Ireland is a neo-colonial state, and that reality must be acknowledged in any consideration of contemporary Irish theatre.[2] Contemporary theatre cannot usefully be ap-

---

[1] In her 'Notes' to P.Freire, *Pedagogy of Hope* (Continuum, 1996), p.205, Ana Maria Araújo Freire writes: 'For Freire, human beings, as beings endowed with consciousness have at least some awareness of their conditioning and their freedom. They meet with obstacles in their personal and social lives, and see them as obstructions to be overcome. Freire calls these obstructions or barriers "limit situations."'

[2] For a detailed discussion of terms such as neo-colonial and post-colonial, as they are applied here, see A. Ampka, 'Drama and the Language of Postcolonial Desire: Bernard Shaw's *Pygmalion*', and V. Merriman's 'Decolonisation Postponed: The Theatre of Tiger

proached as a set of post-colonial cultural practices, in the sense of chronological severance that 'post-colonial' commonly intends. This essay reads postcoloniality as practices and conditions which emerge and are experienced under colonial and neo-colonial conditions. The moment of postcoloniality is a critical occasion, when the capacity to think otherwise is fully engaged, even if the capacity to decolonize – to live otherwise – is not materially present. In such moments are nations, societies and utopias imaginable. At such moments, artists seek to engage the critical faculties of the dreaming public as they contemplate possible worlds.

If, following Yeats's death in 1939, the National Theatre experienced decades of aversion from the struggles of the nation, Irish drama emerged again in rural Ireland to critique 'the leadership of men who freed their nation, but who could never free their own souls and minds from the effects of having been born in slavery'.[3] The spiritual emptiness of the 1950s and its mutation in the first phase of 'new openness' from 1959 on frame Tom Murphy's *On the Outside* and *Famine*, and Brian Friel's *Philadelphia, Here I Come*. Twenty years on, the urban dramas of Billy Roche's *A Handful of Stars (1988)* and *Poor Beast in the Rain* (1989) and Dermot Bolger's *The Lament for Arthur Cleary (1989)*, stage the 1980s as a reprise of the 1950s, accompanied – especially in Bolger – by the violent consequences of two decades of cultural 'openness'. As Irish culture globalizes, and the world wants to come and take a look at the Celtic Tiger, Donal O'Kelly's *Asylum! Asylum!* (1994) and *Farawayan* (1998) include Europe's Others in contemporary Irish dramas of neo-colonial discontent and postcolonial dreaming.

Irish drama's claim to social significance rests on the pledge that in acts of theatre something more than box office, or the aggrandisement of an individual artist, is at stake. Theatre is

---

Trash', in *Irish University Review*, 29 (2), (Autumn/Winter 1999), 294-304, and 305-17 respectively.

[3] M.J. Molloy, 'Preface' to *The Wood of the Whispering* in *Selected Plays of M.J. Molloy*, edited by Robert O'Driscoll (Catholic University of America Press, 1998), p.111.

part of a broader cultural conversation about who we are, how we are in the world and who and how we would like to be. Theatre is a powerful means of constituting and invigorating community. The questioning stance of dramatic artists is essential to the development of critical citizenship, without which no social order can remain healthy. When J.M. Synge released his 'playboy' into the civic space opened up by a national theatre, he demonstrated the critical vigour and political significance of performative images themselves. Far from demanding space to express or enunciate a rarefied 'aesthetic' position, the theatre of Yeats, Gregory and Synge inaugurates a conversation with 'Ireland'. Their use of ambivalent narratives and images of community to critique triumphant nationalism establishes in Irish theatre the commitment of artists to an ethical vision. This critical cultural project engaged with the figure of the Irish peasant and the dynamics of rural community life, not only because of an aversion to a 'filthy modern tide', but because of the ubiquity of the idealized peasant and rural community as human and social models in nationalist rhetoric and iconography. If the stage looked to the West and at rural society, it was because that was where nationalist ideology argued authentic Ireland was to be found.

The playwrights of the National Theatre Society staged the peasant in order to question the social claims of a nationalist monolith bidding to replace colonial personnel, while maintaining intact the social relations of colonialism. Irish theatre is thus created as a site of public conversation on the type of social order emerging in anti-colonial nationalism. Such founding principles are uniquely available as the principled basis to interrogate the neo-colonial conditions of contemporary society, and to critique prevailing theatre practices.

Not all plays staged in Ireland at this time may be understood as the products of postcolonial consciousness. Not all plays are culturally useful, in the sense that they enable spaces for transformative dreaming, for thinking otherwise. Yeats and Gregory, and Synge exposed in dramatic fictions the coexistence of two worlds, a dramaturgical choice which makes it possible to stage liminal states in which desires may be anticipated, even performed. Such dramas are cultural openings which enable participants in theatre to countenance utopian projects such as decolonization. Such plays achieve their effects by subjecting anything which appears to be new, to posit an end to histories either public or personal, to critical questioning. The stance of the artists involved in conceiving and realizing such works is an example of the kind of practices which, following Freire, I describe and valorize as culturally useful. The liminalities I detect in the early Abbey plays, in *The Wood of the Whispering*, in *The Lament for Arthur Cleary* and in Charlie O'Neill's *Rosie and Starwars* (1997), are profoundly the product of social relations in which being, becoming and belonging, are present always as states unresolved. In such dramas, questions of being, becoming and belonging are staged as processes emergent in contemporary experience. The struggles for actualization of the *dramatis personae* of these plays problematize accepted strategies for the narration of the past, the representation of present realities, and the enabling or closing down of dreams of the future.

The Wood of the Whispering, and *The Lament for Arthur Cleary* are dramas forged in the dark days of the 1950s and 1980s. *Rosie and Starwars* appeared at a time when there was a sense of things improving, and acts as a reminder that full citizenship remains to be experienced by many Irish people. Specifically, in this case travellers. Exploiting the symbolic space opened up by Mary Robinson's presidency, Calypso Productions made a bold attempt to undo and critique the theatrical and film text 'Traveller', with all its reductive connotations. *Rosie and Starwars*, in content, form, and exhibition practices, set out to include Irish travellers in public conversations about Ireland. Some years later, Tiger Ireland was resounding to the clamour of the propaganda for 'success', and was undergoing a series of social mutations. In a reflection on the dawn of the twenty-first century, Fergus Finlay remarks:

> Now we are rich beyond our wildest dreams [...] Rich to the point where poverty is beginning to be defined as the absence of a second car. We love to consume, to spend, to have [...] I couldn't help thinking, when the budget caused

such a furore last month, that at last we were beginning to get a taste of what a society without values might look like. That may seem an overstatement, but it seems as if something has died along the way. To be told that the economy was the priority now, that community values had to take second place, and that this was official government policy – there was a rude awakening in that for a great many people who are concerned about the decline of civic life.[4]

Driven by the manifest boom of Tiger Ireland, the state installed the right to consume as the supreme right, the duty to consume as the primary duty. Citizenship is a key concept in republicanism, and a central promise of the libertarian rhetoric of nationalist anti-colonial struggle. For neo-liberal legislators, guaranteeing citizenship comes with unpalatable trappings, such as social responsibility and commitments to egalitarianism and solidarity. In keeping with this political turn, the resurgent neocolonialism of Tiger Ireland manifests itself culturally in the pursuit of local quietism and international success. Finlay points out that national élites seek totems of their achievements in the currency of the international bourgeoisie. They also require of that which is identifiably 'Irish' – and this includes, especially, representations of the past, and of rural society – that it perform new cultural tasks, especially in the matter of domesticating wealth and consumption. The illusion of a new future can also be engendered by staging the past as a place we're all glad to have left behind. The past, and rural Ireland, is up for grabs again, and what is at stake is competing models of present and future.

In the shadow of the Celtic Tiger, Irish theatre demonstrates some confusion about how best to honour its historical responsibility to critique accepted versions of *us now*. Apart from Calypso Productions taking to the streets with *Féile Fáilte*, few were able or willing to confront the construction of *us* at the expense of *them*, in the shape of refugees and economic migrants. Mainstream Irish theatre returned instead to the past and to rural settings in order to interrogate the safer worlds of

---

4 Fergus Finlay, *Cork Examiner*, 31 December 1999.

us then. Such a resort enables theatre to appeal to contemporary urban audiences without placing actual dramas of Ireland now on the stage. In averting the gaze from existing sites of social contradiction, such dramas harmonize with the neo-liberal project of social reconstruction. And so, myth, grotesque and derivativeness appear as distractions from the predicaments of the present. In the case of Martin McDonagh's plays, the past returned to is that of the stage itself. The hoard of variations on Oirishry accumulated over the years is raided again, as familiar 'pot boiler' dramaturgy yields its historical bounty – crowd pleasers.

Marina Carr's *Portia Coughlan* and *By the Bog of Cats…* opt for worlds even more tightly sealed than in McDonagh's. Narrative energy is sought in the psychic disjunctions of narcissistic protagonists haunted by dead brothers. Content which appears to be quintessentially Irish is overlaid with tropes and conventions deriving from Greek cosmology filtered through the pedagogical systems of the Anglo-American world. *Portia Coughlan* and *By the Bog of Cats…* propose a rural Ireland full of self loathing, and dogged not by the events of its own history, but by tropes from Shakespeare and Ancient Greece. The resources of the most successful Irish theatre companies have been deployed in the service of deeply problematic work, to the extent that their theatricality – their ability to operate as spectacle – overpowers engagement with their significance as dramatic art. It is necessary to question the meaning of these representations as constitutive events in the evolution of civil society.

Portia Coughlan (Peacock Theatre, March 1995; directed by Garry Hynes) stages a woman trapped in 'the dungeon o' the fallen world'[5]. Act 1 takes place on Portia's birthday, Act 2 on the day of her funeral, and Act 3 returns us to the day after her birthday, and her last hours. The people encountered live in comfortable circumstances, but there is no doubting their spiritual bankruptcy:

---

[5] Marina Carr, *Portia Coughlan*, in *Plays 1* (London: Faber, 1999), pp.187-255, (p.205).

PORTIA: You're as thick as the rest of them. Thought I'd taken ya out of the slime, but it's still drippin' off ya.
DAMUS: Wasn't far from slime ya were reared yourself, Portia Coughlan.Your aunt the village bike, your father getting auld Tim Lehane drunk and stealin' his land off of him. (p.203)

For the seedy barman, Fintan Goolan, Portia is nothing more than 'trumped-up bog trash' (p.242). During the post-funeral drinks, Portia's grandmother viciously associates her mother's family with whores, tinkers and poverty, in a stream of poisonous invective.

By the Bog of Cats... was staged by Patrick Mason at the Abbey Theatre at Hallowe'en 1998. The Celtic festival of Samhain or Hallowe'en is an in-between time, a moment where the membrane separating this world from that of the dead, of ghosts, visions and the un-nameable becomes permeable. Unquiet spirits wander between worlds at this time. Hallowe'en itself provides a striking example of how the ritual celebration of a culturally sacred moment can be co-opted and transformed into another node in the network of conspicuous consumption. Dreamt and developed in Ireland, it was recognized by the genius of American capitalism as a unique marketing opportunity. Its characteristic emblems are distorted, despised grotesques. Hallowe'en 1998 offered a compelling insight into what crucial wanderings, sightings and unsightings might be assembling to dance a new Ireland into being.

References to Shakespeare in *Portia Coughlan* go no further than attempting to ironize in an unsubtle way the white trash world of Portia against that of the gentle lady of *The Merchant of Venice*. The elaboration of the notion of certain kinds of Irish people as 'trash' is a phenomenon specific to the cultural tone of Tiger Ireland. *By the Bog of Cats...* (Abbey Theatre, October 1998; directed by Patrick Mason) is largely a rewrite of concerns staged in *Portia Coughlan*. The troubled woman as outcast, the incestuous family, the brutal father, the haunting by a dead brother, the corrosive climate of the outcast woman's home. Its frame of reference is that of Euripides' *Medea*, but, again, there is a playful nod toward Shakespeare for good measure: as Act

Two of *By the Bog of Cats…* opens, Carthage Kilbride's mother is found photographing her sequined shoes in deference to the price she paid for them, and the thrift necessary to purchase them: 'I saved like a Shylock for them shoes!' (p.304)

Although few commentators acknowledge it, *By the Bog of Cats…* is primarily a play about travellers, the land, and rural Ireland. The central figure in the play, which dramatizes the last day of her life, is Hester Swayne. Hester is a traveller, 'born on the Bog of Cats'. Carthage Kilbride is father to Hester's child. Mrs. Kilbride is the child's grandmother. As an Irish social type, Mrs. Kilbride is a monster, appalling in herself, and full of prejudice toward others, especially travellers:

> **MRS. KILBRIDE**: […] All tinkers understands is the open road and where the next bottle o' whiskey is comin' from.
> **MONICA**: Well, you should know all about that, and your own grandfather wan!
> **MRS. KILBRIDE**: My grandfather was a wanderin' tinsmith –
> **MONICA**: And what's that but a tinker with notions! (pp.314-5)

This episode reveals a double otherness in the traveller. In a flash of revelation, Mrs. Kilbride's excesses are accounted for: two generations on from the roadside, she is by some distance the most uncouth personage on the stage. In the dramatic world of *By the Bog of Cats…,* the best thing Monica Murray can do by way of mitigating the assault on Hester, as a traveller, is to expose the fact that her most foul antagonist is a traveller too.

In his programme note for the Peacock production of *Portia Coughlan*, Tom Mac Intyre endorses the perceived boldness of Marina Carr's literary achievement. Mac Intyre situates Carr's writing in a line of descent from William Faulkner. In commenting on 'a grotesquerie that aspires to the mythic' in *Portia Coughlan*, Mac Intyre observes, 'the Irish sagas come to mind'. Frank McGuinness's note in the Abbey Theatre's programme for *By the Bog of Cats…* opens as follows: 'I wonder what Marina Carr believes? I think it might be the Greek Gods – Zeus and Hera, Pallas Athena. She knows what the Greeks know.' He continues, 'she has listened to the stern voice of her true literary ancestor, Emily Brontë.' Turning to the kinds of plays Carr writes, McGuinness declares,

> Her theatre is, in the most brutal sense, heroic. Her brave women look into the face of those who have gone before them – Medea, Hedda Gabler, Miss Julie – and they can hold their own in that tough company who took on their world and tore it to ribbons, for that was their destiny.'

He concludes by returning to his opening question, 'I wonder what Marina Carr believes? I can't say for certain, but I am certain in this play she writes in Greek.'

The potential critical limitations of the programme note's form notwithstanding, the tone here is unusually celebratory. In canonizing Marina Carr, these playwrights posit a transcendent lineage of the literary. Mac Intyre states, 'Marina Carr is an original. That means, among other things, it's hard to trace the source of her marvels.'

This framing discourse reasserts, in the name of the National Theatre itself, the notion that writers come from a magnificent but perplexing nowhere. Success admits the writer to a loosely defined pantheon of Western literary 'greats'. All distinctions of ethnicity, class, and even gender, disappear during this rite of passage. The works, and the writer, exist outside history, and are encountered as visitations from a timeless, placeless zone of ineffable creativity.

Others seek to canonize Carr for bringing feminist perspectives to the stage. Victoria White enthuses, '[…] in *By the Bog of Cats…*, [Carr] has recreated the Abbey stage as a national space, and fearlessly put women at the centre of it.' White continues,

> At seven, Hester makes her [First] Communion in a snow-white dress, becomes initiated into a society in which she will have no power, and loses her mother. At seven, her daughter Josie does the same. There are three white dresses around the wedding table of Josie's father (Carthage Kilbride): that of his wife […] his son-adoring mother, and his daughter's Communion dress – a chilling sight. There are still very few Irish women, and almost no little girls, who don't love white dresses […] But Carr spares no feelings in her evocation of

the freedom which is sometimes taken away in return for the joy of being a princess for a day. And seeing those terrible rituals being acted out on the national stage has all the 'shock of the new'.[6]

This paragraph trades heavily on essentializing both women (the universal allure of white dresses) and travellers. White's summary of the fatal symbolism of the dress on seven year old Josie rests on an unsustainable identity of cultural poverty between Hester and her daughter. In the same way that Ireland has changed, the meaning of the text 'Traveller' has changed in the twenty-three years since Hester was seven. Carthage, Josie's father has not absconded, as Hester's father did. He cherishes Josie, he is a man of property, and will acquire even more means by marrying Caroline. He promises financial security both to Hester and, especially to their daughter. Actual travellers experience change over time, but the representative tropes used to depict and to read them, the text, 'Traveller', does not. The consequences extend to erasure of traveller experience as neither White's nor McGuinness even mentions Hester's identity as a traveller. In a compounding irony, both commentators posit essentialized female characteristics as her theatrical raison d'être.

Hester as traveller is unrelentingly the issue in the dramatic world of the play, which before the end of Act One has exposed its primary contest as one in which a traveller occupies land owned by a local bourgeois. If *By the Bog of Cats…* is feminist writing, it is of the kind which has been challenged by those outside the cultural economies of Western bourgeois circulation. Hester Swayne demonstrates, in an Irish context, the limited egalitarianism of such a cultural stance. Figured as the most fully female of all the *dramatis personae* on show, she is also the most comprehensively damned *in and of herself* for her unnaturalness. In a truly ironic inversion of a powerful feminist slogan, Swayne is obliged to play 'nature' to the audience's 'culture'.

---

[6] Victoria White, 'Women Writers Finally Take Centre Stage', *Irish Times*, 15 October 1998.

Carr's superimposition of frames of reference drawn from classical and renaissance drama onto contemporary circumstances is obviously problematic. Such explanatory paradigms were contestable even in the cultural circumstances in which they originally emerged. Portia, the Venetian lady, is not at all congruent with Portia Coughlan. So great is the gulf that the incongruity cannot hope to resonate with ironies which might generate a dramatic dynamic. Fintan Goolan's digression on his hatred of 'poetry shite' in school suggests that, in the world of the play, Portia's name is intended to figure her as someone more susceptible than her peers to a bourgeois account of the refinements of high art, consummated in the literary achievements of William Shakespeare.

The Medea figure submerged in *Portia Coughlan* finally makes it to the stage in the person of Hester Swayne in *By the Bog of Cats…*. In Hester and Catwoman (Teiresias), the trope of women made strange by knowledge – of Shakespeare, sex, songs, people and ghosts – which informs *Portia Coughlan* is elaborated. In *By the Bog of Cats…*, Xavier Cassidy repeats Portia's reference to the small midland community's practice of burning such women as witches, and inaugurates a shorthand reference to intolerance of difference as a generic response to, in *Portia Coughlan*, the wife of a wealthy man who suffers from depression, and in *By the Bog of Cats…*, to a traveller woman who has just put a valuable farmhouse, outbuildings and livestock to the torch.

Medea was an aristocrat, and the daughter of a god. She lived in a palace, in a country which was not her own. She was to be supplanted by royal Jason's strategic marital alliance with a princess. She had actual magical powers, powerful friends, and a safe refuge standing by to which she could resort and claim sanctuary. Ultimately, she could escape the consequences of her murders by means of a chariot supplied by the gods themselves. Hester Swayne is imprisoned in a particularly ugly version of the text 'Traveller', and faces eviction from her home place as a result of Carthage's strategic alliance with Caroline Cassidy. Hester's lifespan is fatally tied to that of the black swan she drags toward its grave in Act One, Scene One. Her transgressive drinking and her guilt for her brother's murder function as explanatory 'character flaws' in the dramatic narrative. It is the basis of the very contemporary social threat of her losing custody of Josie. Like Portia, haunted by her dead twin, Gabriel, Hester is visited by her brother's ghost, and is tortured by neurotic terrors brought on by her mother's desertion. In contemporary terms, Portia's depression, and the catalogue of Hester's 'socio-cultural disadvantage' grounds a chain of cause and effect which damns each of them to inevitable self-destruction. The mobilization of the worlds of the Greeks and the passing references to Shakespeare combine unproblematically to ascribe the inevitabilities of Fate as the explanatory context for the vicissitudes of poor and vulnerable women in these plays. Such a manoeuvre, in which class and entitlement is ignored, and gender defined in reactionary terms, inaugurates at the very centre of the play's dynamic, not questioning, but evasion of the social meaning of their positions.

The movement of the *dramatis personae* of *By the Bog of Cats…* and the *Leenane Trilogy* to central positions in Irish theatre enables such figures to occupy and redefine the co-ordinates of cultural space. When the 'Irishness' of the *dramatis personae* is so compromised by claims for its universality, as in the encomia of Mac Intyre and McGuinness, and is yet so clearly recognizable to audiences in its particularity, it is necessary to question what representational tropes informing 'Irishness' might mean in Tiger Ireland. A review by Laura Hitchcock of the Dublin Theatre Festival in 1998 approvingly disputes Marina Carr's reported remark that *By the Bog of Cats…* is 'a total rip-off of Euripides', citing the play's 'Gaelic ambience [and] totally Irish characters'. A review in *Western European Stages* endorses the Irisness of the dramatic world:

> Perhaps only a young Irish feminist could turn Euripides' *Medea* into a tragi-comedy. Especially one which combines ancient Gaelic beliefs in magic and spells with current agri-

cultural problems in a depressed area John Millington Synge
would have well understood.'[7]

The evocation of Synge is perhaps understandable, but it is
wholly inappropriate. Carr's dramatic project could hardly be
more different, her models less grounded in the lived experiences of contemporary rural life. Where Synge encountered,
critiqued and celebrated actual peasants in the face of their
idealized textualization in the tropes of anti-colonial nationalism, the mapping of Medea on to Portia and Hester plays
into a series of closed discourses around a reactionary social
project. Among those reduced within that project, as *Rosie and
Starwars* makes clear, are women and travellers. The dramaturgical strategies of *Portia Coughlan* and *By the Bog of Cats...*, and
the framing devices within which such productions are presented to the public negate the interrogation of the conditions
in which images of women are produced and have points of
reference in contemporary Ireland. In this way, the plays point
to a turn away from public inquiry, a turn which eases public
acceptance of a divided society. When Irish theatre does this, it
colludes in a fatal refusal of the difficult, postponed, project of
Irish decolonization. Such collusion raises the prospect of a
lesser public role for theatre itself, in which its credentials as
spectacle overpower its ethical obligation to critique and thus
enable renewal of the social order.

---

[7] See Laura Hitchcock's review of the Dublin Theatre Festival 1998
in 'Mad Dogs and Englishmen', and Bevya Rosten, 'Words,
Words, Words' in *Western European Stages* (1998), both in the Abbey
Theatre Archive.

10 | Journeys in Performance :
On Playing in *The Mai* and *By the Bog of Cats...*

[**Olwen Fouéré** responds to some questions on her work in the world premieres of two of Carr's major plays.]

Can you compare the experience of, for instance, playing the Salomé you created in Steven Berkoff's production of Wilde's play (at the Gate Theatre), with that of playing The Mai, *or Hester in* By the Bog of Cats...? *Does Carr create a different structure around her heroines so that the play belongs to them?*

To take the example of Salomé, the difference for me would be similar to the difference between representation and actuality. Or the difference between the performer and the actor. These are fine distinctions, which describe significant differences from my point of view. As Salomé, I would have described myself as a performer, in a highly stylized work, representing Salomé. Of course, at a certain point, these distinctions must break down. It would be part of my job to allow the Salomé I was representing into actuality, like a sort of trans-substantiation, or at least to invite her in at some point. As Hester or The Mai, the task was not so much to create a persona, but rather to find ways of stepping into these women. Hester in particular was already there in front of me. I just needed to step into her. Her inner world was a furnace, and I had no questions about her. We became as one, and I never felt I had to tell the audience anything about her, because she was already so alive. It took me longer to find The Mai, but I had the same experience of stepping into her once she was in front of me. I did not feel the same need to craft the performances in an aesthetic sense as I would with something like Salomé, or with a number of other roles where you're maybe representing something more iconic. Hester is a very mythic character, archetypal in a sense, but I wasn't conscious at all of operating within an archetype. I felt I was living within a person, a role, in which, how can I describe it, the energies were very primal, which I suppose is really what archetypes are about. I didn't feel any need to construct the roles in playing The Mai or Hester; it was about stepping into them. I don't have an answer to 'Does Carr create a different structure around her heroines?' except that, for instance, Oscar Wilde's play is called *Salomé*, but the central figure in the play is really Herod, and Salomé is almost like another side of Herod. Marina allows her heroines to remain central and to totally devour the universe, to rip the fabric of the world around them. Playing them, I never felt like a function of the play. Maybe it's because Marina is a woman, and is writing with a woman in a central role, but I certainly feel that her heroines are extremely central. With Tom Hickey as Red Raftery in *On Raftery's Hill*, Marina's first male protagonist, it's his world. He had that same licence to devour the world around him.

What aspects of Carr's dramatic language interest you or challenge you as a performer?

I will speak later about how important the dialect is, the sound of the language, that it has a music which operates on the performer's psyche, as well as on the audience's psyche, which is beyond words really. Her use of language reminds me to a certain extent of Synge. When you read Synge's language off the page you think 'God, this is an extraordinary construction of images', but in fact he would say that much of what he wrote he heard through the floorboards when he'd be writing in Wicklow, with girls in the kitchen downstairs, or phrases he'd heard on the Aran Islands or whatever. He would probably claim, as Marina has claimed, that the best stuff he wrote was reported speech. Marina's language has a similar poetic magic and it is also very grounded. There is an innate humour too in her language – even in the throes of her tragedies there's a wonderful sort of Beckettian humour and a wild exultation in it. Her language is quite exultant I would say. And the chance to work with that kind of language is both a gift and a challenge to any actor.

Your response to By the Bog of Cats...? *What was it initially, and did it change over time?*

My initial response to the script was a very powerful one. I remember reading an early draft – not the penultimate draft, but the one before that – when Hester was called Angel – I remember reading it and finishing it in bed one morning, and when I got to the end I experienced a very powerful physical release. I remember being in floods of tears. I knew that the play had hit me in a very deep place, and it also seemed to articulate something that I had never fully articulated in anything I'd done before. Some deep grief to do with … yes, some deep grief. I think that deep feeling of grief was brought on by the seamless transition in the play from the intensely personal to the hugely mythic. And the power of this juxtaposition of the detailed and the local against the mythic is that it is not a single action. It's an accumulation of actions which you experience as you're reading or playing. This peaks during the sequence in the final moments of the play. When Josie doesn't want to be left alone, she begs her mother, pleading, 'Take me with you', and it is in order to comfort her that Hester kills her. It is the loving nature of that gesture from Hester, and something about that 'Take me with you' that I find extraordinarily touching, the idea that someone asks to travel with you into death.

My response to the character Angel/Hester was immediate. I immediately connected to her. I felt the greatest difficulty would be to give her a quiet place because the fire of her rage was so hot, and I knew my task would be to contain that rage in some way. Not to repress it but to contain it so that it could burn all the way through two and a half hours, or whatever length the show would be and not to let it burn out too fast. The characters in the play are uncivilized, they have a savage quality. They cut across all the boundaries, and this makes them funny as well. Those were my initial responses to the script and they didn't actually change. When I read the next two drafts and when we started rehearsing, I felt very much the same about the script and the character.

Hester is at once a passionate person, and a mythic figure from Greek tragedy. Does this yoking together relate to your work in the part?

Yes, it does of course. You're dealing with very primal energies, the stuff of myth. I believe that all those Greek mythic figures are classical archetypes, and are representations of the primal energies within us. They are an embodiment of those energies and that's why they survive through time. They're in our DNA, in our physical, spiritual, and psychic DNA. As I said, Hester was there in front of me and I just needed to step into this person who was like a furnace inside, but who was exultant within it as well.

How did you work on the dialogues with the ghosts and with Cat-woman?

I worked on the dialogues with the ghost characters and with the 'real' characters in a similar way. When Hester speaks with the Ghost Fancier, she quickly realizes that he is a form of ghost, but it doesn't particularly alter her conversation with him, except insofar as her curiosity is aroused and she begins to engage more fully. Her last line as he leaves is 'Come back. I can't die. I have a daughter' – recognizing that, in some way, his appearance is a warning that she has one day left to complete her life. I love how the Ghost Fancier is confused by mortal time and gets his dawn and his dusk mixed up!

The Catwoman I regarded very much as a 'real' or local character, who is the midwife or the local witch in the community. I don't know whether those people exist in communities in rural Ireland still. To a certain extent they must. As we know, midwives over the last few centuries were also the healers and the witches. Hester knows that Catwoman tells the truth. A lot of the other characters don't. The truth in the deepest sense.

The appearance of Joseph's ghost at the beginning of Act Three and Hester's conversation with him is the dialogue that disturbs her the most and that scene was the most difficult part of the play from my point of view. I think it was problematic for all of us to find the arc of that scene and I think it was re-written quite a few times during the four week rehearsal period.

How was Monica Frawley's set [for the Abbey production of By the Bog of Cats...*] to work in?*

I found it a superb set. It was classical, stripped down. It was as empty as the bog. It created a mythic space for the play to exist in, and it demanded a nakedness from us on the stage. There was some talk about whether there should be a caravan on the set. In the San Jose production apparently, there was a caravan at several different moments, but I think that the nakedness of our set was right. Also, when I felt the need to mark Hester's more personal territory, as opposed to her larger landscape, I established it by choosing the stage right side, which I imagined to be the steps of the caravan. Monica reinforced this for me by putting stuff around that area, and when I went off stage right, that was the inside of the caravan. So, reading the image of the stage from stage left to stage right, as the audience does, Hes-ter's territory begins stage left (the house) and ends on stage right (the caravan). The stage left area is dominant, since it's known to be where an audience looks first. So you could theo-rize that, at the beginning of the play, the audience and the people from the town share the same world (stage right), and Hester is the intruder on stage left. But Hester's territory moves to stage right, drawing the audience with her, so towards the end of the play Hester shares her world with the audience, and the people from the town all enter from the dominant stage left. Hester never really left that stage right side towards the end as the world of the town came in on her, driving her out. In all those final moments, for instance in that final exchange with Xavier Cassidy, it was very useful for me to be able to cling to that side of the stage, until the Ghost Fancier releases Hester in death. Yes, I think the set expressed and released the mythic dimension of the piece, and the mythic dimension of Hester's space.

How did you manage the dialect in By the Bog of Cats…?

I could see how important the dialect was. When I did *The Mai*, it was written in straight English, (with the exception of Grandma Fraochlán), not in dialect form, and the sound of The Mai, the sound of the characters in *The Mai* was not at all as crucial as it was in *By the Bog of Cats…* The dialect form is a departure that Marina undertook with *Portia Coughlan*, where all of her characters speak with this very particular sound, and it's essential that they speak with that sound. The music of the piece is crucial. I was very anxious to get that right in *By the Bog of Cats…* because I feel it is the key to a number of things that are lurking underneath the language. It is certainly one of the keys to the primal energy that drives Hester, and many of Marina's characters. So what I did was a lot of listening. I was rehearsing another play in Edinburgh before I started rehearsing *By the Bog of Cats…* in Dublin, and I flew over one weekend in order to spend some time with Marina and asked if I could record her saying some of the lines for me, so that I could listen back to the tape and start getting the sound into my head. She also gave me a few guidelines and mentioned certain people who could speak like that. So I think I pretty much had the music of it by the time I came in to day one of rehearsals. When we did the first readings I would simply stop and repeat the sentence if I felt that my sound wasn't right. So I managed the dialect by a lot of preparation beforehand, and by the time I got into rehearsal if I lost the sound it would throw me off my track completely. It was an essential part of the performance. Because the part of your body that this sound needs to come from is a very resonant gut place, the audience then receives the sound in that gut place; (Artaud often talked about this). By the end of *By the Bog of Cats…*, Hester lets out a cry of grief. It was an extension of the sounds I'd been using all evening, so it wasn't hard to go to that place. Marina has talked about the charge the characters must carry, and how playwriting is not about the beautiful sentence. Much of this charge, this unspoken information which the audience receives is through the dialect.

What were the most difficult moments in rehearsal?

The rehearsal period was short and intense. It was four weeks, which is very short for a new play. A lot of new plays get more time than that. It so happened that four weeks was all we had, so I don't remember the most difficult moments [laughing] because it was full on and I never stopped and I don't think I ever had a break – I was on stage for so much of the time. I knew that I could access the end scene, when I would have to murder my child, and so I didn't experience any difficulty about it but I was aware that I had to maintain a trust in myself – that I could tap into that place every time. And Patrick [Mason] was wonderful. I remember a couple of times drawing towards the close of the play when the whole thing would get to me and I would be a bit shaky afterwards, Patrick would come and put his arm around me and we'd have a bit of a laugh, and it was fine. Then there was a period when we started running the play where I realized I was in some sort of overdrive. I was going too fast and it all started to sound the same, at the same pitch. That comes from not properly containing the rage and the drive that I was talking about earlier on (where I knew that was going to be one of my tasks). So when we started running it I was thinking 'Oh my god, it's all up there. What am I going to do?' And Marina and I went out for a meal that night and she gave me a few pointers. She said, yes, you are overdriving it. Just take your time here and there, and she gave me a few pointers like that. Initially, it was hard to avoid overdriving because of the amount of emotional baggage that I was carrying in order to work through the piece, so it was a question of applying a conscious degree of craft to contain it, and to modulate it a little bit more. I suppose that was the most difficult aspect of the rehearsal period, but it was a joyous time because I knew I was being given an opportunity that was rare. I don't think they come around that often – those kinds of roles.

Why does Hester kill her child as well as herself?

In my view Hester kills her child as an act of love. Her child wants to come with her. Her child is otherwise going to enter a world that Hester feels is worse than death. But she certainly does not kill her child as an act of revenge, which is what some people seem to regard the classical Medea as doing. I don't think it's got anything to do with that. I think revenge is a very reductive way of putting it. It has nothing to do with revenge. It has to do with love.

Why does Hester cling to Carthage?

She clings to Carthage because she loves Carthage. He's also the father of her child, and he's her only connection really to the world outside. And it is he who has left her, so of course she clings.

If you were to direct someone else as Hester, what would you be looking for?

That's a difficult one. I would be looking for Hester's dark energy. You usually recognize fairly quickly the people who have it and who have to live with it. Somebody who can see the world at its most reduced and primal and who is in touch with those very primal passions: love, sex, death. Someone who is capable of seeing Hester's murder of her child, and her own suicide, as being born out of great passion, great love, not out of any kind of retaliation. It's interesting that there are a number of people who find that idea very difficult, particularly women. So I suppose if I was to direct somebody I would be looking for someone who would understand that, the heat of those passions. After that I would be looking for a certain animal energy. I think that's all tied up with Hester's way, that you've got to see that feral, animal quality. I don't think Marina titled the play *By the Bog of Cats...* without a reason. I think there's a certain feline grace to Hester, and to the way that she is with her child. I would also look for somebody who was very respectful of the kind of music that is necessary for the delivery of the language.

Do you think the bond between mothers and daughters is the main theme of The Mai?

Actually I don't feel that. Nor do I think those bonds are the most powerful. I think the most powerful drive in *The Mai* is the belief and the longing for everything that is exotic and unattainable. That's in one of Millie's speeches, about Grandma Fraochlán's Moroccan or Spanish father, a passing sailor, '[w]hoever he was, he left Grandma Fraochlán his dark skin and a longing for everything that was exotic and unattainable' (p.116). I think that longing is a huge part of The Mai. And she reaches for it through Robert. She's fairly uninterested in her daughter, in her children. There's something about how she can access her creative power through her sexuality and her relationship with Robert which is her portal to a higher experience. On the other hand, in *By the Bog of Cats…*, Hester's relationship with Carthage is hugely significant, but her relationship with her dead mother and her own relationship with her daughter Josie are the most powerful links. Her mother is also associated with the bog, which is one of the reasons why Hester doesn't want to leave it. If she stays on the bog, she believes she will find her mother again and be reunited with her. If Hester were to die, her terror is that Josie will look for her all her life; that once she goes, Josie will repeat her own anguish. So she takes Josie with her.

What makes home for The Mai or Hester?

I think the bog is home for Hester because it's also her lost mother, which explains how, although she's the daughter of a traveller, she has no desire to leave where she is. Home for The Mai is the house that she has created for Robert. That's home. It's something that she tries to build, tries to make, and it's left empty and will never be filled.

What were the reactions of audiences to The Mai *and* By the Bog of Cats…?

There were two I particularly recall. Firstly, during *The Mai*, I remember the extent to which people, particularly women, felt that The Mai was so hard done by by Robert, and that he was completely the villain of the piece. That always surprised me because I feel that The Mai herself has a strange sort of middle class thing of wanting the perfect home, and she associates her sense of being with the bricks and mortar of this house that she has built for Robert. And there were aspects of her that would certainly have driven me away if I'd been Robert. So I was quite interested by the fact that so many women saw her as being hard done by, and saw him as being absolutely the villain. It was fascinating to me that some women, after the show, couldn't look at or speak to the actor who played Robert, and that they saw The Mai as this great victim. Both actors (Owen Roe and Robert O'Mahoney) were very interested in playing the part, but audience reactions against the character were strong. There's always a filter through which an audience sees a production; there were couples sitting watching the play, the men were embarrassed and squirming, and the women were turning to them and saying, 'Now, see, that's how it is'. I don't think Robert is necessarily underwritten, but it's a difficult role to play. The negative reactions are to do with the stereotypes that audiences bring. Identification with The Mai means there is a reaction against Robert, but look at Grandma Fraochlán – there's so much damage coming from there, from lots of places.

Most people had a very powerful response to the row scene between The Mai and Robert, which I think is brilliantly written, a truly authentic lovers' rage between the two of them. Articulating that kind of female rage is a huge part of Marina's work. I don't know if any other writer in Ireland has confronted it with the same authenticity. At times I feel that she is actually articulating the female rage of the nation. The row scene in *The Mai* functions like the dance scene in Friel's *Dancing at Lughnasa*. It is a moment of dionysian release. The more enraged they both get, the more exultant they become. The exultation is almost like reverse love-making. You could feel it from the audience, that gasp at the back of the throat, and 'Oh god, I know this.' The scene was full of sexual energy. Hester Swane's rage is a bigger thing. *By the Bog of Cats…* is also a deeply political play about the outsider. Carthage is not just marrying another woman; he's entering this land-grabbing, gombeen society. So that Hester's rage is also a cultural rage, of a colonized culture which is being driven out, not allowed to exist, and where her sexuality and creativity are being suppressed.

The other reaction that I recall was during *By the Bog of Cats...* I found it extraordinary how people could not accept that Hester murders her child at the end. One woman came up to me afterwards and said 'But she's deranged'. I said 'How do you mean?' She said 'she's deranged. She kills her child.' I said she doesn't kill her child because she's deranged. She doesn't have to be mad. And there were a couple of other women whose comments I heard at second hand who felt that I hadn't played her mad enough, that Medea had to be mad because she kills her children. I think this is a very reductive way of looking at it.

What do you think are the contrasts or the links between your work in Carr's plays, and your work in Operating Theatre? Does Carr influence you as a writer? Do both types of work feed each other?

First, I wouldn't even begin to compare or link or contrast my work in Marina's plays and my work in Operating Theatre. They're very different things. When I work in Marina's plays I regard myself as an actor, one hundred per cent. When I work in Operating Theatre, that's where I become a performer.

Marina's influence on me as a writer? I wish! No, I don't really regard myself as a writer for a start. I would regard myself as a 'theatre artist', I suppose, if I were to try to define in broad terms what I do in Operating Theatre and other work of that nature. Even if I have written the stuff, I do not quite see it as writing, because I'm writing with my body and with images, I'm not so much writing words on a page which illumine the path for somebody else. If I did begin to write as a playwright or novelist, I've no idea where my influences would be. But if Carr's influence were in there I'd be delighted.

As a performer/actor do both types of work feed one another? Very much so. The work that I make, and the work that I work with are two streams of my life that run parallel and nourish one another. The work that I do as an actor in the theatre in general develops my craft, my openness to other ideas, and my love of the ensemble. Whereas my work with the likes of Operating Theatre, which is 'my own' work, is lonelier and less accessible for a lot of people, it does develop my creative courage, a certain fearlessness in me I suppose, and it develops my hunger for travelling that world of imagination, that country that we call the imagination. Having to travel there alone is a very good thing.

Coda

Looking back on my work in *The Mai* and *By the Bog of Cats...* a couple of images have formed around the sense of difference between the writer and the actor, what makes one, and what makes the other. If imagination is a country, then Marina's maps bring me to a stretch of land and water that I recognize. The interior landscape of the bog, the colours of rage and passionate love. This place is dark, deep and conversant with the world at its most reduced and primal, a place of great anguish and great exultation: twin truths that rise and fall with parallel intensity.

If imagination is a country it is as infinite as the cosmos in its dimensions. The playwright goes there utterly alone, and returns with a map. The actor, equipped with the map, sets off once more, for the most part travelling alone although in close communication with her fellow actors, to that eternally undiscovered country. Perhaps they both die and come back reborn, who knows, but each task certainly brings us a little closer to our death. The writer gives her map to the actor, the words illumine the path, blazing a trail through to the next encounter, or pathway, or river, or dead-end.

11 | 'One bog, many bogs':
Theatrical Space, Visual Image and Meaning in Some Productions of Marina Carr's *By the Bog of Cats....*[1]

Enrica Cerquoni

> The present epoch will perhaps be, above all, the epoch of space. We are in the epoch of simultaneity: we are in the epoch of juxtaposition, the epoch of the near and far, of the side-by-side, of the dispersed. We are at a moment, I believe, when our experience of the world is less that of a long life developing through time than that of a network that connects points and intersects with its own skein. (Michel Foucault)[2]

> Because we no longer have one shared place, one Ireland, we can no longer have a naturalistic theatre of recognition [...] We must instead have a theatre of evocation in which strange worlds, not our own, are in Yeats's phrase, 'called to the eye of the mind'. [3]

---

[1] For this article I wish to thank Monica Frawley and Joe Vanek for kindly allowing me to discuss with them some aspects of their work in performance in relation to Carr's *By the Bog of Cats....*

[2] Michel Foucault, 'Of Other Spaces', *Diacritics,* 16, (1986), 22-27 (p.22).

[3] Fintan O'Toole, 'Irish Theatre: The State of the Art', in *Theatre Stuff: Critical Essays On Contemporary Irish Theatre*, ed. by Eamonn Jordan (Dublin: Carysfort Press, 2000), pp.35-46, (p.45).

Now [...] there is a sense of people not belonging to a territory anymore, but belonging to a state of mind. People would make their home less in terms of territory now.[4]

As a woman I have no country.[5]

Inspired perhaps by Michel Foucault's assertion that 'the present epoch will perhaps above all be the epoch of space', cultural theory in the last decades of the twentieth century has recognized space as a seminal category in critical and cultural studies. What Liam Harte defines as a 'spatial turn which has occurred under the aegis of postmodernism'[6] has shown the radical potential of spatial analysis in re-thinking both the methodology and the subject-matter of cultural discourse. It has also questioned the older critical reliance on time as a key analytical category. Human experience belongs as much to space as to time.

It could be argued that the invisibility of space-based studies in the established cultural scenario for most of the twentieth century stretches back to ossifying gender divisions perpetuated by a masculinist discourse based on unity, fixity and exclusion: in classical mythology the story of Odysseus and Penelope has always told people from different times and different places how man, moving actively outside the house from one adventure to another, is a free agent of time, whereas woman, waiting and waiting within the four walls of the house, is an element of space. In William Blake's allegory in 'A Vision of the Last Judgement' (1810) that connection is, alas, openly stated: 'Time is a Man, Space is a Woman'.[7]

---

[4] Anne Devlin, 'Anne Devlin in Conversation with Enrica Cerquoni', in *Theatre Talk: The Voices of Irish Theatre Practitioners*, ed. by Lilian Chambers[et al], (Dublin: Carysfort Press, 2001), pp.107-123, (p.119).

[5] Virginia Woolf, *Three Guineas*, (London: The Hogarth Press, 1943), p.197.

[6] Liam Harte, 'significance of Space', *Irish Times*, 3 November 2001, p.8. Further references to this article are given after quotation in the text.

To re-evaluate spatial analysis then becomes a way of giving voice to differences and complexities, and not just gender-related ones. It points to the creation of a constructive dialogue between issues of 'otherness', be they related to gender, class, ethnicity, culture and so on. It also re-opens the stiffness of cultural categories, re-shuffling them and asking us to refocus our vision.

Space seems to be a particularly significant measure of analysis in the Irish context due to the 'highly contested nature of space on this island from colonial to contemporary times' (Harte, p.8). Under the influence of this spatial 'lens', the question of 'who one is and who one can be' appears to become a 'function of where one is and how one experiences that place'[8]. The imbrication of space, place and identity has proved crucial in shaping questions of national historical experience, and this is so even more now, in post-millennium European Ireland, where to the existing divisions between Northerners and Southerners, urban and rural, 'settled', half-settled and traveller, an influx of immigrant arrivals has added further complexity. This growing presence of non-nationals has re-opened questions of who people are, of where people belong, of how fractured and slippery the borders of territory are, and of how margins need to be enlarged to make space for the multiplicity of society, for anomalous and liminal spaces, for the co-presence of diverse and often conflicting world-views and 'hybrid' identities. As Steve Pile and Nigel Thrift argue, the

---

[7] William Blake, 'A Vision of The Last Judgement', in *The Complete Writings of William Blake*, ed. by Geoffrey Keynes, (Oxford: Oxford University Press, 1966), pp.604-617, p.614.

[8] Una Chaudhuri, *Staging Place: The Geography of Modern Drama* (Ann Arbour: University of Michigan Press, 1995), p.22. Further references to this edition are given after quotation in the text.

absolutism of

> 'root' metaphors, fixed in place, is replaced by mobile 'route'
> metaphors which can lay down a challenge to the fixed iden-
> tities of 'cultural' insiderism[9].

What is home/homeland, by the way? Is it one or more
than one? Is it a possible or impossible space, a dystopic or
utopic notion? And how do woman and man redefine it in
today's Ireland?

In response to these issues, in this article I intend to explore
the perceptual and conceptual articulations of theatrical space
as defined by Carr's play *By the Bog of Cats...* and accomplished
in the Irish premiere in 1998. I will also look, in less detail, at
two American productions both staged in the United States in
2001. Occasionally, this analysis will journey through articulations of space in Carr's previous plays *The Mai* and *Portia Coughlan*, so as to contextualize the dramatic designs of *By the Bog of
Cats...*by reference to these earlier works by the same author
and specifically set in the Midlands.

This interpretation will attempt to highlight how, in differently rendered visual images of space, a multifaceted and always
diverse notion of landscape is foregrounded. Nonetheless, in
each uniquely presented 'bogland', the relation between female
and landscape inevitably reopens the debate on what homeland
is, and how to redefine it in woman's terms. It will also underscore the inherent theatricality of Carr's *mise en scène* as well as
the playwright's and stage designers' key-roles in reinventing
Irish theatrical locations less burdened by national traditions.
These locations are both real and imagined, present and absent,
familiar and unfamiliar, home and not-home. One bog, many
bogs; one Ireland, many Irelands.

---

[9] Steve Pile, Nigel Thrift (eds.), *Mapping The Subject: Geographies of
Cultural Transformation* (London: Routledge, 1995), p.10. Further
references to this edition are given after quotation in the text.

II

Given the central role played by space in the theatrical presentation, it is particularly challenging to apply spatial analysis to it. As an art form that is ephemeral and shifting as well as real and concrete, theatre becomes a unique apparatus for reaching out towards differences, for broadening, through the creation of actual and imagined spaces, plural notions of identity and states of mind.

The space of the stage, being both a physical and imaginative realm, is at once here and elsewhere. As spectators we don't just imagine or dream of an 'elsewhere': the 'elsewhere' is indeed 'here', before us, as tangible and material as it could be. Yet, it is not. This continual and engulfing slippage between the physical and the fictional space in theatre keeps spectators in a continual suspension between the 'here' and the 'not-here'. Gaston Bachelard's notion of the mysterious imaginary potential of the interior spaces of chests and caskets becomes an excellent image to express theatre and the secret powers of its visual evocation. Chests and caskets, as objects that 'may be opened' and closed, are 'fraught with unknown and possible elements'[10], thus engendering a series of limitless possibilities. Similarly, the stage is at once a space of closure and revelation, a liminal place, a border zone where spectators, alongside performers, journey through spaces of alternative possibilities and hidden realms. The spatial conception of a play is filled out and enriched in the visual aspects of a stage production. Undoubtedly, theatre is about word, sound and silence. But it is also about image, movement and presence.

In 1998, Marina Carr's play *By the Bog of Cats…* premiered at the Abbey Theatre as part of the Dublin Theatre Festival. This was the first play written by a woman dramatist to be produced on the main stage of the national theatre for decades. In a country where, in Robert O'Byrne's words, 'cultural idols are

---

[10] With particular regard to Bachelard's notions of chests and caskets see Gaston Bachelard, *The Poetics of Space* trans. by Maria Jolas (Boston: Beacon Press, 1969) (1994), pp.74-89.

far more likely to be male than female'[11] this choice would instead potentially represent a wider and plural notion of Ireland based on difference and innovation. Besides, the play could certainly answer Fintan O'Toole's partly justified preoccupation with the idea of Irish theatre as bogged down by words and stories, and less prone to enhanced visual presentation.[12]

Criticism has widely acknowledged Carr's extraordinary ability in using narrative drama and her powerful mastery of the verbal, to the extent that Eileen Battersby has claimed how 'language dominates her approach to writing'.[13] What criticism has explored less is Carr's strong visual consciousness, her power as 'image-maker, as creator of striking pictures that illuminate the stage and [...] animate the inner stage of the audience's imagination'[14]. Marina Carr's *By the Bog of Cats...* is particularly vibrant in visual components. In it, the verbal imagery successfully meshes with the powerful visual image thus epitomizing that 'theatre of evocation' that O'Toole's opening quote recalls.

III

From the opening stage directions, Carr invites practitioners and audiences to see landscape as a dominating and elemental force: '*Dawn. On the Bog of Cats. A bleak white landscape of ice and*

[11] Robert O'Byrne, 'Reviving Lost Literary Luminaries', *Irish Times*, 4 January 2002, p.15.

[12] In an article on the state of Irish theatre Fintan O'Toole sees it as 'a theatre besotted by words and stories that is still alive to the need of going beyond them.' In other 'words', he sees the Irish play as still distant from a notion of total theatre where all the forms – visual, verbal and musical – meet. See Fintan O'Toole, 'Getting Back to the Story', *Irish Times*, 12 October 2001, p.12.

[13] Eileen Battersby, 'Marina of the Midlands', *Irish Times*, 4 May 2000, p.15.

[14] Patrick Mason, 'Introductory note to the radio version of *By the Bog of Cats...*', RTE Radio One, April 1999.

snow[15]. In this first immediate, vividly physical image what catches the eye is a Beckettian expanse of water and mist, frozen, surreal, harsh and wild. Indeterminate and open, it is also shifting, mutable and vast, as one of characters explains to us quite early in the play: 'this auld bog, always shiftin' and changin' and coddin' the eye' (*BBOC*, p.15).

The surrounding landscape is, for Carr, another character: 'it needs to be present, to have a presence' (Battersby, p.15). This assertion also sounds true of her previous 'Midlands' plays. In *The Mai* (1994) the inside space of the dream-house is located on the edge of Owl Lake, a presence embodying darkness and unhappiness; in *Portia Coughlan* (1996) the presence is that of the Belmont River, a physical location but also and especially the personification of Portia's obsession with her twin-brother, with her lost half self.

As J. Hillis Miller remarks 'there is always a figure in the landscape'[16] that will always try and have an impact on it; it will walk it, claim it, resist it. In the immense, undefined and shapeless landscape of *By the Bog of Cats...*, the figure is that of Hester Swane, a forty-year-old female itinerant wandering a Midland bog.

As Carr says in an interview, 'I chose to make her a traveller because travellers are our national outsiders, aren't they?' (Battersby, p.15). The status of Hester's character as the definitive outsider is also sanctioned by her mythical ascendancy: literary references throughout the play relate her not just to Medea, the half-goddess /half-human inhabiting a foreign land, but also to Dido the wanderer, the archetypal figure of the outsider. Thus, through the character of Hester, Carr has taken a mythical situation and made it relevant within the contemporary Irish and non-Irish context. Hester's unresolved condition of settle-

---

[15] Marina Carr, *By the Bog of Cats...* (Oldcastle: Gallery Press, 1998). Further references to this edition are given after quotation in the text.

[16] J. Hillis Miller, *Topographies* (Stantford: Stantford University Press, 1995), p.4.

ment, her scattered sense of place and of self, becomes emblematic of what Pile and Thrift define as

> the 'unhomely' [...becoming] the norm, replacing the sovereignty of national cultures, or the universalism of national cultures [such that] new subjectivities are needed. (Pile, p.18)

The connection between female and landscape is immediately established: in the opening visual image the figure crosses the solitary space, dragging *'the corpse of a black swan after her, leaving a trail of blood in the snow'* (BBOC, p.13). That actual and unmarked space of white snow is now transformed in a realm that suggests darkness and death. The transition to the surreal is the otherwordly presence of the Ghost Fancier, who '*stands there watching her*'. The melancholic undertones of '*a lone violin*' (BBOC, p.13) accompanies the poetic expressiveness of the whole unrestful image.

This picture establishes a series of visual connections, of visual 'hooks' so to speak, which will accompany the audience throughout their journey. The first example is when, in the first scene, the Ghost Fancier hints at Hester's complementary relationship with the dead swan, 'What're you doin' draggin' the corpse of a swan behind you like it was your shadow?' (BBOC, p.13). In the following line, this specularity is re-enforced when Hester herself describes the difficulty in separating the dead swan from the frozen bog: 'found her frozen in a bog hole last night, had to rip her from the ice, left half of her underbelly' (p.13). When later on Hester claims:

> I was born on the Bog of Cats and on the Bog of Cats I'll end my days. I've as much right to this place as any of yees, more, for it holds me to it in ways it has never held yees (BBOC, p.35)

the audience's earlier perception of those visual correspondences bonds character to environment. The powerful backdrop, invested with human association, advocates a suspension between memory and imagination. As spectators, we are in a shifting and permeable land which moves between contrasts: openness and closedness, reality and myth, actuality and imagination.

If Carr's earlier 'Midland' plays *The Mai* and *Portia Coughlan* are, on the surface, partly set within the restrictive confines of an indoor space, (thus deceptively giving a semblance of resting within the tradition of realism and its staging of three-walled rooms), here something different catches the viewer's eye.

Completely disrupting the realistic conventions of the fixed theatrical space, that claustrophobic interior space from which female characters have tried to release themselves in a century of Irish and non-Irish drama (remember Synge's Nora in *The Shadow of the Glen* and Ibsen's Nora in *A Doll's House?*), Carr's radical choice of an outdoor space is fraught with possibility and change.[17] It could be argued that the close association of the plot with the Greek myth of Medea requiredly channels the playwright's dramatic design towards an obligatory path, as in Greek plays the visible action usually takes place outdoors; or might it be that the open and wide outdoor space is the consequence of writing a play for a big stage like the main stage of the Abbey[18]?

Without overlooking the arguable validity of the last two assumptions, it is valuable to emphasize the role of the writer's creative process and also how Carr's 'Midland' plays before *By the Bog of Cats...* reveal a gradual but radical distancing for women characters from 'the old discourse of home which equated [...it] with a sense of entrapment within naturalism's famous four walls' (Chaudhuri, p.xiii).

The notion of the inside space as unstable and unsafe began to be explored in *The Mai* and in *Portia Coughlan*. At a certain

---

[17] In Ibsen's and Synge's dramatic works the female characters at the end of both play exited the visible inside space of the house and entered a potential and imaginative outside world, thus becoming emblematic of the woman's efforts to escape the restraining space and role in which she had been confined.

[18] This second assumption was foregrounded by Christopher Morash during a research seminar entitled 'Performing Irish Space: A Historical Perspective on Theatre Architecture', UCD, Belfield, 29 January 2001.

point in *The Mai*, the eponymous central character, looking around the space which she has built, claims:

> this house – these days I think it's the kind of house you'd see in a corner of a dream – dark, formless, strangely inviting. It's the kind of house you build to keep out neuroses, to stave off nightmares. But they come in anyway with the frost and air bubbles in the radiators. It's the kind of space you build when you have nowhere to go[19].

The traditional notion of the inside space as a protection, as a shelter is, in *The Mai*, seriously questioned; its foundations are as unstable and shaky as The Mai's absolutist visions of love, life and family turn out to be in the play. In the following play, *Portia Coughlan*, this already permeable structure is completely deconstructed. The space of the house is for Portia a 'psychic' inferno, a monstrous limbo, in which she, and the spectator with her, experience the weak and inhuman side of people around her. The house, as Portia says, 'is creachin' liche a choffin, all thim wooden duurs an' fluurs sometimes ah chan't brathe anamore'[20]. The house is no longer home.

In *By the Bog of Cats…* the onstage space has taken on different connotations. The interior as a domestic space has been erased from the audience's main visual perspective, and has been replaced by an open space (which would traditionally have been positioned offstage and as such, have been envisaged only through the seductive power of language). Now, that imaginative outside, where Synge's Nora and Ibsen's Nora entered more than a century ago, is brought centrestage. The unseen has become visible, the absent has become present.

Unlike The Mai and Portia, whose search for identity was partly still marked by a departure from a unfulfilling domesticity, Hester's quest for selfhood follows a different path: she moves from itinerancy, to an attempt at domesticity, to itinerancy again. She has lived in a house for a while, but as she explains to the Ghost Fancier, she 'has never felt at home'

---

[19] Marina Carr, *The Mai* (Dublin: Gallery Press, 1995), p.51.
[20] Marina Carr, *Portia Coughlan*, in *The Dazzling Dark*, ed. by Frank McGuinness (London: Faber and Faber, 1996), p.255.

(p.14) in it. That house, as Hester asserts, 'should never have been built in the first place' (*BBOC*, p.63). In a crucial offstage moment at the beginning of Act Three, Hester burns the house; 'the bed and the whole place' (*BBOC*, p.59) go up in flames. According to the stage directions, the other interior setting required in the play is in the second act, to host Carthage and Caroline Cassidy's 'wedding'. Yet, appearances are deceptive: the interior of Xavier Cassidy's house is no ordinary home, but a mock version of it. As will be explored later in the analysis of performance, due to the presence of an interior, the staging of this scene is an interesting point of contention; it could deceptively drag practitioners into a realistic representation which could bear visibly upon the impact of the whole conceptual image. In other words, to set this scene in a rural domestic environment is to completely miss the point.

Since the beginning, Hester's association mainly with open or unfixed spaces such as the swan's lair, the caravan, the yard and the bog seems to suggest a whole reconceptualization of the notion of home/homeland for female characters. This new idea moves on from a restrictive notion of indoors as a 'natural' space' for women characters, and embraces placelessness and displacement not as the absence of place or as the wrong place, but as an alternative kind of 'placement' (Chaudhuri, p.138) which involves a combination of many distinct places. Home/homeland becomes a manifold figure, far from being 'circumscribed and clearly defined' (Chaudhuri, p.138), and is less linked to attributes of territorial rootedness and continuity that formed the traditional idea of belonging.

Visually, such a move releases the audience's gaze from what Bert O. States spots as one major consequence of realist theatre's use of a single set in one or two rooms. He calls this 'the imprisonment of the eye [by which] … one of the two senses through which theatre comes to us is locked into a hypnotic sameness'[21]. Now, like in a non-realistic painting, where picto-

---

[21] Bert O. States, *Great Reckonings in Little Rooms: An Essay on the Phenomenology of Theatre* (Berkley: University of California Press, 1985), p.69.

rial space extends beyond what is presented to the viewer, likewise with theatrical space: unwilling to remain enclosed, it transcends any confinement and fixedness to open up into the 'elsewhere', into inward realms of dreams and memory. This is the place where Hester's memories of her mother Josie Swane belong, and where Hester last saw her before she vanished for good beyond the endless stretch of the bog. The space of the bog then is characterized by loss and longing, yet it also represents her only site of connection and survival.

IV

In the majestic, basically monochrome and barren vastness of icy bogland created by Monica Frawley, (designer of set and costumes for the Patrick Mason production of *By the Bog of Cats...* in the Abbey Theatre in 1998, with Olwen Fouéré in the main role of Hester Swane), suggestiveness, movement and desolation were the main features. Frawley stresses the power of the opening description: 'I found it extraordinary. It was the fact that it was covered in snow and hugely immediate'[22].

So snow became for her a central image. Representations of snow in artists as diverse and distant in time and aesthetics as the painter Pieter Bruegel The Elder, and the photographer-painter Cartier-Bresson, potently fuelled her imagination.

Undoubtedly, a major inspiration was the physical beauty and the spectral extra-ordinariness of the Midlands landscape where the viewer's eye spaces out in the flatness of the bog. As Frawley says when interviewed, it 'could go on for ever', interspersed by sudden appearances of pools of water reflecting the sky.

> All you could see was the sky, the variety of it and the pitch black colour all around. The landscape fed into me and what struck me was the amount of people living in caravans –

---

[22] Monica Frawley, 'Unpublished interview with Enrica Cerquoni', Dublin, 21 November 2001. Further references to this interview are given after quotation in the text.

there were loads of caravans on the bog and clothes hanging outside them – it all had a kind of ethereal beauty.

So the main artistic drive in the design process was to bring the physical and the surreal together, to get that sense of extensiveness, of people suddenly appearing in the distance and then suddenly vanishing, along with a deep sense of human isolation within such a vastness. The challenge was, of course,

> to get all this within the physical confines of the Abbey stage. I wanted the image to travel from the physical to the inner; it is about an inner landscape and I wanted everything to be cold and frozen so as to convey that connection. The idea of snow is almost like the 'petrifaction' of Hester's mind. (Frawley)

Fusing the inner and outer landscapes of Carr's wintry outdoors, Frawley's finished product was an imposing snow-clad rise of terraced ground, gouged out in levels from the misty and icy earth and extended horizontally as if in continuous slow-motion. Evoking an overwhelming feeling of chill and human solitude, the raked terraced platform stage, reminiscent in its structure of the cut-up Irish bog and of its Greek ascendancy, confronted the audience with an unfixed image that 'didn't rest at the edge of the eyes' (Frawley). Instead, it was perceived as devoid of stable contours and as projecting itself endlessly in both directions and towards the horizon. Erasing any safe sense of spatial dimensionality, the image had a dream-like quality, in the sense of literally being like an image from a dream, completely edgeless, and where, as Frawley underlines,

> people loom out of emptiness: take for example the image of Xavier Cassidy, performed by Tom Hickey, in his black coat, looming out of this dark and smoky ambience. Suddenly he was there, and when he was there he was incredibly there.

The atmospheric and suggestive construction potently conveyed the strong link between place and female subject: it was held in gloomy colourings, glaring under a Blakian sky, and lit by an interplay of light and shadow. Indeed, as lighting changes throughout the performance became less realistically motivated and more symbolically expressive of this eerie quality, of this in-between dimension, the scenic composition reflected the permeability and the ever-shifting facets of both environment and main character.

The conceptual stylization of the play's outer landscape was, in this production, reflective of Hester's pliability, of the doubleness of her experience, of the dark and light side of her inner world. At one moment it denoted attachment, and as such was nurturing and vulnerable, and at another moment harshness and brutality, and connoted separateness. Like Olwen Fouéré's performance of Hester Swane, Frawley's setting unfolded a specular visual narrative of resistance that defied any linear model, eschewing consistency of interpretation and easy classifications on the spectator's part.

The stylized and slow-motion pacing of some of the actors in performing characters such as the Ghost Fancier (Pat Kinevane), or Joseph Swane (Ronan Leahy) or the Catwoman (Joan O'Hara) heightened the ominous atmosphere of brooding shadows and ghostly silhouettes and evidenced the theatricality of Carr's dramaturgy in offering performers the possibility to cross realistic boundaries of representation. The wooden structure of stepped, unevenly-cut platforms broke the proscenium line of the Abbey stage, thus jutting the performers' space across the audience's space. The usual separation between the stage and the audience which characterizes the Abbey Theatre space was, in this production, partially reduced: there was a threatening closeness and the effect of constant motion was as much horizontal as frontal, in a resulting image which was dynamic and fluid.

The audience could not remain at a safe distance from what was happening onstage. They were drawn to share Hester's quest and her displaced condition. Such an experience, strengthened through the changed relationship between the stage and the auditorium, is already present in Carr's dramaturgy, which undoubtedly questions a 'theatre of recognition', and introduces crisis: the spectator views actions and characters from Hester's perspective, through the woman outsider's mind. The audience partakes of Hester's crossing of spatial boundaries, of her darker vision of a marginalized existence, where ties are severed and connections to one's fellow beings are damaged. Indeed Carr's disruption of a 'single' vision goes even further and actualizes a double projection for the audience as they 'are in the picture, beholding, yet part of it'.[23]

Saintsbury's words could be used here to allude to the audience's twofold experience: their perception is filtered through Hester's, yet their engagement doesn't prevent them from 'ironically observing themselves'[24]: they could be part of those fellow beings, of those savage members of the 'settled' community seen in the close spatial reality before them. This effect was successfully achieved in the wedding scene of the Mason production, where it was decided to have the long wedding table out in the snow. As Frawley explains, this was quite a disputed aspect of the stage composition among the artists involved in the production:

> I knew I didn't want the idea of a naturalistic kitchen; we talked about the dropping in of a wall; we explored different possibilities. To have a table out in the snow might seem insane but you don't have ghosts wandering around either. (Frawley)

In the blackly comic wedding space of 'celebration' all traditional structures of society were subverted. Church, State, family and marriage, they were all under attack and exposed as false icons. Fouéré's entrance as Hester in the world of 'others' (or was it her own world?) in her 'spoiled' and 'unfit' dress ultimately defied and disrupted the ideology of the established order. This was no space of celebration: the Hogarth-like image of the long wedding table with its grotesque guests, half awake and half asleep, rested on a shaky ground which burst open on Hester's sense of exclusion as on 'the suffering of individuals

---

23 H. A. Saintsbury, quoted in Gay McAuley, *Space in Performance: Making Meaning in the Theatre* (Ann Arbor: Michigan Press, 1999), p.235.

24 Melissa Sihra, 'A Cautionary Tale: Marina Carr's *By the Bog of Cats...*', in *Theatre Stuff*, pp.257-268, (p.262).

[…and stood] in for the shifting of a floor of a whole civilization'.[25]

The destabilizing effect that Carr's dramaturgy and Frawley's
powerful stage design remade the relationship between the
performers' space and the audience space as a two-way mirror
in which the interplay of perspectives, like in an optical game,
created a multiplicity of focus.

It can't be forgotten that the re-workings of the fictional and
physical reality of the theatre space in achieving these de-
framings of experience was taking place on the Abbey stage, the
National Theatre in Ireland, which, in Garry Hynes's words, is
'one of the hottest stages in the world because of the link between it and the growth of the country"[26]. In view of this, one
can't help seeing the political and ideological significance of
such a transformation in the representation of the relationship
between woman and home/homeland as offered by the 1998
production of *By the Bog of Cats…* in the Abbey, by tradition a
male site of theatrical expression. As Victoria White has noted,
it 'recreated the Abbey stage as a national stage and fearlessly
put women at the centre of it"[27].

Not all critics have been positively impressed by the play.
Victor Merriman and Bruce Stewart, for instance, exploring in
different articles the political resonances of the play for an
Abbey audience, have seen the piece as conservative, reactionary and supportive of a new bourgeois Irish mentality[28]. Such
critical responses illustrate how the playing of women's experi-

---

[25] Samuel Beckett, 'The Essential and the Incidental', in *Sean O'Casey:
A Collection of Critical Essays*, ed. by Thomas Kilroy (Englewood
Cliffs: Prentice Hall, 1975), pp.167-168 (p.167).

[26] Garry Hynes, 'Garry Hynes in conversation with Cathy Leeney', in
Theatre Talk, pp.195-212 (p.207).

[27] Victoria White, 'Women Writers Finally Take Centre Stage', *Irish
Times*, 15 October 1998, p.16.

[28] With regard to these controversial critical contributions see Victor
Merriman, 'Decolonisation Postponed: The Theatre of Tiger
Trash', *Irish University Review*, 29 (1999), pp.305-319 and Bruce
Stewart, ' "A Fatal Excess" at the Heart of Irish Atavism', *Iasil
Newsletter*, 5 (1999), pp.1-2.

ences and of other less represented groups is usually welcomed
as innovative and subversive when it is acted out within alternative theatrical structures. However, when experiences of 'otherness' get inside the structures of official power, (for such is the
role of the Abbey Theatre in Ireland), they become differently
charged.

Here is a play, in the official space of the national stage,
woman-authored, and where the main female character is a
traveller – metaphor of the definitive outsider; here is a play
where the main action unfolds in an open space (no domestic
centre, but a realm of limitless possibility) and where the only
glimpse of an inside space as home is completely dismembered
and mocked. These are attributes that pose perhaps more than
one question. Is this not a move irreversibly progressing towards an alternative theatrical image of nationhood, which is
less recognizable and self-explanatory, more fragmented, complex and open to what has always been on the borders in Ireland? Does it not foreground a notion of the National Theatre
as freed from the threat of becoming 'hostage to one or other
version of being Irish' (Hynes, p.207)? And does this not more
broadly revise the notion of what Ireland as homeland is or
perhaps what Ireland as homeland no longer is for women?
Virginia Woolf's quote from *Three Guineas* significantly continues 'As a woman I want no country. As a woman my country is
the whole world' (Woolf, p.197).

V

What happens when the telling and powerful visual image
enhanced by the original production of *By the Bog of Cats...* is
transferred by a non-Irish company to a non-Irish stage, into a
completely different country and culture? Does it lose its political and ideological connections because of the trans-national
move, or paradoxically, does the move reinforce them?

In the tall, stark and cold stage re-presentation designed by
Joe Vanek for the West Coast premiere of *By the Bog of Cats...*
at the San Jose Repertory Theatre under the direction of Timothy Near (with Holly Hunter in the role of Hester Swane),

abstractedness, verticality, angularity and free associations re-
imagine the physical locations of an Irish land and its native
traditions. The characters' costumes seemed to temporally
locate the *dramatis personae* in an ambiguous somewhere between
the 1950s and the 1970s and Hunter's Hester was in Vanek's
words a 'reborn hippie'[29]. In reply to a question about the
Irishness of his decor Vanek remarked:

> It was as Irish as it could be, given that I am a half Eng-
> lish/half Czech living in Ireland and interpreting Ireland for
> an American director who was very specific in wanting
> something.

In his artistic vision, the haunted and haunting bog land was
an impressive 'architectural void', a wasteland where, like in
'Beckett's *Waiting for Godot*, nobody ever arrives and nobody
ever leaves' (Vanek). Vanek's place and non-place imploded in
height and depth, characterized by a dynamic and diverse exploration of forms, of simplified, basic structures and atmospheric motifs. In this controlling scenic expression, striving
towards height and verticality, I couldn't help thinking of Henry
Levebre's comment that those co-ordinates 'have ever been the
spatial expression of potentially violent power'[30].

The opening image featured a raked stage space, an 'open
box' comprised of a flat, furrowed ground of snow and ice and
with sides of two revolving panels, sixteen feet high, which, like
old bog walls rising into cuts, revealed 'a more epic, nearly
geological cross section, their bases frozen into sheets of crazed
ice' (Vanek). On this structure a black curtain, measuring fifty
feet, went up, flapping in the wind, with snow falling on it to
evoke the form of the bog as well as the brutality of this cold

---

[29] Joe Vanek, 'Unpublished interview with Enrica Cerquoni', Dublin,
4 January 2002. Further references to this interview are given after
quotation in the text.

[30] Henry Lefebvre, *The Production of Space*, transl. by Donald Nichol-
son-Smith (Oxford: Blackwell, 1991), p.143.

environment – on windy Irish bogs 'the drying turf is covered with huge sheets of black plastic that snap to the wind'[31].

The image, atmospherically lit, revealed the transient, ancient and powerful presence of this extra character onstage. Most of the bogs in Ireland stretch back thousands of years, and they are all different in shape and size: if in the Midlands they are vast expanses of flat, in the West 'they rise majestically as angular, cut walls – often the height of a human, and sink into dank, waterlogged ditches'. (Vanek)

The shifting quality of Vanek's set, which, as opposed to the horizontal stress of Frawley's construction, was vertically oriented and reminiscent of Craig's abstract models of stage settings, unveiled an immediate association between place and female character: when the black curtain went up and the back wall was raised, the 'open' frontal box revealed a smaller framing 'inner' box with Holly Hunter as Hester Swane coming from inside it, and dragging the black swan downstage onto the snowy field.

The 'open', more external box, like Bachelard's 'casket', extended further into the depths of the theatre, to disclose the woman character's inner realm. The physical and the fictional depth of the stage seemed here to overlap, becoming a transparent metaphor for Hester's state of mind. Visually, the effect was of a sudden revelation: an unseen world was potently brought onstage and the audience was now being sucked into Hester's perspective.

> That inner boxed landscape that engulfs spectators until the end is also a closed world, hermetically sealed. It takes you all the way from A to Z and never releases you for a moment [...] Characters are held captive behind the four walls.' (Vanek).

This last statement could convey the sense that the concept behind the stage composition aimed to recreate a semblance of

---

[31] Timothy Near, 'Notes From the Director', in the Programme to San Jose Repertory Theatre, *Performing Arts Magazine*, September (2001), p.3.

the four walled structure typical of realist theatre but nothing could be farther from that. Those four walls were completely abstract. Despite the apparent logic of 'total visibility' (Chaudhuri, p.27) whereby stage directions were more literally followed and all the spaces mentioned in them – the caravan, the yard and the outside of the house – visualized onstage, Vanek's abstract forms removed the audience's gaze from any realistic reference. Those forms were architectonic frames, bone structures, exterior shapes completely deprived of any non-essential and naturalistic detail.

Vanek's visual response to the representation of the caravan, for instance, was based on an idea of a traditional travellers' wagon (maintained in its external form with a set of steps and the seats on the side) but was then completely conceptualized by its skeletal frame, with its arch of frozen glass, reminiscent of motifs from Renaissance sculptural works (Michelangelo's 'La Pietà'). The same arched frame was also slightly bloody and rusty, thus visually recalling that conflict in the play's theme between Catholicism and Paganism, between forces of the established order and the subterranean powers beneath it. For the wedding scene, the whole set changed: very slowly a wall dropped in, trying to stave off the unruly, frosty field of the bog and stretching the action across the forestage. The geometrical wall revealed, at its centre, a carved window with frosty glass, recalling in form the arched frame of the caravan; the rest of the wall presented an ancient Chinese painted motif, an 'amorphous' blending of cloudish shades which suggested a visual impression of movement, – 'the atmospheric movement' (Vanek) – and created a subtle correspondence with the shade motifs on the central window frame. The decision to recreate an indoor space for the scene by no means marked a shift to realistic representation. In this case, it seemed to create a strong sense of visual continuity with the whole conceptual image proposed by Vanek's spatial concept: all the diverse visualized locations emphasized by Near's production became part of a single yet unfixed continuum, the mutable bog, from which the characters never escaped.

The long wedding table stood on a ground half covered with material whose effect was of greyish cobblestones and half retaining the snowy and icy qualities of the bog field: in spite of the wall, there was no real separateness between the outside and the inside, between public and private space. The suggestiveness of the 'atmospheric movement' painted on the wall rendered the latter a frail barrier, a permeable structure, a defenceless means of protection which blurred any divisions and favoured a spreading of forces. The visual presentation had so far exiled all the conventional associations between interior and exterior space, that they were, in this scene, very much in the same realm. The image was an in-between zone, where the distinction between public and private dimensions was erased.

In Vanek's abstract visual composition the isolated figures at the table sat on a wobbly structure thus suggesting a sense of instability and of slowly being drained into the sucking space of the bog or into the understage. These amphibian creatures of the wedding group, (for whom the back wall created no interior, but an undefined and fluid precinct, like in a '"Last Supper" image' (Vanek)), formed a pictorial composition that abounded in plastic eloquence. And in Carr's play, this is the last supper indeed, as no other meal will be consumed before the tragic final resolution.

Unlike Leonardo's painting, however, where Jesus provided the centre of the visual image, here Hester, as the female Christ figure and the controlling visual trope of the play, had been taken out of the picture. As a witness to the wedding scene brought much closer, the viewer's gaze experienced a sense of existential dislocation and of a power vacuum. The architectural frame of the back wall could then be seen – appropriating Belsey's Lacanian assertion on architecture – 'as a way of enclosing emptiness [...and] containing a void'[32]. The architectural structure tried to close in upon the menacing vacancy of the human condition in a failed attempt to keep it in place.

---

[32] Catherine Belsey, 'Making space: perspective vision and the Lacanian real', *Textual Practice*, 16 (2002), 31-55, (p.32).

Disrupting the unified visual centre of the image, the designer's composition displayed representations that were drained of fixed and absolute signification. The hegemonic occupancy of that critical space was interrogated: with Hester/Hunter re-entering the wedding party ('crawling in' in Vanek's words) and dismantling the male space of legitimacy, the stage was transformed into a realm of instability and visual disorder. Four white dresses were onstage and two audiences were watching – the Fellinian wedding guests onstage, and the audience in the playhouse as the offstage guests to the wedding. Thus the stage was remade as a location of refracted images, in a breakdown of conventional oppositions that had traditionally defined sanctified structures of social power. Through this multiplicity of images – each of the brides onstage were ironically as much legitimated as the other – the stage picture became a visual metatext to Hester's spoken claim: 'this is my weddin' day be rights and not wan of yees can deny it. And yees all just sit there glarin' as if I'm the guilty one.' (*BBOC*, p.54).

In terms of theatrical space and visual image, the transposing of a play from culture to culture requires, on the scenographer's part, an attempt to disclose 'differentness' to the onlooker. For the viewer, then, the act of perceiving becomes an attempt at making that experience of 'differentness', with its own particular memory and associations, part of her/his world of experience.

In Vanek's visual response, that sense of 'differentness' was never compromised but heightened and deepened. In Vanek's re-focalization of the vision for a non-Irish audience, none of the play's political and ideological connections – so resonant on the stage of the Abbey – were lost. American audiences were faced with a scenic image of an Irish location which embodied an empowering association between female subject and landscape. It was a visual physicalization of the woman character's inward dimension, that vast realm of the mind that is buried between the conscious and the unconscious.

Such a visual critique defied the limiting paradigms of nationhood as male, unitary and indivisible. It emphasized the possible co-existence of contrasting visual images: framework and deviation, centre and border, absence and presence, unity and multiplicity, advancing and yielding, rising and falling, all became equally important components of the same broader image.

VI

In the Irish Repertory North American premiere of *By the Bog of Cats…*, produced in Chicago in 2001, directed by Kay Martinovich and designed by Michelle Habeck, (with Tracy Michelle Arnold in the role of Hester Swane), the guiding principle in the scenic transposition seemed to be in line with Mies van der Rohe's dictum 'less is more'.[33] A simplified platform stage provided a flexible space and became a visual commentary on the thematic flow of the play.

What was particularly striking from an audience's perspective was the semi-dark, utterly empty expanse of monochrome greyish flatness that – with the exception of a few selected props – occupied the full extension of the platform stage. Shafts of light partly infused the stage surface with the snowy and frozen appearance of a winter landscape. Such a visualization, characterized by bareness and sparseness, seemed to be completely and interestingly at odds with the logic of 'total visibility' adopted by the San Jose production.

Habeck's stark dematerialization of the Irish physical location was rested on an adaptable oblong thrust-shaped structure, with three distinct playing areas symbolizing the caravan, the yard and, most extensively, the bog. The bog became a shadowy, contourless, protruding area that encapsulated characters and audience: the bog was around, below and within.

The deployment of the thrust stage – a stage unenclosed by any frame that projects forward from its background and is open to the spectators on three of its sides – achieved here some major effects. The main one was to bring the audience space menacingly close to the performers' space leaving both

---

[33] Mies van der Rohe, quoted in Robert Ballagh, *Robert Ballagh on Stage* (Dublin, Project Press, 1990), p.13.

unsafe and unprotected. There was a strong sense of this fluid stage image moving forward and coming closer to the onlooker both physically and metaphorically. Due to this emphasis on proximity, the true focus of the composition became not its ground but the figures on it, as performers were being drawn closer in what was the theatrical equal of a cinematic close-up. Two small lights on the black back wall of the stage (like cat's eyes) softened the harshness of the designer's spatial solution. They functioned as two small openings or fissures through which we and they, spectators and performers, were being looked at throughout the unfolding of the performance. Furthermore, they extended the spectator's visual field and the characters' fictional world beyond the confines of the stage into an invisible but contiguous offstage realm of hidden energies and unspoken meanings.

Stage and auditorium could have achieved an effect of wholeness if the raked auditorium had not kept in place the separation between the two areas of the theatre space, thus reminding the onlookers of the stage's mythical dimension and its connection to Greek tragedy: we, as the spectators/Gods, were watching the performers/characters/humans from above.

Habeck's visual metaphor of enveloping bleakness and formlessness – reminiscent of a Beckettian limbo space – conjured up rawness and primitiveness but also captured the fluid emotional geography of the landscape, its unresolved and irresolvable ambiguity as a place poised between dark and light, real and surreal, ordinary and extra-ordinary, outward and inward. Through the interplay of light and shadow, the stage surface acquired at one moment the elemental quality of a fossilized ground, invested with the actions and the emotions played on it, and at another moment it shifted to suggest an unlived-on amniotic surface, unmarked by experience. Habeck's scenic response evoked an image as mutable and multifaceted as the main woman subject in the play. It became a visual extension of Hester's closeness to other spaces and possibilities, of the interrelated presence of light and dark in her personality. As she says to Caroline Cassidy at a certain point in the play:

[...] there's two Hester Swanes, one that is decent and very
fond of you [...]. And the other Hester, well, she could slide
a knife down your face, carve ya up and not bat an eyelid.
(*BBOC*, p.30)

With regard to this dynamic interaction of female subject
and environment a very telling visual image is established at the
very outset of the play, when the disquieting figure of Tracy
Michelle Arnold as Hester Swane emerged from the smoky
upstage for the ritual of the burial of Blackwing, the black swan.
Arnold's well physicalized act of cutting and opening the frozen
turf to make space for the broken body of the bird revealed at
once emotional turbulence and vulnerability. It appeared as a
physical and symbolic act of 'occupation', a struggle to assert
a(n) (under)world shelter which could secure for her visual
counterpart – the black swan – a personal space. This perturb-
ing act reverberated as a haunting mark throughout the performance. At the end of the play everything that belonged to
Hester/Arnold in her dramatic life will be re-claimed into the
sucking space of the bog hole.

Habeck's thrust-out platform seemed to present some problems for the staging of the wedding scene. Ideally, the radical
choice of a thrust stage would appear appropriate and particularly convincing for conveying the sense of exposure and human collapse that the scene requires. Practically, instead, it
worked less successfully than it did for the rest of the performance. Because of the complete lack of any physical boundary,
the dinner table seemed rather randomly positioned and the
actors – despite their efforts – appeared to struggle in their
movements and groupings in the performing space. The making of meaning was then affected in that scene: the dominant
image was visually confusing and Hester's focal confrontation
didn't have the impact it could have had. From an audience
perspective the stage space became, all of a sudden, too popu-
lated, the table overpowered the rest of the space – the bog; the
conflict of forces and power relations was obliterated along
with the tone of grotesque tragi-comedy. It was as if the physical arrangement of Habeck's scenic solution, totally exposing
characters and actions to the viewers, had paradoxically flat-

Illustration 14

Mary Ann Thebus (Catwoman), *left*, and Tracy Michelle Arnold (Hester)
in *By the Bog of Cats...* at the Irish Repertory Theatre of Chicago (2001)

Illustration 15

Tracy Michelle Arnold (Hester), *far right*, enters in Act Two of *By the Bog of Cats...* at the Irish Repertory Theatre of Chicago (2001)

Illustration 16
Holly Hunter (Hester) in *By the Bog of Cats...* at the San Jose Repertory Theatre, San Jose (2001)

Illustration 17
Jillian Lee Wheeler (Josie) in *By the Bog of Cats...* at the San Jose Repertory Theatre, San Jose (2001)

Illustration 18

Holly Hunter (Hester), *left* and Joan MacIntosh (Catwoman) in *By the Bog of Cats...*
at the San Jose Repertory Theatre, San Jose (2001)

Illustration 19

Act Two of *By the Bog of Cats...* at the San Jose Repertory Theatre, San Jose (2001)

Illustration 20

Sanneke Bos (Portia) in *Portia Coughlan* at the RO Theater,
Rotterdam (2002)

Illustration 21

From left to right: Rogier Philipoom (Fintan), Ditha van der Linden (Blaize), Paul R. Kooij (Sly), Marc De Corte (Senchil), Goele Derick (Maggie May) in *Portia Coughlan* at the RO Theater, Rotterdam (2002)

Photo by Pan Sok, courtesy of RO Theater

Illustration 22

Nadia Dijkstra (Josie), *left*, Anneke Blok (Hester), *centre*, and Rogier Philipoom (Fintan) in *Kattenmoeras [By the Bog of Cats...]* at the RO Theater, Rotterdam (2002)

tened the main significance of the scene, that is, the sense of human disintegration and breakdown.

Though we are talking about space, I believe Brecht's point about illusion could be apt here: his realization that to break the illusion it is necessary first to re-create an illusion exemplifies my point about the effect of a total exposure[34]. The absence of any barriers may have obstructed the possibility of experiencing a stronger atmosphere of breakdown, a visual sense of conflictual forces being torn to shreds.

The concerns expressed above with regard to the wedding scene didn't spoil the overall success of the production's conceptual stage image. The designer's visual strategy of a dematerialized setting, conceived more as a place of interiority rather than a physical reality, communicated double-edgedness and complexity despite sparseness and economy of design. Completely stripped to its bare essentials, Habeck's bleak rendering channelled the audience's focus to the actors' corporeality, pointing primarily to that of Hester/Arnold. The actress' dominant presence mapped the symbolic topography of the performance: it brought forward the multiplicity of Hester's spatial experience and the self-division of her human journey. Her movement across the non-representational areas of the designer's scenic arrangement evoked for the spectators an alternative and uncomfortable vision of an Irish home/homeland which, in conflict with traditional cultural expectations, reintegrated lost aspects and dimensions of the self.

VII

Given the multiple visual possibilities conjured up by each production's unique theatrical vision, it seems to me that there is something more to Irish theatre than just 'words'. Besides, the three productions' alternative uses of theatrical space and visual images have proved the boundless possibilities within physically limited confines.

---

[34] See Bertolt Brecht, 'Notes on Stanislavski', *Drama Review*, 9 (1964), pp.155-166.

In the diverse and unique realizations of the Irish bog, the designers' stage expressions explored in this article all seem to reinforce the aesthetic of resistance of *By the Bog of Cats...* to fixed and exclusionist notions of home/homeland. All of the three theatrical re-presentations also deployed platform structures that broke with the proscenium frame, be it in a more or less radical form. This makes visual the exigency implicit in Carr's dramatic design, of getting rid of the picture frame – the fractured shell of domesticity for women characters in theatrical realism – and of moving towards theatre as a place of openness, as an unframed canvas where spectator and performer can attain a more direct and intimate communication.

The three scenographers' conceptual images, moving away from any realistic re-presentation, foregrounded theatrical locations characterized by inclusiveness, open-endedness, non-linearity and multi-dimensionality. As Jaroslav Malina has put it, 'stage design, just as other areas of national culture, seeks its own national identity'[35]. In the hybridity of our current world this becomes a space of impossibility if thought of according to dogmatic and inherited categories of interpretation. Through an idea of stage design willing to move beyond the stiffness of a realistic representation, as the three productions in the difference of their visual strategies achieve, an alternative and fragmented notion of Ireland as home/homeland could emerge for woman and man. This notion is more of a possible and open space, whose boundaries are permeable and provisional and whose identity is in a constant state of flux, being continually (re)-invented and (re)-negotiated.

Carr's Hester Swane transgresses the normative categories of the established system. Through Hester's re-claimed sense of ownership, and feeling at home in the vast and uncircumscribed space of the bog, and in her moving amid a plurality of varied and less traditionally defined female spaces, Carr's implosive

---

[35] Jaroslav Malina, 'Theatrical Space in Postmodern Times: Concepts and Models of Space Analysis', in Irene Eynat-Confino, Eva Sormova (eds), *Space and the Postmodern Stage* (Prague: Prague Theatre Institute 2000), pp.15-17 (p.16).

dramaturgy of space and the set designers' different artistic transpositions encourage the spectator to suspend the old habit of seeing the relationship between space and gender as responding to immutable and unshakeable laws. Their representations envisage a re-made image-concept of an Irish home/homeland for women characters as one containing within it many diverse and even incompatible places. It becomes more of an inward place, an inner condition, 'a state of the mind' (Devlin, p.119).

This shift in perception inevitably dislodges assumed ideas of belonging and identity for women: an expanded idea of subjectivity seems to take shape and new notions of self and 'other' step forward.

Through Carr's theatrical imagination and through the artistic vision of theatre practitioners, the Midlands now inhabits a theatrical present at the intersection between places, 'a metaphor for the crossroads between the worlds'[36], a symbol of other spaces.

---

[36]Marina Carr, 'Afterword' to *Portia Coughlan* in *The Dazzling Dark: New Irish Plays*, ed. Frank McGuinness (London: Faber, 1996), pp.310-311.

12 | Always the Best Man, Never the Groom:
The Role of the Fantasy Male in Marina Carr's Plays

Matt O'Brien

'Never fear. You're all descended from the ancient kings: I know that.'[1]

My four-year-old son Sam has recently decided that he must have another father. Not *instead* of me, but *in addition* to me. Having already assumed the male characteristic of not letting a little science get in the way of personal ambition, Sam is absolutely convinced that his 'other daddy' is the genuine article, as important, as corporeal, and as factual as I am, but with a few key differences.

My doppelganger, the 'other daddy' is a fairly impressive figure. He's a firefighter (rather than a theatre director) who owns horses (instead of a car), and was a soldier in the army (as opposed to an acting student in tights and a dance belt). His name is John.

And whether Sam recognizes it or not, John has two distinct advantages over me. One is the absolute fantasy of his very existence, when anything and everything is allowed. The other is that he's already in the past, died in a tragic firefighting accident of some flexible detail. Since 'John' will never actually

[1] Broadbent to Doyle in *John Bull's Other Island*, by G.Bernard Shaw.

appear again, there's no danger of him losing the power of absolute enchantment over a four-year old's mind.

Now if, for whatever reason, I were to start taking 'John' as seriously as Sam does, I might begin to feel inadequate. Anecdotally, that seems to be common enough in life, men who secretly feel (and they'll be damned if they'll admit it) threatened or inferior to other men they've never really known, such as their wives' or girlfriend's ex-lovers. This feeling of inferiority to a more powerful 'alpha male' seems incumbent in the male experience, and is something that Marina Carr has recognized, without ridiculing the inferiority complexes of her men. But it's easy – too easy – for directors, actors and critics to occasionally miss this point, leading to productions of her work that miss out on a key element in her writing.

When Carr's work is written about, it's often done so from a necessarily 'female' perspective. For example, in looking at three recently published collections of essays about contemporary Irish drama, I'm seeing five pieces specifically about Carr's work, all of them written by women. With the exception of the Abbey premieres of *The Mai* and *By the Bog of Cats...*, the directors of the highest-profile productions of her work in Ireland and the U.S. have likewise been women (Garry Hynes, Kay Martinovich, Timothy Near, and Emily Mann). And when Carr is put into context (including by my own company in Chicago), the publicity shorthand used is often along the lines of 'the first major Irish female playwright'. To quote a famed Seinfeld line 'not that there's anything wrong with that'; except that it can tend to set up, in the mind of audience members, theatre journalists and practitioners, the idea that somehow Carr is writing 'women's plays', and that the female characters should be the primary focus of her plays.

Well, to an extent, yes, there's no question that Portia Coughlan, Hester Swane, and The Mai are the central characters in their respective plays – but in order for the plays to work as *dramatic creations*, it's necessary that any producer or director focus just as clearly on the men in Carr's works, most of whom share a problem – to wit, the 'Best Men' in their women's lives.

In Carr's dramatic worlds, as in my four-year-old's heart, there is often a key male character, 'the Best Man' – who isn't on stage. This 'Best Man' will have a number of characteristics desired by the female protagonists, a combination of gentleness, faithfulness, strength, heroism and, in the case of Portia Coughlan and her dead twin Gabriel Scully, artistic spirit. But these 'Best Men' are never direct players in the on-stage action. They've vanished before the lights go up, leaving those men who *are* on display to deal with the idealized worlds hanging back in the shadows around them. When confronted with these 'ideal men', the on-stage men find themselves puny in comparison. This feeling of inferiority, when exacerbated by the supporting characters in the plays, leads eventually to expressed incidences of drunkenness, anger, physical attack, and emotional or physical withdrawal. Not a pretty picture, but one that's familiar to many of us, particularly when seen in an Irish cultural context.

While I can't speak for contemporary Ireland, here in America, 'the absent male' is a common and key element in our Irish-American ethnic legacy. Many of us have at least one sordid tale of familial woe in our past, feckless and reckless Irish men abandoning our grandmothers, aunts, cousins, etc, or fathers who died too early, leaving their broods to fend for themselves in the new land.

One interesting aspect of this situation is how often these absent men, in Irish America certainly, are seen in a split light. We abhor their irresponsibility, we admire their independence. For example, in Act IV of Eugene O'Neill's explicitly autobiographical *Long Day's Journey Into Night*, James Tyrone lays into his famine-immigrant father as a coward who abandoned his wife and children in a strange country and went back to Ireland to die. But if we visited the Tyrone house the next morning, there's every good chance we'd encounter Tyrone telling his incredulous (and hungover) sons the story of a great fight his father won in the old country, or the huge estate that he left in Cavan in order to give his children the chance of a better life in Baltimore (indeed, Tyrone constantly swings back and forth between disparaging his fellow Irishmen and indignantly defending the honour of the island of his birth). These speculative stories would have a germ of truth, in the same way that television movies are sometimes 'based' on the stories ripped from today's tabloid headlines. The names are usually right. Past that, a certain amount of fantasy is assumed to hold sway. This split-revisionist story-telling and self-deluding mythological worship of the past is a key element in Carr's plays, with characters lying in absolute abeyance after fathers, husbands and brothers have left them behind. From the nine-fingered fisherman in *The Mai* to the sweet voiced Gabriel Scully in *Portia Coughlan*, the women in Carr's plays often have 'perfect' men in their pasts (imaginary pasts, quite possibly), leaving the men depicted at a distinct disadvantage when it comes to negotiating successful relationships with the women.

The conflict of the idealized past versus the commonplace present is a powerful one in contemporary drama. It's a key element in many of the major plays, from Tennessee Williams's *The Glass Menagerie* to Chekhov's *The Cherry Orchard* and Beckett's *Waiting for Godot*, whose twin protagonists remember fondly their days of picking grapes in the warm sun.

As with Williams's Wingfields (abandoned by their husband and father) and Chekhov's faded family of aristocrats (abandoned by their wealth, their influence and their youth), Carr's characters are longing for pasts that either never were or have been seriously over-romanticized, desperately grasping for anything that will make the old days re-appear, destroying themselves in the process. The central conflict between imperfect present and unattainable dream-past plays itself out, in her mature plays, in the course of a male/female relationship at the centre of the play. But just as we need the past fully created in the play in order for that conflict to exist, we likewise need a fully created man, equal in every way to the female protagonist, in order to make the drama, so carefully crafted by the author, come to life in front of an audience.

Because of her position as a 'female playwright' (one feels that the phrase should almost be capitalized), a common tendency is to believe that Carr is somehow writing 'women's plays'. As noted by Mary Trotter, '[a]udiences, trained to understand and appreciate male discourses, are often reluctant to embrace feminist forms, or they regard dramas with female protagonists as the theatrical equivalent of "chick flicks".[2] One problem with the 'female playwright' angle is that it can lend itself to productions of Carr's plays that put *so* much focus on the female characters that the men in the plays, all of whom are necessary to move the dramatic action forward, get short shrift, or are treated as plot devices with a single defining characteristic. But this misses one of the most important features of Carr's plays, the fact that she's gone to great lengths to present some redeeming, or at least empathetic, aspects of her male characters.

By way of example, I've seen several productions of *By the Bog of Cats...* since the original production at the Abbey in 1998. In two of these productions, Carthage Kilbride, the weak-willed farmer who forsakes Hester Swane in favour of the younger, wealthier Caroline Cassidy, was clearly depicted as a 'bad guy'. In one case, the director chose to have the actor play Carthage as an empty-headed dullard (emphasizing his 'smallness' in comparison to Hester's tribal atavism and the muscular crudity of Xavier Cassidy, his rapacious new father-in-law). In the other production, the actor played him as an unfeeling automaton, totally unsympathetic to the pain his actions are causing Hester and the desperation that is obviously rising in her.

The play still worked, but in both cases, the audiences were robbed of a key level of dramatic development. Because these two Carthages were less than appealing to begin with, Hester's overwhelming obsession with him made less than perfect sense, and, more damaging, the choices robbed the audience of the possibility that Carthage might actually accede to Hester's desires. By reducing Carthage to a one-note figure, Hester was bereft of a worthy partner, one who can and does, on occasion. aspire to some sort of 'goodness'. Both of these productions shortchanged the audience from the full realm of the play, and

---

2 Trotter, Mary, 'Translating Women Into Irish Theatre History', *A Century of Irish Drama*, Stephen Watt, Eileen Morgan, and Shakir Mustafa (Bloomington: Indiana University Press, 2000).

missed some of the complexities that can cause audiences to think long and hard about productions well after the lights have gone up.

To understand Carthage in production, we should look at what we know about him from the script. We know that he was involved with Hester for fourteen years. He met her when he was still a teenager. He was with her the day she killed her brother, Joseph Swane. He was going to marry her at one point – he went so far as to buy a wedding dress, so he does (or at least did) have the capacity for romantic feelings for her. He has an overbearing mother, but also has the ability to deal with her firmly, if needed.

But it's what we don't know about Carthage that has to be filled in by the actor and director in order to make him fully human. For example, there's only passing mention of him having a father. Why don't we ever hear about Mr. Kilbride? In Elsie Kilbride's rambling and embarrassing speech at the wedding banquet (one of the show's comic highpoints), she speaks of a little boy who loved to sleep in bed with his mother, who built a replica of Calvary on a muddy hillside as a birthday present for his sainted mother – but she never mentions any *detail* about his father, unlike Xavier Cassidy who makes reference to Caroline's dead mother in his wedding toast. If we start filling in the blanks, as an actor and director should do in this situation, we can make some assumptions that will lead to greater possibilities in motivating Carthage's behaviour during the course of the play.

A safe bet is that as a family of a widowed mother and young boy, Carthage grew up without any male guidance. He tries for his mother's sake, as best he can, to cover some of the emptiness created by his missing father, but probably knows that he'll never be able to really fill the role. Behind Carthage's adult actions is the shame of an impoverished childhood, as he seeks respectability and approval from his 'better', Xavier Cassidy. If we take all of this into account, then Carthage's situation is exactly as pathetic as Hester's – she's hoping desperately for her mother and her lover, both of whom abandoned her, to return to her. Carthage is hoping desperately for alpha male approval and to be seen for once as a man of substance – even if it means driving off the mother of his child to get those things.

Carr has given the actor playing Carthage a tremendous opportunity to underscore his conflicted situation, in a scene between him and his daughter early in Act One. Entering the scene where Elsie Kilbride, his overbearing mother, is disparaging Hester to Josie, he chastises Elsie for her actions:

> **CARTHAGE**: I don't know how many times I tould ya to lave the child alone. You've her poisoned with your bile and rage.
> **MRS. KILBRIDE**: I'm saying nothin' that isn't true. Can't I play a game of snap with me own granddaughter?
> **CARTHAGE**: Ya know I don't want ya around here at the minute. G'wan home Mother. G'wan!
> **MRS. KILBRIDE**: And do what? Talk to the range? Growl at God?
> **CARTHAGE**: Do whatever ya like, only lave Josie alone, pick on somewan your own size. (*He turns Josie's jumper the right way around.*) You'll have to learn to dress yourself.[3]

This exchange can be played with impatience on the part of Carthage, a busy man having to fight off his mother *and* properly dress his daughter on his wedding day. I've seen it done that way, and it made sense, given the circumstances. But a more interesting approach was utilized by director Kay Martinovich and actor Mark L. Montgomery in the American premiere production in Chicago. Carthage's attitude toward his mother could be described as confidently expressed exasperation, rather than anger, and when he shifted gears for the line toward his daughter, Carthage looked at Josie with great patience and compassion, not scolding her for her incompetence, but rather letting her know, in a somewhat tremulous voice, that the world was going to be different for her from that afternoon forward. There was, in his delivery, the echo in his voice of a boy who sounded less than sure of his own situation, afraid of the step he was about to make even as he tried to

---

[3] Marina Carr, *By the Bog of Cats…* in *Plays 1* (London: Faber, 1999), pp.257-341 (p.281).

encourage her to take it with him. Rather than a cold hearted bastard of a father who was angry that his brat was a clod when it came to dressing herself, we saw a fully grown man facing both the possibility of escape from his miserable past and the fear that he wouldn't be quite good enough for his new surroundings. It established, early on, that Carthage was not a villain, but a victim, in his own way, and revealed a layer of complexity to the script that other readings and directions had missed.

But there are two more absent fathers in *By the Bog of Cats…*, one of whom is actually a female. There is Hester's biological father (mentioned in passing, for all intents and purposes), but more importantly her 'real' father – who was in fact, her mother. I say her 'real' father because the character of Big Josie Swane, Hester's mother, has, as described by Catwoman, Xavier Cassidy, and even Hester herself, characteristics that are traditionally ascribed to men. Big Josie is sexually possessive and willing to become violent in protection of her 'property'; Xavier says she once 'bit the nose of a woman who dared to look at her man, bit the nose clean off her face.'(*BBOC*, pp.294-5). She is a cigar smoking drunk who neglects her offspring with disregard rarely seen in women but commonly ascribed to men in both fictional and real worlds. Her absence weighs on Hester every second of the day pictured in the play.

Watching rehearsals for the Chicago production, it became very clear that one of the beauties and complexities in *By the Bog of Cats…* is that this abandoning 'father', Big Josie Swane, is actually the single most important character in the play. If not for her actions years ago, none of this would be happening. Her absence is actually a presence (neat trick, that). So in this, the author has taken one of the touchstones of literature and lifestories and, by changing the gender, paid homage to the icon while making it even more universal, moving firmly away from the 'women good/men bad' mentality. The fact that she creates new versions of iconic figures is refreshing and intriguing, but without directors and actors who are willing to pursue those revisionist characterizations, the audience might never know it.

As another example, the character of Robert, the on again/off again husband of the title character in *The Mai* has been described as 'not a fully developed character'[4] (and, on a more anecdotal level, by audience members as 'a bastard'). If we only take into consideration the facts and circumstances of the play, there's no question that he'd be a less than desirable husband for almost any woman. He's a philanderer, a so-so composer/musician and provider, a diffident father to the children – but key to all of this is firmly looking at the issue of perspective in this play.

The Mai is a series of flashbacks as relayed by a character in the drama, in this case, Mai and Robert's daughter Millie. In these flashbacks we see the passage of months following the time when her father, a middling composer and cellist, returned to his family after a five year absence. In the period leading up to the opening flashback, her mother, The Mai of the title, has saved for and built an improbably beautiful home on the banks of Owl Lake in the Midlands, a beautiful home on a beautiful site, with a huge window overlooking all, where she can sit and wait for her man to return.

Over the course of the play, a series of scenes depicting the reunion, gradual fading, and finally the cataclysmic end of the marriage are seen. While Robert starts off romantically and spiritually connected to Mai, he gradually reverts to form, leaving the house for weekends with his new lover (while pretending to be off playing concerts in the country). Everything leads to a drunken spat between the couple, after which the relationship is marked by silences, a permanent silence coming when The Mai finally drowns herself in Owl Lake.

In the middle of all of this action sits Mai's ancient grandmother, Grandma Fraochlán, who worships the memory (over and over again) of her long dead husband, the nine-fingered fisherman, an incredibly passionate, strong, and resilient man, if her memory is to be believed (again, allow for perspective). Her recollections have an obvious effect on the younger generation;

---

4 Christiansen, Richard, Review of *The Mai* , *Chicago Tribune* 14 April, 2000.

at one point, The Mai tells her, 'You make our men seem like nothing.' (*TM*, p.143) Here then we have three generations of women, grandmother, grandaughters (and through recollection, The Mai's mother Ellen) all of whom long for some sort of White Knight. Grandma Fraochlán thinks she found hers before he was taken from her. Ellen (the mother) was turned against her husband by Grandma Fraochlán because she believed he was not a suitable match for Ellen's aspirations. And The Mai is trying like hell to keep a man she believes is the only one for her, even though a more perceptive woman would see the clues that he was stifled by the demands her absolute love puts on him.

Since the story is necessarily coming from Millie's point of view, her take on Robert is the one we'll be working with. But is it really the full perspective? What didn't she see that he did? Again, a situation where director and actor need to explore the possibilities and find those things about him that are so redeeming that the audience goes home not with an understanding of who was 'right' or 'wrong', but simply of a relationship that was doomed from the first. Greek in origin, perhaps, but common enough in real life.

So why does Robert do what he does? In the purely structural sense of the play, it really doesn't matter why; it's simply important that he do it in order for the action to play itself out. But for the actor working on the character, that's not much of a help.So he has to be able to find things in the man that aren't explicitly mentioned in the script to allow him to make sense of the piece. So forget Millie for a second, and look at the situation from his perspective. First, he has a wife who could only be described as 'perfect'. She's brilliant, warm, beautiful, openly sexual with him – in short everything most men would desire. But add to this her greatest single flaw – an incurable and at times overweening romanticism – and you could see how living with her could be a problem for any average man – and there's his key – his abject 'average-ness'.

I mentioned the final blow-up between Mai and Robert, but there's an earlier argument between them, following his return from a weekend trip when it's apparent that he's been with another woman. During the fight, Mai grabs his cello and plays, violently, a few phrases of music '*expertly*', according to the stage directions:

> THE MAI: Not bad, hah? For someone who hasn't played in over fifteen years. With a bit of practice I'd be as good as you. Now there's a frightening thought – for both of us. How dare you throw ten pounds at me on my fortieth birthday!
>
> ROBERT: What you want me to do, take you to Spiddal and pretend everything is wonderful?
>
> THE MAI: Just because we're not in the first flush of passion doesn't mean we're pretending. And for your information, I don't read Cosmopolitan!
>
> ROBERT: Fine.
>
> THE MAI: Do you know what I did this weekend, Robert, or do you care?
>
> ROBERT: Could you cut out the headmistress tone? You're not addressing Assembly now. (*TM*, p.155)

At this point in the relationship, as Millie is recalling it, it's obvious that he's already fallen off the wagon from a fidelity standpoint. But there's also the sense, as this scene develops, of a *pattern* of argument – it's possible to see that this fight is typical of the types of battles this particular couple may have had before. She knows where and how to get him – by pointing to his impotence as a musician, something which, in the back of his mind, he very well could fear to be true. Later in the same scene, the argument turns to money, at which point she says 'keep your f***in' mouth shut about your paltry little contribution.'(p.156) So we see her belittling his professional talents and his competence as a breadwinner. She's doing it out of anger over what appears to be his weekend tryst, but the fact that she knows where his 'buttons' are indicates that she's figured out his own insecurities as a man, and is willing to use them when necessary.

She figured him out. Arguably, because of that, the relationship could never have worked anyway. Robert apparently needs to be in a relationship where his lover assesses his traditional masculine qualities as sufficient – which The Mai, subconsciously or not, can't do. She wants to, *needs to* have him be her

'Best Man', but Robert is simply incapable of fulfilling the role. 'The Mai' – obviously The Chieftain of her clan on the banks of Owl Lake – requires a man suitable for a Queen. Robert must recognize that he'll never be that man; he simply isn't up to the task.

Olwen Fouéré, the actor who first played Mai, says 'I think the sexual relationship between her and Robert was probably extraordinary'.[5] No doubt. And in that 'extraordinary' relationship, how do we know that Robert isn't feeling a bit intimidated? If he is, then yes, it is a sign of weakness on his part – but that's the point – he's weak, not cruel. From his perspective, he really is trying to be part of this relationship, but is constantly feeling relegated to being junior partner to his mate. His pride (again, a weakness) is such that offers of help from her family only build resentment within him. Those things being true, there's no way to make him a hero in this play, but there's also no reason to rush to label him an ass. If anything, he's the one who's able to escape, in his own way, the dangerously impossible world that Mai and Grandma Fraochlán have constructed for themselves.

On Raftery's Hill (2000) is one of Carr's more controversial plays, explicitly depicting the sort of physical and emotional squalor only hinted at in *By the Bog of Cats*.... Set in the Midlands, the action takes place in the house of Red Raftery, a coarse and brutal sixty-ish widowed farmer living with his three children and his senile mother. His only son, Ded Raftery, is depicted as something of an idiot savant, a gifted musician who nonetheless lives in the cowshed out of fear of his father, eating his meals among the cowdung rather than facing the withering eye of his father (*'beaten to a scut'*, according to the stage directions,[6]). Raftery's oldest daughter, Dinah, acts as his caretaker, cleaning his house and providing his meals for him. The relationship resembles nothing so much as that of a constantly arguing married couple. Raftery's aged and senile mother Sha-

---

[5] Olwen Fouéré, Interview with Melissa Sihra, *Theatre Talk*, (Dublin: Carysfort Press, 2001), p 162

[6] Marina Carr, *On Raftery's Hill* (Oldcastle: Gallery Books, 2000), p.13.

lome is always seen on her way out the door, trying to walk back to her native Kinneygar to be with her (dead) father again. And the youngest daughter Sorrel is presented as a relative innocent – at least in the beginning. We have, in essence, a family that could have easily just walked in off the set of a *Jerry Springer Show* taping.

Midway through Act One, we see the entrance of Sorrel's suitor Dara Mood, greeted by Raftery with the line 'Well, if ud isn't the young fancier come to plunder the heart a me daugher.' (*ORH*, p.21) Mood is, in some ways, a gentle revision of Carthage Kilbride. A small farmer, but with modest ambition, primary among them marrying Sorrel. His gentleness and modesty are in stark contrast to the brutality and crudity of Red Raftery, so a clear conflict for the heart of Sorrel is set up. Mood enters with news from the Valley of a local girl, a classmate of Sorrel's, who has just died following the stillborn birth of a baby that is now known to have been sired by her own father. Raftery refuses to believe Mood's reportage of the father's confessed guilt, saying, 'Ud's only your word again our beliefs, thah righ Sorrel?' (*ORH*, p.23) The hints of a separate moral code in the Raftery household are made explicit at the end of Act One, when Raftery rapes Sorrel at knife point on the kitchen table, saying, 'I'll show ya how to gut a hare.' (*ORH*, p.35)

Act Two is set several weeks after the rape scene, and sees Sorrel transformed (as would be expected) by the violence visited upon her. She's now listless and depressed, and given to frequent bathing in an effort to cleanse herself. During this act, she also discovers that her older sister Dinah is, in fact, her mother, and that Dinah and Raftery are still having sex on occasion. All of the illusions of 'normalcy' in this family disappear from her, with a sordid reality clearly established, requiring her to find a new paradigm for understanding the world.

Dara Mood re-enters, sensing that something is wrong with Sorrel, but anxious and confused over the secrecy of what it is. Raftery enters the scene, and disdainfully tosses Mood the offer of £20,000 and fifty acres as a 'wedding present', which Dara pridefully turns down.

> **DARA**: I'll noh touch your river field Red Raftery, noh if ud was harvestin nightingales and gold.
> **RED**: Big words from the small farmer. Raftery's Hill fed yees all through the Greah Hunger, sould yees yeer fifty acre a scrub and marsh, 1923. You'll take me river field young Mood and me churchyard field and me daugher, for the Moods was ever opportune, and you're wan a them.
> **DARA**: You'll never see my plough on your cursèd land.
> **RED**: (*As he exits*) You may see mine on yours. (*ORH*, p.52)

In turning down the money and the land, Mood maintains his independence from Raftery, but to Sorrel's mind, maintains his 'smallness' as well. Mood's refusal to take part in Raftery's expiation of his guilt fails to strike Sorrel as anything other than her fiancé clinging to his small world. She rebukes him for his stance, shaking the cheque at him saying '[…] wud this […] we'll be rich and have standin in the communihy instead a bein scrubbers from the Valley.' (*ORH*, p.53) She needs Mood to be heroic, and wealthy, and powerful – because she needs him to be like her father. But instead, she breaks with him, turning away the only man who could have potentially saved her *from* her father.

This odd turn of events might strike audience members as puzzling or unsatisfying, but the author clearly contextualizes Sorrel's refusal of Dara Mood within *this* particular family, and this particular universe. In the final moments, the ancient Shalome scoffs at Red Raftery's memory of his grandfather's funeral, saying, 'Daddy dead? What a lark. Daddys never die, they just fake rigor mortis, and all the time they're throwing tantrums in the coffin, claw marks on the lid.' (*ORH*, p.57)

Unlike *The Mai* and *By the Bog of Cats…*, public response to *On Raftery's Hill* has been somewhat reserved. Describing the opening night reception in Washington, D.C., Fintan O'Toole said, 'By the time the interval came, [the audience] was sitting in shocked silence.'[7] Likewise, the anonymous critic for the *Irish Emigrant* noted that the opening night performance at the Town Hall Theatre in Galway was greeted with 'polite applause but

---

[7] O'Toole, Fintan, 'Arts at the Crossroads', *Irish Times* 9 June, 2001.

not the standing ovation it deserved.' The piece itself is unsparing, showing a particular type of sickness without suggesting that there is any way out of the situation. The nihilistic attitudes of the central characters creates, as a byproduct, a world where ugliness and pain are so inevitable that hope is never allowed to grow for the audience.

I suspect that one reason for audience coolness toward the play is because in *On Raftery's Hill*, the 'Best Man' – the legendary and fanciful offstage figure in the other plays – is actually *on*-stage, in the person of Red Raftery. Unlike the other two cited plays, we *see* the Fantasy Male here – and he's horrifying. His need for self satisfaction, his domination of the situations and rooms he enters, his disregard for the feelings and needs of his children is perfectly in line with Big Josie Swane, and, for all we know, Grandma Fraochlán's nine-fingered fisherman. After all, according to her, '[t]here's two types of people in this world [...] them as puts their children first and them as puts their lover first and for what it's worth, the nine-fingered fisherman and meself belongs ta the latter of these.' (*TM*, p.182) Not just her – but *him* as well. The romantic past becomes a horrifying and disturbing situation once it's not a memory but an actual event happening in front of the audience's eyes. The unfulfilled longings of The Mai and Hester Swane are shown to have a root in a pathetic need for outside validation. Traditionally, these types of doomed or unrequited loves are seen as tragic; *On Raftery's Hill* suggests that they are instead a form of sickness.

In many ways, *On Raftery's Hill* completes a cycle of plays for Carr, taking the romantic notions of the White Knight (mentioned by the three sisters in *The Mai*) and allowing that ideal to grow and fester until it's revealed that he may well have been Red Raftery all along. Carr reveals herself to be an anti-romantic poet, recognizing the folly of hopes and 'happy endings' for those who lay victim to their own longings, and presenting audiences with a challenge to re-consider the 'ideal' characterizations of lovers in popular culture. The 'down endings' of the plays mentioned here take the common cultural notions of doomed romance and turn them on their ears, strip-

ping them of the possibility of positive outcomes, hence moving them instead to their logical, yet compassionate, conclusions: real men, and real women, dealing with a general inability
to see things for what they really are.

13 | Rising Out Of The Miasmal Mists:
Marina Carr's Ireland

Claudia W. Harris

Playwright Marina Carr seems to be answering a resounding 'Yes' to Marianne McDonald's question: 'Does there come a time in a nation's history – a crisis of identity, of cultural and political consciousness – where recourse is made naturally to that literature which most radically investigates and establishes national identity: fifth-century Attic tragedy?'[1] In her essay 'Dealing with the Dead', Carr compares 'the rest of us who write' with 'royal writers' whose 'ink is supplied from the blue veins of God, from the lyre strings of Orpheus, from the well spring of another world'. Carr refers to Homer and the Greek ghosts who she imagines surrounding his desk as 'these warriors of the desk, these songstitchers, these myth finders, while scaring you with their formidable gifts, do also bolster the heart, especially in this anti-heroic age when the all-consuming intellectual pursuit seems to be that of demystification.'[2] Carr seeks instead to re-mystify, to elevate the anti-hero in a reinscribed Irish heroic age, to recover her desolate, polluted Ireland from

---

[1] Marianne McDonald, 'Classics as Celtic Firebrand: Greek Tragedy, Irish Playwrights, and Colonialism' in *Theatre Stuff: Critical Essays on Contemporary Irish Theatre* ed. by Eamonn Jordan (Dublin: Carysfort Press), p.16.

[2] Marina Carr, 'Dealing with the Dead', in *Irish University Review* 29 (1) (Spring/Summer 1998), pp.190-191.

the stench of poisonous vapours. She is defining her own writing project while describing 'what these royal writers do. They talk back and forth across the centuries and in a way you could define literature as one endless conversation among kinsmen and kinswomen.' (*DWTD*: 193-194). Carr has joined that 'royal' conversation but has not always been understood by her eavesdropping critics or audiences.

Myth-finder Carr, born in 1964, is a relatively new voice in Irish drama. Frank McGuinness describes her as 'a writer haunted by memories she could not possibly possess, but they seem determined to possess her. This haunting is a violent one, intensified by the physical attack on the conventions of syntax, spelling, and sounds of Standard English.'[3] Carr's characters speak the 'flavour' of her native County Offaly, although she claims that 'the real midland accent is a lot flatter and rougher and more guttural than the written word allows.'[4] (*BBOC* 1998: p.8). Along with the 'rough exoticism' of the language, Carr recognizes, in an 'Afterword' to *Portia Coughlan*, the harshness of the Midlands landscape – 'the open spaces, the quicksand, the biting wind, the bog rosemary'; nonetheless, Carr is irresistibly drawn in 'nightly forays back to that landscape', despite not having lived there for fourteen years. 'I find myself constantly there at night: lights off, head on the pillow and once again I'm in the Midlands. I'm wrestling, talking, laughing, reeling at the nocturnal traffic that place throws up.Now I think it's no accident it's called the Midlands. For me at least it has become a metaphor for the crossroads between the worlds.' (pp.310-311). If Carr is a writer 'haunted by memories she could not possibly possess', as McGuinness claims, this nocturnal 'wrestling' she describes might offer a clue. Inhabited by the ghosts that surround her writing desk, Carr's Irish Midlands are her passageway into an ancient new imaginative world.

---

[3] *The Dazzling Dark: New Irish Plays* (London: Faber and Faber, 1996) introduced and ed. by Frank McGuinness, p.ix.

[4] Marina Carr, *By the Bog of Cats…* (Loughcrew: Gallery Press, 1998), p.8.

On Raftery's Hill (9 May 2000) was Marina Carr's next step in re-mystification set in the Midlands, following her highly successful trilogy from the 1990s: *The Mai* (5 October 1994), *Portia Coughlan* (27 March 1996), and *By the Bog of Cats...* (7 October 1998). Both *The Mai* and *Portia Coughlan* premiered at the Peacock; *By the Bog of Cats...* premiered at the Abbey, an indication of Carr's progression to mainstage attention. Unlike these four plays, where Carr has developed her strong individual voice, are two earlier plays – *Low in the Dark* (1989, Crooked Sixpence at Project Arts) and *Ullaloo* (1991, Peacock) – influenced by her academic interest in Samuel Beckett; 'Carr's early work', according to Anna McMullan, 'discards realism altogether, and is characterized by non-naturalist setting, non-psychologized characters and a non-linear structure.' [5]

On Raftery's Hill, after premiering 9 May 2000 at Galway's Town Hall Theatre, received its American premiere 18-21 May 2000 at the John F. Kennedy Center for the Performing Arts, Washington D.C., during an Irish arts festival: 'Island: Arts from Ireland'. Following the Kennedy Center performances, the play opened 4 July 2000 for a successful run at the Royal Court Jerwood Theatre Downstairs, London. The play's poor reception during the Kennedy Center festival raises pertinent questions about the probability of any widespread understanding of Carr's particular dramatic 'conversations' as well as more general questions about the exportability of Irish drama. A description of the festival's atmosphere and goals, however, accounts for the inevitable unenthusiastic audience reaction to this demanding play.

The two-week arts festival (13-28 May 2000) was not just a bow to the interests of forty-four million Americans who claim Irish ancestry but was also a recognition of American arts which trace their roots to Ireland. For the seventeen free concerts, American and Irish artists shared the Kennedy Center

---

[5] Anna McMullan, 'Gender, Authorship and Performance in Selected Plays by Contemporary Irish Women Playwrights: Mary Elizabeth Burke-Kennedy, Marie Jones, Marina Carr, Emma Donoghue' in *Theatre Stuff*, 34-46, (p.41).

Millennium Stage. May 2000 was clearly the month to explore all things Irish without the necessity of a body-numbing flight across the ocean. Luminaries on hand for the celebration included Seamus Heaney, Mary Black, Sharon Shannon, Ricky Skaggs, Emmylou Harris, Elvis Costello, 'Riverdance', and the band Coolfin. Irish film, dance, music, storytelling, poetry readings, visual art exhibits, an arts education program, and an academic conference all intensified the spotlight on Ireland. Sponsored in part by the Governments of Ireland and of Northern Ireland, the festival was first proposed by Jean Kennedy Smith, former United States Ambassador to Ireland (1993-98) and a member of the Kennedy Center Board of Trustees, as a cultural exchange which would highlight arts from the entire island, north and south. At the 23 September 1999 press conference announcing the festival, Smith remarked 'the exceptional cultural renaissance that is now evident in every part of Ireland.'

The festival quickly acquired in Ireland the additional impetus of being an artistic expression of appreciation to the United States for the Clinton administration's role in supporting the peace process. With rich Irish irony, this festival, planned to celebrate peace in Northern Ireland, took place during yet another crisis in the peace process. May 2000, David Trimble's Ulster Unionist Party was deciding whether or not to accept the IRA's promise on 6 May to put its weapons 'beyond use' and thus again share governmental power with Sinn Fein. In February 2000 when disarmament talks broke down, England suspended the ten-week-old Protestant/Catholic executive rather than risk First Minister Trimble's resignation. The Ulster Unionists' close but affirmative vote (459 to 403) which kept Trimble in power and allowed devolved government to continue in Northern Ireland finally came 27 May during the last days of the festival. So the threat of a complete governmental breakdown with its concomitant renewed crisis in Northern Ireland created a particularly Irish undercurrent of tension throughout the Kennedy Center festivities.

The three Irish plays receiving their American premieres during the festival demonstrated the wide range of Irish social/political issues and provided audiences with fairly representative examples of contemporary Irish drama: *Catalpa* (17-21 May), written and performed by Donal O'Kelly, capitalizes on the performative possibilities of traditional Irish storytelling; Stewart Parker's *Pentecost* (23-27 May) typifies both the lyrical qualities and political implications of Irish urban drama; and Carr's *On Raftery's Hill* (18-21 May) is a violently compelling, absurdist drama set in rural Ireland. The festival audience could have gained background understanding had they attended a three-hour panel discussion – 'An Unpredictable Past: Theater and History in Contemporary Ireland' (20 May) – consisting of Irish theatre artists and critics and chaired by Fintan O'Toole. Participants were Nicholas Grene, Paul Mercier, Donal O'Kelly, Karen Fricker, Garry Hynes, and Colm Tóibín. The entire cast of *On Raftery's Hill* took part, reading short scenes from various Irish plays referred to by the panel participants.

O'Kelly based *Catalpa* (1995) on the true story of a whaling ship out of New Bedford, Connecticut, captained by George Anthony who in 1875 rescued six Irish political prisoners from Fremantle Penal Colony in Australia. Serving up this American hero to Kennedy Center audiences was a brilliant choice. Originally titled *Catalpa: The Movie*, the play uses a film-framing device; O'Kelly, as screenwriter Matthew Kidd, imagines the artistic possibilities of his recently rejected screenplay. On the small American Film Institute stage with only a bed, table, chair, and white curtain, fluidly doubling as a sail or shroud, O'Kelly provided all the sound effects and portrayed without confusion and with rare nuance more than twenty characters, performing an amazing range from Captain Anthony, to his wife Gretta, their baby daughter Pearl, the ghost of his deceased mother-in-law, the Fenian John Devoy, a bluff Dublin conspirator, a bored clerk pining for the sea, a cynical whaling agent, an Irish port commissioner, the Scottish First Mate, the ship's crew, a drowning Indian, a pregnant French maid, a British colonial governor, an awkward Australian, the six prisoners, as well as seagulls, an angry whale, and a fierce storm. Kennedy Center audiences rewarded O'Kelly's dazzling performance with standing ovations night after night.

Parker set *Pentecost* (1987) during the 15-29 May 1974 Ulster Worker's Council strike which crippled Belfast, brought down the power-sharing executive on 28 May, and instituted twenty-six years of direct rule from England. This 1974 governmental initiative in Northern Ireland had lasted only five months and was the first and last Protestant attempt to share power with Catholics until the present government. So *Pentecost* is unmistakably still relevant to the present political situation and was a fitting dramatic conclusion to the festival. Lynne Parker directed the fine ensemble cast with subtlety and strength. This restaged Rough Magic 1995 production transformed the intimate Terrace Theatre stage into a finely-detailed, East-Belfast parlour house where four desolate people collect: Marian (Eleanor Methven) whose baby has died, her estranged husband Lenny (Brian Doherty), her friend Ruth (Morna Regan) whose policeman husband has battered her again, and Lenny's chum Peter (Paul Hickey) who has been drawn back from England by the terrifying television broadcasts showing Belfast under siege. The ghost of Lily (Carol Moore), the house's last tenant, haunts Marian who is trying to make sense of her own life by sorting through Lily's possessions. The best scenes occur between Marian, a lapsed Catholic, and the staunchly Protestant Lily. Each of Parker's characters, including the house, reveal desperate stories, relating the outside conflict to their internal strife. But despite the political and personal difficulties explored, the play exhibits a heightened, poetic language which adds pure pleasure to the stories; in fact, *Pentecost* seemed upbeat in comparison to *On Raftery's Hill*. Parker's work reflects the only possible hope – the warmth and wittiness and humanity of Northern Irish individuals.

If *Catalpa* was the most accessible of the three festival plays to American audiences, *On Raftery's Hill* was clearly the least. Carr's bleak tale of incest and insanity seemed out of place in the celebratory atmosphere of the festival. Commissioned by Galway's Druid Theatre and co-produced by Druid and London's Royal Court, the play was planned for small theatre spaces, but even on the Kennedy Center's large Eisenhower Theater stage, the realistic farmhouse box set with its black walls and dingy lighting conveyed the claustrophobic tone of the play. The terse Kennedy Center programme note offered little help for bewildered audience members compared to the detailed explanations of the other two plays. After mentioning Carr's trilogy and territory – 'women, history, rage, dangerous love, tragedy' – the note quotes director Garry Hynes: 'There is a growing and evolving maturity in Marina's work. She is really creating an extraordinary imaginative world in her plays – she's not bound by naturalism or spurious authenticity. She has a poetic world of her own.' Although Hynes' statement is no doubt true, even if abstract, the frightful Raftery family would remain inexplicable regardless of a careful reading of the programme note. What, for example, does Hynes mean by 'spurious authenticity'? Without specific detail of Carr's project to re-mystify, to reinscribe her Midlands society in terms of fateful ancient tragedy, Carr's 'imaginative world' as well as the play itself is obscured by the miasmal mists.

Four generations of Rafterys occupy the Hill. Red Raftery (Tom Hickey) exacts a shocking price from his family: his elder daughter Dinah (Cara Kelly) was sent in to him at twelve by her now dead mother, but she continues to submit because she is protecting her sister/daughter Sorrel and because she and her Daddy are 'just like children playin in a field ah some awful game, before rules was made.'[6] Dinah never admits to being Sorrel's mother, even when asked directly: 'Our mother died givin birth to you … now stop all a this, for your own sake' (*ORH*, p.39). Red's crazed son Ded (Michael Tierney) lives in the cow shed in constant fear of his father's wrath, haunted still by the blood flowing when Red forced him to deliver Dinah's child – 'And I says Daddy I don't know what to do and Daddy says she's only calvin' (*ORH*, p.48). Red's senile mother Shalome (Valerie Lilley) tries repeatedly to leave, strewing flowers in her wake: 'Goodbye Raftery's Hill. I shall not miss you. Goodbye disgusting old kitchen and filthy old stairs' (*ORH*, p.15) – but she never gets farther than the front gate. Red's

---

[6] Marina Carr, *On Raftery's Hill* (Loughcrew: Gallery Press, 2000), p.56 (all references are to this edition).

daughter/granddaughter Sorrel (Mary Murray) tries to escape by marrying farmer Dara Mood (Keith McErlean), but her drunken, raging father rapes her brutally, cutting off her clothes with his hunting knife and pushing her down on the kitchen table: 'Now, this is how ya gut a hare' (*ORH*, p.36). Red has forced himself then on all three Raftery women, including, according to rumour, his mother (*ORH*, p.42). Sorrel breaks off her marriage plans, not because of the rape but because the unaware Dara refuses to accept the dowry Red offers; she seizes the deed for fifty acres and the £20,000 cheque, saying, 'They're mine and dearly paid for' (*ORH*, p.50).

Like his savage behaviour inside the house, Red strides around his 300 acres slaughtering wild game and farm animals alike, raising a stench all smell except the Rafterys. Sorrel does not believe Dara when he tells her about Red's killing spree: 'I seen him cut the udders off a cow noh two wakes ago. Down in the river field. And then he shoh ud, and then he dragged ud to the river wud a rope, a job should take three men to do. And then he pushed ud over the bank into the river. Cows is the most beauhiful creatures, gentle and trustin and curious and they've these greah long eyelashes. This wan walked up to him and starts nuzzlin him and he goes ah her wud a knife' (*ORH*, p.33). Only the outsiders Dara Mood and Red's hunting buddy Isaac Dunn (Kieran Ahern) seem to be fully aware of his strange behavior. 'Ya don't hunt fair, Red', says Dunn, describing to Sorrel the seven baby hares Red strangled; 'Ud's not the hares has the land ruined and you wud a stinking carcass in every field. You'll turn this beauhiful farm into an abattoir' (*ORH*, p.19). One of the most unnerving aspects of this poetic play is the denial of perversion; this caged family largely ignores what appears to be an ancient pollution. Dinah even makes the absurd claim to Sorrel in the final moments of the play that they are a 'respectable family, we love wan another. And whahever happened ya happened ya be accident' (*ORH*, p.56).

The Rafterys show no similarity to the picture-perfect Irish farm family Americans romanticize. Perhaps this is what Hynes means by 'spurious authenticity'. Carr is not bound by others' romantic expectations. But does it necessarily follow then that

Carr's view of rural Ireland is authentic as opposed to other spurious views? Lloyd Rose, reviewing *On Raftery's Hill* for the *Washington Post* (19 May 2000, p.C2), argues that because of the production's superb acting and exquisite direction 'the almost ludicrous grotesqueness of the Raftery family comes to seem not merely natural but almost matter-of-fact, a curse of nature, like drought, or locusts'. True, but by recognizing the curse without noting the Greek-like fate inherent in the play, he misses an opportunity to explain the classical underpinnings of Carr's work. Rose adds, 'It's a mark of playwright Marina Carr's considerable talent that this excess of awfulness, which should be laughable, is instead surreally powerful'. He further asserts that Hynes 'and her cast bring to this dark, compelling script naturalness, inevitability and a scary *humanness*' (my emphasis). Yes, Hynes presents the play with a chilling and, considering her programme note, apparently an unintended naturalism, but that Rose could find 'humanness' in Carr's characters implies a misunderstanding of the play. Instead of human qualities, each displays animal characteristics; in fact, animalism saturates the play's metaphors, pervasively undercutting every character and action. So, like Greek tragedy, the play often displays the antithesis of humanness, but Raftery's Hill is not Mount Parnassus. No gods these, although they do look down on 'scrubbers from the Valley' (*ORH*, p.53). Also absent from Rose's analysis is an appreciation for Carr's Irish black humour; *On Raftery's Hill* is, at times, hilarious.

Some of this comedy results from Shalome's innocent craziness. After she makes yet another escape to the front gate, this time wearing Sorrel's ruined wedding dress, Red tries to convince Shalome she cannot go home because her daddy is dead; she answers like the wise fool she is: 'Daddy dead? What a lark. Daddys never die, they just fake rigor mortis, and all the time they're throwing tantrums in the coffin, claw marks on the lid' (*ORH*, p.57). Early in the play, Shalome shares with Dinah and Sorrel a funny memory from her childhood which shows an unconscious animalism:

> Once a man with a gorilla came to our house and the gorilla
> licked me all over as if I were its baby and the old man told
> me about the language of gorillas, how they encompassed
> the poetry of the sea . . . I didn't know what he meant … still
> don't. […] And Mother came and saw me in the arms of the
> gorilla and was terrified it would harm me and shouts at the
> man and the gorilla runs down the verandah with me gripped
> tightly in its armpit. Next thing myself and the gorilla are
> looking down at Mother and the old man. We're up an or-
> ange tree. We pick orange blossom and throw them down on
> Mother and the old man. Nothing will make us come out of
> that orange tree … it was a wonderful, wonderful time. I
> couldn't have been more than three, for Mother died at the
> end of the summer (*ORH*, pp.17-18).

The image comes full circle at the end of the play when
Dinah is extolling the respectability of the family and then asks,
'D'ya honestly think we'd harm wan another?' Sorrel answers,
'spare me your Legion a Mary canter. We're a band a gorillas
swingin from the trees' (*ORH*, p.56).

So what can be made of Carr's band of gorillas, the Rafterys,
especially in light of the Kennedy Center venue? Frankly, I
hesitate to contemplate what sense of Ireland festival audiences,
full of school children, gleaned from *On Raftery's Hill*. Without
question, Carr was not well served by the choice of this play for
an event many attended with as little thought as they would a
St. Patrick's Day parade. The misunderstanding was on both
sides. Before the play was even written, Kennedy Center planners leapt at the chance to premiere a new play by a young Irish
female playwright. And Irish planners more familiar with Carr's
work may have been under the impression that the Kennedy
Center was the type of national theatre they were used to on
Dublin's Abbey Street or London's South Bank. But aesthetic
issues were not the festival's main focus. Overall, the Kennedy
Center met its brief to 'demonstrate the roots and development
of Irish arts', but I wonder how any of Carr's plays, however
staged or prepared for, could have contributed meaningfully to
this particular festival with its carnival atmosphere and its overt
goal of cultural sharing. Nonetheless, to characterize simply as a

mistake the choice of *On Raftery's Hill* for the Kennedy Center performances is unfairly dismissive of Carr's difficult vision and would appear too much like censorship. And yet, the expectation remains that theatre from a distinct place acts out its culture on stage. How then does Carr's work serve Irish culture?

Given the right circumstances, theatre can be particularly useful in developing cross-cultural understanding, offering a dramatic means of expression that bridges cultural and language barriers. In fact, theatre is distinctive as a cultural product because it dramatizes much of what is true about that culture. Kennedy Center audiences, as led by festival advertisements, expected to see performances of Irish cultural truths: 'The world's gaze has long been focused on this remarkable land, and America's center for the performing arts finds it fitting to honor its lasting contributions to world culture'; the brochure specifically characterizes the three plays, which range from 'hilarious to heartbreaking', as 'windows into the heart of the people'. In a book about the politics of Ireland's 'self-conscious stage representation', Nicholas Grene claims that 'Ireland, from at least as far back as Boucicault, was a marketable phenomenon, a space, a place which *needed* to be represented and represented truly'.[7] Grene may be right about the uniqueness of the way the idea of Ireland has been marketed. Some cultures do seem driven to stage their stories. Should audiences, therefore, expect from these self-conscious representations a certain level of theatrical truth or cultural recognition? After a Kennedy Center matinee of *On Raftery's Hill*, several Irish actors, male and female, expressed concern about what they believed to be a skewed view of their culture; they worried especially that Americans would get an inappropriately dark view of rural Ireland. Several mentioned 'poor' Tom Hickey – such a nice man playing such a despicable character. Then they laughed, wondering out loud where the farm inspectors had been. Regardless of cultural associations, though, any audience would

---

[7] Nicholas Grene, *The Politics of Irish Drama: Plays in Context from Boucicault to Friel* (Cambridge: Cambridge University Press, 1999), p.2.

find problematic Red Raftery's brutality toward his family and his wholesale killing of animals.

If theatre has traditionally been used to showcase Irish culture, setting up expectations then about the truth of that representation, what view of Ireland did *On Raftery's Hill* offer Americans attending the play? Or is that an unfair question? After all, whose view of a given culture should take precedence? Rather than simply exploring their own truth, must writers answer to an overarching cultural understanding? Writers may not have much choice in the matter. Although Carr's aim may be primarily non-representational, she does use Irish idioms and settings and thus inescapably participates in the process of cultural definition. Grene argues persuasively that 'Irish drama is outward-directed, created as much to be viewed from outside as from inside Ireland'[8]; this sense of 'otherness' then creates an 'estranging' effect even when the plays are performed only within Ireland. If true, a self-consciousness about Ireland being a place apart would permeate a playwright's perspective, whatever the play's story or however commonplace or exotic the setting. Through its theatre, Ireland has become not merely a dramatized place but – 'as subject' – has taken on the power of metaphor, of archetype. Writers carry the weight of this enlarging, distancing effect and must reconcile conflicting interpretations and multiple representations. The Irish actors leaving *On Raftery's Hill* were caught up in this culture-conscious phenomenon, and their view of Ireland as subject clashed with Carr's view. These actors expressed no corresponding concerns about *Catalpa* or *Pentecost*, plays which presented Irish culture as quirky but not demented.

In contrast to the self-consciousness inherent in the representation of Ireland is the unconsciousness of the creative process. The act of writing itself could propel the likely clash between cultural and artistic re-creation. Writers cannot anticipate possible responses to their work without compromising creativity; they write from their own experiences – experiences which may or may not conflict with prevailing views. Carr must,

---

[8] Grene, p.3.

in the end, be true to the intense hauntings, to the 'wrestling' with 'nocturnal traffic'[9] which drives her work. Theatre never simply mirrors life but is an intensification of life. The dark demons Carr is exorcizing are rooted in abusive relationships from which no one would argue Ireland is immune. McGuinness claims that 'the unhappy, unholy family is the only constant in [Carr's] universe, and it is in the process of tearing itself to pieces'[10] – both on Carr's stage and in actuality. Nearly every possible family permutation or dysfunction is played out in her work. Melissa Sihra argues that 'for Carr the family is central to the drama' and from this 'microcosm' come 'implications for culture and nation.'[11] If Sihra is right, then Carr's 'unhappy, unholy family' is a symbol for larger cultural issues. According to Richard Schechner, 'the interactions played out in the theater are those which are problematical in society, interactions of a sexual, violent, or taboo kind concerning hierarchy, territory, or mating. [...] drama is not a model of all human action, but of the most problematical, difficult, taboo, liminal, and dangerous activities.'[12] Schechner's statement is an apt description of the dangerous, taboo interactions in Carr's *On Raftery's Hill*. Given this interpretation, her vision, rather than being an embarrassing betrayal of her culture, is instead central to the purpose of performance.

Carr brings to light what any culture might want to keep hidden, especially from the neighbours. But what is the possible danger in staging these violent and taboo interactions? Does explicit abuse on stage shock enough to make audiences question the wide-spread practice, or do Carr's well-written, disturbingly funny plays aptly referred to by Grene as 'black pastorals' (Kennedy Center panel comment) simply make abuse seem a natural and even tolerable part of Irish life? Do her depressed

---

[9] Marina Carr, 'Afterword' in *The Dazzling Dark*, p.310.

[10] Frank McGuinness, 'Introduction', *The Dazzling Dark*, p.ix.

[11] Sihra, Melissa, 'A Cautionary Tale: Marina Carr's *By the Bog of Cats...*' in *Theatre Stuff*, 257-268, (p.257).

[12] Richard Schechner, *Performance Theory* (New York: Drama Book Specialists, 1988), p.213.

characters, often left in degradation and misery, offer audiences a cautionary tale, or do they give audiences an out, a way to distance themselves rather than engage with a culture which seems too foreign to understand? Jill Dolan argues that plays 'still caught in the representational systems'[13] to which they refer offer little possibility for radical change; performances can lead to further debasement rather than providing a viable critique of abusive practices. Carr's Dinah certainly models denial more than confrontation. On the other hand, Sihra believes that

> the genre of the Fantastic, which does not invent other worlds but inverts elements of the *known* world, allows for a distance that affords oblique access to the culture and society in question. By entering spaces outside the frame of the real, Carr replaces familiarity and comfort with estrangement and unease, thus offering the necessary objectivity for self-scrutiny[14].

By exploring the benighted lives of these exotic characters in all their strangeness, according to this interpretation, Carr is allowing audiences to engage in healthy self-critique. I wonder. Even though Dolan may be too pessimistic, Sihra might be much too hopeful.

True, by imbuing Red Raftery with godlike power over family and nature, Carr is reinscribing Greek tragedy onto her Midlands landscape, but she is also recalling onto the stage the terrifying, larger-than-life, abusive father – the immortal father-figure, only faking rigor mortis while 'throwing tantrums in the coffin, claw marks on the lid' (*ORH*, p.57). Rather than provide critical distance from real-world situations, *On Raftery's Hill* may plunge victims back into an all too painful reality. Her women characters, given Carr's gender and youth, are surprisingly limited, damaged women, unable to transcend their circumstances. No feminist in any traditional sense, Carr writes women more problematic than her men; these women are not conquering the world or even surviving, for that matter. The

---

[13] Jill Dolan, *The Feminist Spectator as Critic* (Ann Arbor: University of Michigan, 1988), p.67.

[14] Sihra, p.264.

central female figures in Carr's trilogy all commit suicide, and that the women in *On Raftery's Hill* are alive at the end of the play prompts the question, 'Why'? Clare Wallace argues that along with their 'sexual freedom, passion, and independence', Carr's 'strong-willed women' are 'haunting because of their chronic inability to imagine freedom'[15]. In the end, both genders are inescapably caught in endless violence, in fated, circumscribed lives, scratching claw marks on the lid. So can the bizarre stretch the limits of acceptability in helpful ways or merely render a given culture too obscure to comprehend? Norma Jenckes announces in an *Irish Times* article[16] that 'blood is flowing on the legitimate stage again' and asks, 'Never known for their pacifism or aversion to violence, are the Irish just trying to amuse their English and American cousins with their profound sense of cultural difference?' Are the Irish leading a trend, as Jenckes seems to believe, where stage violence has simply become an entertaining substitute for real violence?

Claiming that 'some Irish plays have travelled better than others', Grene explains that Irish drama 'as a commodity of international currency has produced mixed results'; even though allowing 'early success to very talented writers such as McGuinness, Barry, McPherson', this commodity mentality 'has enabled McDonagh, a playwright of much more doubtful originality, to achieve quite astonishing success by manipulating the formulae of the Irish play'[17]. Although Carr is not included in Grene's list of talented writers, she certainly stands alongside Sebastian Barry and Conor McPherson. But Carr should not be lumped together with the jokester Martin McDonagh, as Vic Merriman does. First, acknowledging them as 'the most celebrated Irish playwrights of the late nineteen nineties', Merriman then asserts that 'at a time of unprecedented affluence, Carr and McDonagh elaborate a world of the poorly educated, coarse and unrefined.

---

[15] Clare Wallace, 'Tragic Destiny and Abjection in Marina Carr's *The Mai, Portia Coughlan* and *By the Bog of Cats...*', *Irish University Review* 31 (2) (Autumn/Winter 2001), pp.431-449, (p.435).

[16] Norma Jenckes, *Irish Times* 13 July 2000, p.14.

[17] Grene, p.262.

The focus is tight, the display of violence inhering in the people themselves, grotesque and unrelenting'[18]. True, perhaps, but I believe the differences in their intentions makes the comparison unfair. How can Carr's fierce pursuit of her own truth be compared to McDonagh's parodies? Nevertheless, *On Raftery's Hill* did not travel well to the Kennedy Center; the 'international currency' Carr has enjoyed along with her early success was clearly not born out by the festival performances. This 'mixed result' is in itself worth noting.

Writing about the Irish Repertory of Chicago's successful production of *By the Bog of Cats...* at the Victory Gardens Theater (1-24 June 2001), Enrica Cerquoni seems to counter Merriman's criticism: 'In an age in which materialism and consumerism are so often made the subject of drama, Carr bravely goes against the grain by writing about the poor'[19]. The Victory Gardens, winner of the 2001 Outstanding Regional Theatre Tony Award, has built the type of involved audience Carr's work requires; Cerquoni refers to the 'admittedly baffled audience' anxious to ask questions during an after-show discussion. She worries, though, about a significant change Carr apparently made, causing Hester Swane to regret her brother's death: 'Is Carr trying to make this character more likeable to a non-Irish audience, or does the playwright now see it differently? Nonetheless, Cerquoni calls Carr's willingness to re-examine Hester Swane 'admirably adventurous' and says the production provides 'a gateway for cultural dialogue'.[20] But Cerquoni's review still raises the general question of exportability: can Irish drama transfer successfully to the American stage? Yes, of course, barring certain exceptional situations. This Victory Gardens production also raises the more specific question addressed in

---

[18] Merriman, Vic, 'Decolonisation Postponed: The Theatre of Tiger Trash', *Irish University Review* 29:2, (Autumn/Winter 1999), pp.305-317, (p.312).

[19] Cerquoni, Enrica, 'Review of *By the Bog of Cats...*', *Irish Theatre Magazine* 2:9, (Summer 2001), p.70.

[20] *ibid.*, p.2.

this essay: can Carr's unique vision be translated into under-standable dramatic conversations? Also, yes. And careful, re-spectful critical analysis is a necessary part of this rich conversa-tion. Carr does despair because few read plays and few play-scripts are reviewed: 'theatre seems to have been demoted to the scum end of literature' (*DWTD*: p.194). Carr certainly wants to interact meaningfully with both kinsmen and kinswomen as well as insiders and outsiders. Why else would she participate in ongoing discussions and write so eloquently about her craft?

Since theatre is inherently so powerful a medium, what fi-nally is a writer's responsibility? The 'incredible bravery' the writer must have, Carr insists, is 'about the courage to sit down and face the ghosts and have conversations with them, [...] about going over to the other side and coming back with some-thing, new, hopefully: gold, possibly' (*DWTD*: p.191). Truth in art, as in life, is cumulative; once the impossible has been achieved – once all the pictures are painted, all the stories are told, all the dramatic narratives are performed – an understand-ing of a given culture is possible. These mythic stories a people tell to themselves and to others have value apart from any agreement about their relative truth; these endlessly repeated narratives reveal the deep issues that drive a culture. And Carr's individual voice is a crucial component of the cumulative, cultural story. In her work, Carr cracks open a window onto the ghost world that troubles her sleep and allows her audiences to overhear the tumult. Imagining the contentious Rafterys crowd-ing around Carr's writing desk, elbowing each other, wailing out their story is not difficult; anti-heroes all – the Rafterys belliger-ently occupy Carr's inverted heroic age, her ancient new world 'before rules was made' (*ORH*: p.56). And Carr, the interpreter, stands at the crossroads between these worlds, buffeted by the biting wind blowing across the Midlands bog, dispersing the mists for only a brief moment. May the scary hauntings con-tinue.

Selected Bibliography

Published Plays

Low in the Dark, in *The Crack in the Emerald: New Irish Plays,* ed. by David Grant, (London: Nick Herne Books, 1990), pp.63-140.

The Mai, (Meath: The Gallery Press, 1995).

Portia Coughlan, (London: Faber & Faber in association with the Royal Court, 1996).

Portia Coughlan, in *The Dazzling Dark,* ed. by Frank McGuinness, (London & Boston: Faber & Faber, 1996), pp.235-311.

Portia Coughlan, Revised Edition, (Meath: The Gallery Press, 1998).

By the Bog of Cats..., (Meath: The Gallery Press, 1998).

Plays 1, (London: Faber & Faber, 1999).

On Raftery's Hill, (Meath: The Gallery Press, 2000).

Ariel, (Meath: The Gallery Press, 2002).

The Mai, Portia Coughlan, By the Bog of Cats... and *On Raftery's Hill* are also published in acting editions by Dramatists Play Service, Inc. (New York)

Articles:

'Dealing with the Dead', *Irish University Review,* 28.1, Spring/Summer 1998), pp.190-6.

Interviews:

'A Playwright's Post-Beckettian Period', interview with Marina Carr by James F. Clarity, *New York Times*, 3 November 1994: C 23.

'Interview with Marina Carr', in eds Heidi Stephenson and Natasha Langridge, *Rage and Reason: Women Playwrights on Playwriting*, (London: Methuen, 1997), pp.146-155.

'Marina of the Midlands', Interview with Marina Carr by Eileen Battersby, *The Irish Times*, 4 May 2000.

Interview with Marina Carr in ed. Cliodhna Ní Anluain, *Reading the Future: Irish Writers in Conversation with Mike Murphy*, (Dublin: The Lilliput Press, 2000), pp.43-57.

Marina Carr in conversation with Melissa Sihra, in, ed. Lilian Chambers et al.,*Theatre Talk: Voices of Irish Theatre Practitioners*, (Dublin: Carysfort Press, 2001), pp.155-166.

Selected Critical Bibliography on Carr

Becket, Fiona, 'A Theatrical Matrilineage?: problems of the familial in the drama of Teresa Deevy and Marina Carr', in eds Scott Brewster, Virginia Crossman, Fiona Becket and David Alderson, *Ireland in Proximity: History, Gender, Space*, (London: Routledge, 1999), pp.80-93.

Burke, Pat, 'A Dream of Fair Women: Marina Carr's *The Mai* and Ní Dhuibhne's *Dún na mBan Trí Thine'* in *Hungarian Journal of English and American Studies*, 2.2, (1996), pp.123-27.

Kurdi, Maria, 'Alternative Articulations of Female subjectivity and Gender Relations in Contemporary Irish Women's Plays: The Example of Marina Carr', *Codes and Masks: Aspects of Identity in Contemporary Irish Plays in an Intercultural Context*, (Frankfurt: Peter Lang, 2000), pp.59-72.

Leeney, Cathy, 'Exiled at Home: Teresa Deevy and Marina Carr' in *Cambridge Companion to Twentieth Century Irish Drama*, ed. Shaun Richards (C.U.P., 2003)

McMullan, Anna, 'Marina Carr's Unhomely Women', *Irish Theatre Magazine*, 1:1 (Autumn 1998), pp.14-16.

McMullan, Anna, 'Gender, Authorship and Performance in Selected Plays by Contemporary Irish Women Playwrights: Mary Elizabeth Burke-Kennedy, Marie Jones, Marina Carr, Emma Donoghue' in *Theatre Stuff: Critical Essays on Contemporary Irish Theatre*, ed. Eamonn Jordan (Dublin: Carysfort Press, 2000), pp.34-46.

Merriman, Vic, 'Decolonisation Postponed: The Theatre of Tiger Trash', *Irish University Review* 29:2 (Autumn/Winter 1999), pp.305-317.

Morse, Donald E., 'sleepwalkers along a Precipice: Staging Memory in Marina Carr's *The Mai*', *Hungarian Journal of English and American Studies*, 2.2 (1996) pp.111-22.

Murray, Christopher: *Twentieth Century Irish Drama: Mirror up to Nation*, Manchester & New York: (Manchester University Press, 1997), pp.235-8.

O'Dwyer, Riana, 'The Imagination of Women's Reality: Christina Reid and Marina Carr' in ed. Eamonn Jordan, *Theatre Stuff: Critical Essays on Contemporary Irish Theatre*, pp.236-248.

Roche, Anthony, 'Woman on the Threshold: J.M. Synge's *The Shadow of the Glen*, Teresa Deevy's *Katie Roche* and Marina Carr's *The Mai*, *Irish University Review*, 1995, Spring/Summer; Vol.25, No 1; pp.143-162.

Sihra, Melissa, 'A Cautionary Tale: Marina Carr's *By the Bog of Cats…*, in ed. Eamonn Jordan*, Theatre Stuff: Critical Essays on Contemporary Irish Theatre*, (Dublin:Carysfort Press, 2000), pp.257-268.

Wallace, Clare, 'A Crossroads between Worlds': Marina Carr and the Use of Tragedy' in *Litteraria Pragensia: Studies in Literature and Culture*, 10.20, (2000), pp.76-89.

Wallace, Clare, 'Tragic Destiny and Abjection in Marina Carr's *The Mai, Portia Coughlan* and *By the Bog of Cats…*, *Irish University Review* 31:2 (Autumn/Winter 2001), pp.431-449.

Selected Carr Productions

A: Irish Premieres of Marina Carr's Published Plays

Low in the Dark, presented by Crooked Sixpence Theatre Company at the Project Arts Centre, Dublin on 24th October 1989.

Curtains	Bríd Mhic Fhearai
Bender	Joan Brosnan Walsh
Binder	Sarahjane Scaife
Baxter	Peter Holmes
Bone	Dermot Moore
Director	Philip Hardy
Designer	Liz Cullinane
Costumes	Leonor McDonagh
Lighting	Brian O'Rourke
Music	Bunna Beo Ensemble

The Mai, presented at the Peacock Theatre, the National Theatre Society Ltd, Dublin, on 5th October 1994.

The Mai	Olwen Fouéré
Millie	Derbhle Crotty
Robert	Owen Roe
Connie	Michele Forbes
Grandma Fraochlán	Joan O'Hara
Beck	Bríd Ní Neachtain
Agnes	Máire Hastings
Julie	Stella McCusker
Cellist	John O'Kane
Director	Brian Brady
Designer	Kathy Strachan
Lighting	Aedín Cosgrove
Music	Michéal O Súilleabháin

Portia Coughlan, commissioned by the National Maternity Hospital, Dublin, and presented at the Peacock Theatre, Dublin, on 27 March 1996.

Portia Coughlan	Derbhle Crotty
Raphael Coughlan	Seán Rocks
Maggie May Doorley	Marion O'Dwyer
Senchil Doorley	Des Keogh
Damus Halion	Don Wycherley
Stacia Doyle	Bronagh Gallagher
Fintan Goolan	Charlie Bonner
Marianne Scully:	Stella McCusker
Blaize Scully	Pauline Flanagan
Sly Scully	Tom Hickey
Gabriel Scully	Michael Boylan / Peter Charlesworth Kelly

Director	Garry Hynes
Designer	Kandis Cook
Lighting	Jim Simmons
Music	Paddy Cunneen

By the Bog of Cats...presented at the Abbey Theatre, Dublin on 7th October 1998.

Hester Swane	Olwen Fouéré
Josie Kilbride	Siobhan Cullen / Kerrie O'Sullivan
Carthage Kilbride	Conor MacDermottroe
Monica Murray	Pat Leavy
Mrs Kilbride	Pauline Flanagan
Xavier Cassidy	Tom Hickey
Caroline Cassidy	Fionnuala Murphy
Catwoman	Joan O'Hara
Ghost Fancier	Pat Kinevane
Ghost of Joseph Swane	Ronan Leahy
Young Dunne/Waiter	Conan Sweeny
Father Willow	Eamon Kelly
Waiters	Gavin Cleland, Kieran Grimes

Director   Patrick Mason
Designer   Monica Frawley
Lighting   Nick Chelton

On Raftery's Hill, co-production of Druid Theatre, Galway and the Royal Court Theatre, London. First presented at the Town Hall, Galway, 9 May 2000. Presented at the John F. Kennedy Center for the Performing Arts, Washington D.C., during an Irish arts festival: 'Island: Arts from Ireland', 18-21 May 2000. Opened at the Royal Court Jerwood Theatre, London, 3rd July 2000.

Red Raftery   Tom Hickey
Dinah Raftery   Cara Kelly
Sorrel Raftery: Mary Murray
Ded Raftery   Michael Tierney
Shalome Raftery   Valerie Lilley
Dara Mood   Keith McErlean
Isaac Dunn   Kieran Ahern

Director   Garry Hynes
Set Design   Tony Walton
Costume   Monica Frawley
Lighting   Richard Pilbrow
Sound   Rich Walsh
Music   Paddy Cunneen.

Ariel, produced by the Abbey Theatre in association with Fiach Mac Conghail on 2 October 2002.

Fermoy   Mark Lambert
Frances   Ingrid Craigie
Ariel   Elske Rahill
Elaine   Walsh
Stephen   Dylan Tighe
Boniface   Barry McGovern
Sarah   Joan O'Hara

Hannafin	Des Cave
Verona	Caitríona Ní Murchú
Young Stephen	Paul McGovern / Shane Murray Corcoran
Young Elaine	Lydia Rahill / Siobhan Cullen
Cameramen	Michael McCabe / Pepe Roche
Director	Conall Morrison
Set Design	Frank Conway
Costume	Joan O'Clery
Lighting	Rupert Murray
Sound	Cormac Carroll
Dramaturg	Jocelyn Clarke

B: Selected Productions Outside Ireland

Maja [*The Mai*], presented at the F.X. Salda Theatre, Liberec, the Czech Republic, 23rd November 2001.

Mai	Markéta Tallerová
Millie	Martkéta Zárubová
Robert	Martin Polách
Grandma Fraochlán	Eva Lecchiová
Beck	Dana Sedláková
Connie	Štipánka Prýmková
Julie	Milena Šajdková
Agnes	Michaela Lohniská
Translator	Jan Hanèil
Director	Lída Engelová
Dramaturg	Johana Kudláèková
Stage/Set Design	Ivo Žídek
Costumes	Ivana Brádková
Music	Zdenìk Zdenik

Portia Coughlan (a co-production with the Wiener Fest-wochen) presented by RO Theater, at the RO Theater Rotterdam on 2nd November 2002.

Portia Coughlan	Sanneke Bos
Raphael Coughlan	Herman Gilis
Maggie May Doorley	Goele Derick
Senchil Doorley	Marc de Corte
Damus Halion	Tom Van Bauwel
Stacia Doyle	Fania Sorel
Fintan Goolan	Rogier Philipoom
Marianne Scully:	Sylvia Poorta
Blaize Scully	Ditha van der Linden
Sly Scully	Paul R. Kooij
Gabriel Scully	Eelco Smits

Kattenmoeras [*By the Bog of Cats…*] presented by RO Theater, at the RO Theater, Rotterdam, on 2nd November 2002

Hester Swane	Anneke Blok
Josie Kilbride	Nadia Dijkstra / Ruby Schmelzer
Carthage Kilbride	Paul R. Kooij
Monica Murray	Sanneke Bos
Mrs Kilbride	Goele Derick
Xavier Cassidy	Jack Wouterse
Caroline Cassidy	Fania Sorel
Catwoman	Sylvia Poorta
Ghost Fancier	Eelco Smits
Ghost of Joseph Swane	Eelco Smits
Father Willow	Marc de Corte
Fintan Goolan	Rogier Philipoom
Translator	Peter Nijmeijer
Director	Alize Zandwijk
Designer	Thomas Rupert
Costumes	Valentine Kempynck
Lighting	Marc Heinz

| Music | Wim Selles |
| Dramaturgs | Erwin Jans, Herman Gilis |

Portia Coughlan, presented by The Pittsburgh Irish and Classical Theatre Company at Chatham's Eddy Theatre, USA, on March 22, 2001

Portia Coughlan	Deirdriu Ring
Raphael Coughlan	Douglas Rees
Maggie May Doorley	Kate Young
Senchil Doorley	E. Bruce Hill
Damus Halion	Christian Rummel
Stacia Doyle	Catherine Moore
Fintan Goolan	John Yost
Marianne Scully	Susan MgGregor-Lane
Blaize Scully	Ginger Lawrence
Sly Scully	Alex Coleman
Gabriel Scully	Michael Karas

Director	Timothy Douglas
Designer	David M. Maslow
Lighting	Matthew J. Kopans
Music	Jennifer Fritsch
Dramaturg	Melissa Sihra

By the Bog of Cats... presented by Irish Repertory of Chicago, USA, 3I May 2001.

Hester Swane	Tracy Michelle Arnold
Josie Kilbride	Susan Wiltrakis/ Zoe B Kanters
Carthage Kilbride	Mark L. Montgomery
Monica Murray	Marilyn Bogetich
Mrs Kilbride	Caitlin Hart
Xavier Cassidy	David Darlow
Caroline Cassidy	Amanda Archilla
Catwoman	Mary Ann Thebus
Ghost Fancier	Ed Zeltner
Ghost of Joseph Swane	Christopher Grobe

Young Dunne/Waiter	Geoff Rice
Father Willow	Brendan Gregg
Director	M.K. Martinovich
Designer	Michelle Habek
Lighting	Jaymi Lee Smith
Dramaturg	Melissa Sihra

By the Bog of Cats... presented by the San Jose Repertory Theatre, 14th September 2001.

Hester Swane	Holly Hunter
Josie Kilbride	Jillian Lee Wheeler
Carthage Kilbride	Gordon McDonald
Monica Murray	Wanda McCaddon
Mrs Kilbride	Carol Mayo Jenkins
Xavier Cassidy	J. G. Hertzler
Caroline Cassidy	Gretchen Cleevely
Catwoman	Joan MacIntosh
Ghost Fancier	James Carpenter
Ghost of Joseph Swane	Matt Tufman
Young Dunne/Waiter	Alex Moggridge
Father Willow	Stuart Rudin
Director	Timothy Near
Designer	Joe Vanek
Dramaturg	Melissa Sihra
Lighting	Peter Maradudin
Sound Design	Jeff Mockus

Index

Contributors

Bernadette Bourke holds a Masters Degree in Modern Drama Studies from N.U.I., Dublin. She teaches English at Donahies Community School, where she also directs plays with the Donahies Drama Group, specializing in the works of Synge and O'Casey.

Enrica Cerquoni teaches at the Drama Studies Centre at N.U.I., Dublin, where she is currently completing her Ph.D. research on the plays of Marina Carr and Anne Devlin. She has published articles on Augusta Gregory, J.M. Synge, and Anne Devlin. She contributed an interview with Anne Devlin to *Theatre Talk* (2001), published by Carysfort Press.

Olwen Fouéré was born in west Galway of Breton parents and became an actor in 1976 after an initial training in the visual arts. She has performed and toured internationally with many theatre companies in Ireland and the U.K. including the Abbey Theatre, the Gate Theatre, Dublin, the Royal National Theatre, the R.S.C., the Royal Lyceum, the English Shakespeare Company, Druid Theatre Company and Field Day. Highlights include creating the title role in Steven Berkoff's production of Wilde's *Salomé* at the Gate Theatre, Dublin, and her roles as The Mai, and as Hester Swane in *By the Bog of Cats...* She is co-director (with Roger Doyle) of Operating Theatre, where her solo performances have included the widely acclaimed *The Diamond Body*, (written for her by Aidan Mathews), which she performed internationally in English and in French, *The Pentago-*

nal Dream by Sebastian Barry, and *Angel/Babel* and *Chair* (both written and developed in collaboration with Operating Theatre). She has also performed and collaborated on several works by artist James Coleman, which continue to be exhibited internationally.

Claudia W. Harris is Associate Professor in the English Faculty at Brigham Young University. As an academic, a freelance journalist, and theatre critic, she has developed over the years an abiding interest in Ireland, which takes her there several times every year. As co-chair of the International Committee of the American Theater Critics Association, she serves as delegate to the International Association of Theater Critics. These roles enable her to see and write about theatre from around the world. She is a correspondent/theatre critic for the *Salt Lake Tribune* (Utah) and is Utah correspondent for *Back Stage* (NYC).

Cathy Leeney is interested in twentieth century and contemporary Irish theatre, in gender and performance, and in directing. She edited *Seen and Heard: Six New Plays by Irish Women* (Carysfort Press, 2002), and has published articles on contemporary and twentieth century Irish theatre, including contributions to the *Cambridge Companion to Twentieth Century Irish Drama* (CUP, 2003), and to *Amid Our Troubles: Irish Versions of Greek Tragedy*, edited by Marianne McDonald and J. Michael Walton (Methuen, 2002). She is currently writing a book on Irish women playwrights from 1900 to 1939. She lectures at N.U.I. Dublin Drama Studies Centre.

Frank McGuinness was born in Buncrana, Co. Donegal, and now lives in Dublin and lectures in English at N.U.I., Dublin. He is best known for *The Factory Girls, Observe the Sons of Ulster Marching Towards the Somme, Innocence, Carthaginians, Someone Who'll Watch Over Me, Mutabilitie, Dolly West's Kitchen*, and *Gates of Gold*. His adaptations of Sophocles, Ibsen, Chekhov, Strindberg, Lorca, and Brecht have been internationally acclaimed. His work for film and television includes *Scout, Henhouse* and *Dancing at Lughnasa*. He has published two volumes of poetry with Gallery Press, *Booterstown* and *The Sea with No Ships*.

Tom Mac Intyre was born in Cavan in 1931 and still lives there. He has written many plays for the Abbey Theatre, most notably *The Great Hunger*, which toured internationally. Other Abbey productions include *Sheep's Milk on the Boil, Good Evening Mr. Collins, The Chirpaun, Jack Be Nimble,* and *Find the Lady*. Recently, his *The Gallant John-Joe*, written specially for actor Tom Hickey, enjoyed rave reviews nationally and in Edinburgh and New York. His selected stories, entitled *The Word for Yes*, are available from Gallery Books. He has also published several volumes of poetry, including two in the Irish language. The most recent collection, *Stories of the Wandering Moon*, is available from Lilliput Press. Tom Mac Intyre is a member of Aosdána.

Anna McMullan is Director of the M.Phil. in Irish Theatre and Film at the School of Drama, Samuel Beckett Centre, Trinity College Dublin. Main areas of research include contemporary Irish theatre, feminism and theatre, and the drama of Samuel Beckett. Her book, *Theatre on Trial: Samuel Beckett's Later Drama* was published by Routledge in 1993, and she has contributed to several collections of articles on Beckett. She has published widely in Ireland and internationally on contemporary Irish theatre, including a chapter on 'Irish Women Playwrights Since 1958' in *British and Irish Women Dramatists Since 1958*, edited by Trevor Griffiths and Margaret Llewellyn Jones (Open University, 1993). She co-edited, with Caroline Williams, the contemporary drama section of the fifth volume of the *Field Day Anthology*, devoted to Irish women's writing (Cork University Press, 2002).

M.K. Martinovich completed her M.Phil. in Irish Theatre and Film at Trinity College Dublin. She works as a freelance theatre director in Chicago, where she directed the American premiere of Marina Carr's *By the Bog of Cats...*, and the Chicago premiere of Carr's *The Mai*, both for the Irish Repertory of Chicago. For eight years she was the owner and operator of the Actors' Center, a professional acting studio in Chicago, where she also taught acting in the Meisner technique. Other companies she has directed for include Apple Tree Theatre, Buffalo Theatre Ensemble, and Famous Door Theatre.

Victor Merriman lectures in contemporary Irish theatre at Dundalk Institute of Technology. He is a regular contributor to critical fora, including academic conferences, periodicals, and print and broadcast media. A member of An Chomhairle Éalaíon/The Arts Council (1993-1998), he chaired the Council's Review of Theatre in Ireland 1995-1996.

Eilis Ní Dhuibhne is a fiction writer. Born in Dublin, she is a graduate of N.U.I, Dublin, from which she holds a Ph.D. in Irish Folklore. She is the author of plays, collections of short stories, and novels.

Matt O'Brien is the founder and artistic director of Irish Repertory of Chicago, where he has produced the American premiere of Marina Carr's *By the Bog of Cats...*, and the Chicago premiere of *The Mai*, along with plays by Friel, Shaw, O'Neill, Leonard, Beckett and Murphy, among others. He was the Artistic Director of Chicago's 'Buckets O' Beckett' Festival in 1996, presenting eighteen of Beckett's plays over four weeks with artists such as Frank Galati, John Mahoney, and Academy Award winner Estelle Parsons in the festival company.

Fintan O'Toole is one of Ireland's leading political and cultural commentators. He has been drama critic for *In Dublin* magazine, the *Sunday Times* and the *New York Daily News*, and Literary Advisor to the Abbey Theatre. He edited *Magill* magazine and since 1988, has been a columnist with the *Irish Times*. His award-winning work has appeared in many international newspapers and magazines, including the *New Yorker*, the *New York Review of Books*, *Granta*, the *Guardian*, the *New York Times* and the *Washington Post*. He has also broadcast extensively in Ireland and the U.K. Books include *The Irish Times Book of the Century* (1999), *A Traitor's Kiss: The Life of Richard Brinsley Sheridan* (1997), *The Lie of the Land: Selected Essays* (1997), *The Ex-Isle of Erin* (1996), *Black Hole, Green Card* (1994), *Meanwhile Back at the Ranch* (1995), *A Mass for Jesse James* (1990) and *The Politics of Magic* (1987).

Anthony Roche is Senior Lecturer in the English Department at N.U.I., Dublin. He is the author of *Contemporary Irish Drama:*

From Beckett to McGuinness (1994), and is currently completing a book entitled *Synge and the Making of Modern Irish Drama*. He was editor of the *Irish University Review* from 1998 to 2002.

Medb Ruane is a journalist and critic. Currently writing for the *Sunday Times*, the *Evening Herald*, and as guest columnist for *Newsday*, she has published extensively on contemporary Irish culture and on women's history.

Sarahjane Scaife is an actress, director, and teacher of theatre. She graduated in English and Philosophy from N.U.I., Dublin, and studied movement and dance in New York with Stephan Niedialkowski and Eric Hawkins for four years. She was movement director on the series of W.B. Yeats Festivals at the Abbey Theatre in the 1990s, and is founder member of the experimental theatre company Throwin' Shapes. She has a particular interest in the work of Samuel Beckett, which she had directed and taught in many countries.

Melissa Sihra is Lecturer in Drama at Queen's University Belfast. Her doctoral dissertation, from Trinity College Dublin, is on the plays of Marina Carr. Her work as a dramaturg includes American productions of Carr and Brian Friel, including the U.S. premiere of *By the Bog of Cats...* for Irish Repertory in Chicago. She is currently writing a book on the theatre of Marina Carr.

Clare Wallace is a lecturer in the Department of English and American Studies at Charles University in Prague, in the Czech Republic. She co-edited (with Louis Armand) *Giacomo Joyce: Envoys of the Other* (Bethesda: Academia, 2002), is an advisory editor for the online journal *Rhizomes: Cultural Studies in Emerging Knowledge*, and has written on Marina Carr, Patrick McCabe and James Joyce.

Carysfort Press was formed in the summer of 1998. It receives annual funding from the Arts Council.

The directors believe that drama is playing an ever-increasing role in today's society and that enjoyment of the theatre, both professional and amateur, currently plays a central part in Irish culture.

The Press aims to produce high quality publications which, though written and/or edited by academics, will be made accessible to a general readership. The organisation would also like to provide a forum for critical thinking in the Arts in Ireland, again keeping the needs and interests of the general public in view.

The company publishes contemporary Irish writing for and about the theatre.

Editorial and publishing inquiries to:

CARYSFORT PRESS

58 Woodfield, Scholarstown Road,
Rathfarnham, Dublin 16,
Republic of Ireland
T (353 1) 493 7383   F (353 1) 406 9815
e: info@carysfortpress.com

www.carysfortpress.com

NEW TITLES

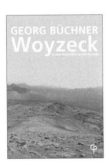

GEORG BÜCHNER: WOYZECK
A NEW TRANSLATION
BY DAN FARRELLY

The most up-to-date German scholarship of Thomas Michael Mayer and Burghard Dedner has finally made it possible to establish an authentic sequence of scenes. The wide-spread view that this play is a prime example of loose, open theatre is no longer sustainable. Directors and teachers are challenged to "read it again".

ISBN 1-904505-02-3
€8

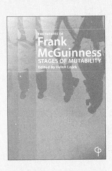

THE THEATRE OF FRANK MCGUINNESS
STAGES OF MUTABILITY
BY HELEN LOJEK

The first edited collection of essays about internationally renowned Irish playwright Frank McGuinness focuses on both performance and text. Interpreters come to diverse conclusions, creating a vigorous dialogue that enriches understanding and reflects a strong consensus about the value of McGuinness's complex work.

ISBN 1-904505-01-5
€15

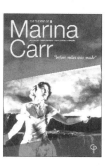

THE THEATRE OF MARINA CARR
"BEFORE RULES WAS MADE"

EDITED BY ANNA MCMULLAN
& CATHY LEENEY

As the first published collection of articles
on the theatre of Marina Carr, this volume
explores the world of Carr's theatrical
imagination, the place of her plays in
comtemporary theatre in Ireland and
abroad and the significance of her highly
individual voice.

ISBN 0-9534-2577-0
€20

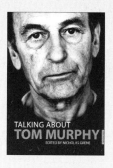

TALKING ABOUT TOM MURPHY
EDITED BY NICHOLAS GRENE

Talking About Tom Murphy is shaped
around the six plays in the landmark Abbey
Theatre Murphy Season of 2001, assembling
some of the best-known commentators on
his work: Fintan O'Toole, Chris Morash, Lionel
Pilkington, Alexandra Poulain, Shaun
Richards, Nicholas Grene and Declan Kiberd.

ISBN 0-9534-2579-7
€10

HAMLET
THE SHAKESPEAREAN DIRECTOR

BY MIKE WILCOCK

"This study of the Shakespearean director as
viewed through various interpretations of
HAMLET is a welcome addition to our
understanding of how essential it is for a
director to have a clear vision of a great play.
It is an important study from which all of us
who love Shakespeare and who understand
the importance of continuing contemporary
exploration may gain new insights."

From the Foreword, by Joe Dowling,
Artistic Director, The Guthrie Theater,
Minneapolis, MN

ISBN 1-904505-00-7
€18

THEATRE OF SOUND
RADIO AND THE
DRAMATIC IMAGINATION

BY DERMOT RATTIGAN

An innovative study of the challenges that
radio drama poses to the creative
imagination of the writer, the production
team, and the listener.

"A remarkably fine study of radio drama –
everywhere informed by the writer's
professional experience of such drama in
the making…A new theoretical and
analytical approach – informative,
illuminating and at all times readable."

Richard Allen Cave

ISBN 0-9534-2575-4
€20

THEATRE TALK

VOICES OF IRISH THEATRE PRACTITIONERS

EDITED BY LILIAN CHAMBERS, GER
FITZGIBBON & EAMONN JORDAN

"This book is the right approach - asking
practitioners what they feel."

Sebastian Barry, Playwright.

"... an invaluable and informative collection
of interviews with those who make and
shape the landscape of Irish Theatre."

Ben Barnes, Artistic Director of the Abbey Theatre

ISBN 0-9534-2576-2
€20

IN SEARCH OF THE
SOUTH AFRICAN IPHIGENIE

BY ERIKA VON WIETERSHEIM
AND DAN FARRELLY

Discussions of Goethe's "Iphigenie auf
Tauris" (Under the Curse) as relevant to
women's issues in modern South Africa:
women in family and public life; the force of
women's spirituality; experience of personal
relationships; attitudes to parents and
ancestors; involvement with religion.

ISBN 0-9534-2578-9
€10

THE STARVING
AND OCTOBER SONG

TWO CONTEMPORARY IRISH PLAYS

BY ANDREW HINDS

The Starving, set during and after the
siege of Derry in 1689, is a moving and
engrossing drama of the emotional journey
of two men.

October Song, a superbly written family
drama set in real time in pre-ceasefire
Derry.

ISBN 0-9534-2574-6
€10

SEEN AND HEARD (REPRINT)

SIX NEW PLAYS BY IRISH WOMEN

EDITED WITH AN INTRODUCTION BY
CATHY LEENEY

A rich and funny, moving and theatrically
exciting collection of plays by Mary
Elizabeth Burke-Kennedy, Síofra Campbell,
Emma Donoghue, Anne Le Marquand
Hartigan, Michelle Read and Dolores
Walshe.

ISBN 0-9534-2573-8
€20

THEATRE STUFF (REPRINT)

CRITICAL ESSAYS ON CONTEMPORARY
IRISH THEATRE

EDITED BY EAMONN JORDAN

Best selling essays on the successes and
debates of contemporary Irish theatre at
home and abroad.

Contributors include: Thomas Kilroy, Declan
Hughes, Anna McMullan, Declan Kiberd,
Deirdre Mulrooney, Fintan O'Toole,
Christopher Murray, Caoimhe McAvinchey
and Terry Eagleton.

ISBN 0-9534-2571-1
€19

URFAUST

A NEW VERSION OF GOETHE'S   EARLY
"FAUST" IN BRECHTIAN MODE

BY DAN FARRELLY

This version is based on Brecht's irreverent
and daring re-interpretation of the German
classic.

"Urfaust is a kind of well-spring for German
theatre… The love-story is the most daring
and the most profound in German
dramatic literature." *Brecht*

ISBN 0-9534257-0-3
€7.60

UNDER THE CURSE

GOETHE'S "IPHIGENIE AUF TAURIS",
IN A NEW VERSION

BY DAN FARRELLY

The Greek myth of Iphigenie grappling
with the curse on the house of Atreus is
brought vividly to life. This version is
currently being used in Johannesburg to
explore problems of ancestry, religion, and
Black African women's spirituality.

ISBN 0-9534-2572-X
€8.25

HOW TO ORDER

TRADE ORDERS DIRECTLY TO

CMD
Columba Mercier Distribution
55A Spruce Avenue
Stillorgan Industrial Park
Blackrock
Co. Dublin

T (353 1) 294 2560
F (353 1) 294 2564
E cmd@columba.ie

or contact
SALES@BROOKSIDE.IE